Without Embarrassment
The Social Coward's Totally Fearless Seduction System

by Michael Pilinski

Copyright © 2010
All Rights Reserved

All Rights Reserved. No part of this publication may be reproduced, stored in a retrieval system, or transmitted in any form or by any means, electronic, recording or otherwise, without the prior written permission of the Author. Revised 2010 version. First electronic publication: October, 2002 by Michael Pilinski

Contact: mikepil@highstatusmale.com for more information.

Readers are raving about Without Embarrassment...

"This is one good book. I have been amazed to learn about toxic shame -- and have finally come to understand what my real weaknesses are. **Just being exposed to this radical idea has made a huge improvement in my self-esteem.** Very different from what I'd expected." ~ Larry

"Within one week of reading Without Embarrassment I can honestly say that my life has taken a solid turn for the better. I have already connected with 2 beautiful ladies and planted seeds in 4 or 5 other encounters with some cool, laid-back HSM attitude and conversation. **I feel like I've been re-born!** I appreciate so much that you didn't sugar-coat anything in the book -- just the brutal truth, and a masterpiece of truth it is. This is one formerly clueless forty-something guy who is truly grateful." ~ JZ

"This is by far the greatest investment I've ever made for myself. Your details on how to execute the first kiss is worth many times the price of your book - **the simplicity of it is just beautiful.** I was clueless on this ONE critical aspect of the seduction dance." ~ Bill

"Mike, I'm 'on to' you... you've disguised a book on how to be a better man under the pretext of teaching us how to seduce women. I now understand that by becoming the best man you can be, everything else just falls into place. **By simply switching my attitude and presenting myself with class it seems like a new world has opened up for me."**~ Steve

"I must say that I found your book immensely enlightening and insightful on the same scale that I found physics books such as Steven Hawking's *A Brief History of Time,* Feyman's *Quantum ElectroDynamics* and Lederman's *The God Particle* enlightening. **I was humbled by your intellect and your knowledge of this material on a MASSIVE scale.** You Sir are THE MAN" ~ Rick

"Really intelligent, really brutal, really funny **and really true!** I recommend this book to every guy who wants to be more in control of his life." ~ Eric

"Giovanni Casanova himself couldn't have written a better book." ~ Greg

Introduction 6

Chap 1: Is Your Ego Roadkill Yet?

Stop Trying to Get Lucky, *Get Informed* 12
Romantic Ratings 16
Four Types of Rejection Sensitivity 18
My Sad and Pathetic Story 20
Becoming Fearless is a Learned Skill 25
The Female Mating Call 27

Chap 2: How the Game is Played

Establishing Yourself as a Player 31
It's All Subconscious with Her 34
The Nice Guy Blues Explained 36
Nice Guys on Parade 40
Instant Charisma and Classy Courage 44
How Does Your Blood Smell? 47

Chap 3: The Male Dominance Scale

Are You a 2.5 or a 9.5? 51
High Status Males vs. Low Status Males 53
The Way Women Want Men to Act 60
The Seven Attributes Women Love to See 64
But None of this Works for You 72

Chap 4: Comfortable Wimps Tough Men

Toxic Shame Keeps You in a Straitjacket	73
Your Secretly Shamed Affection Needs	80
Anchors Aweigh	89
The Zone of Discomfort	94
Why You End Up Friends and Not Lovers	99

Chap 5: Essential Flirting

Seek Adventure, Not Outcome	109
Pretending You Don't Want it	119
The Rejection-Proof First Contact	123
On Rejection Sensitivity	135
Instant Rapport?	136
Visuals, Auditories and Kinesthetics	141
Romance is a Trance	147
Five Minute First Contact Scenario	157

Chap 6: Closing the Sale

Escalate When the Time is Right	168
You Must Disclose Sexual Interest	172
Be the First One to Touch Her	175
The Assumptive Attitude	182
The Deep Look	186
Deliver a Knockout First Kiss	188
Putting it All Together	196

Chap 7: The Big Picture

Delivering on *Her* Primary Emotional Needs 201
Your Four Primary Emotional Needs 210
The "Right One", defined 213
Getting Her Addicted to You 217
Your Perfect Pad for Shagging 221
Play Nice You Evil Bastard 226

Appendix A 233
Cayman Magic – (A fictional pick-up story)
      On Closer Examination 245

Appendix B 263
Mike's 7 Mega-Rules of Men / Women Relations

Appendix C 266
The Dominant Male Test

Appendix D 275
Scoring the DM Test & Interpretation of Results

Without Embarrassment

Introduction | A Tiger Outside My Gate

Are you socially withdrawn? Is "nerd" how you would describe yourself? Can you remember a horrible, mocking, humiliating event in your past that still haunts you to this day?... see it as vividly as when it first happened? (Oh, I can remember quite a few of them!...). What kind of mechanism does it take to control you? Are you the sort of person who's motivated by the idea of seeking pleasure... or are you all about *avoiding pain* and psychic harm at all costs?

Here's the Great Wonder of being alive... lurking inside every rotten situation there exists a seed of infinite possibility. If you can find this seed and nurture it somehow, what the great philosophers refer to as a *catharsis* can occur in your life. *A **monumental change** which walls off all possibility of going back to the way that you used to be.* This process is accessible to anyone interested in taking up the personal challenge of living Life to its fullest. And no going to the mountain required – just simple but specific **Knowledge** is all that's necessary.

> *I know a man who was out of touch...*
> *And he'd hide in a house and he didn't say much...*
> *Dee da lee do...*
>
> Crunchy Granola Suite
> Neil Diamond, 1972

I remember being 18 years old hiding up in my room... listening to these heart-wrenching songs from Neil Diamond's *Love at the Greek* album. Yeah, I know I'm dating myself as an old fart for a lot of you guys. If I am then you can substitute your own sad songs from your own musical era... I'm sure they're similar. Both our stories of growing up with the forlorn frustration of not being able to connect with the opposite sex is one for the ages: it never changes much from generation to generation. All our experiences are just as relevant despite the passage of time and style and fashion, because the *issues that lie beneath them* are universal and eternal. You can read this as a light of **hope** for yourself.

We are all awkward when those funny urges first begin to grab hold of us in our early teens – when we start to look at the girl down the street, our teacher, maybe even our own *sister* (yuk!) in a strange way that we'd never considered before. It isn't long before we begin to experience the massive discontinuity between our bursting sexual-physical maturity and our social awkwardness. Our bodies lurch far out ahead of our minds and emotions!

Then suddenly, you're supposed to switch gears in mid-childhood and go from being a kid to a young adult – instantly knowing how to charm these... *girls* (who you didn't even want on your ball team last summer!...) and somehow get them to do *something* that everyone expects you to *somehow* know how to do. And if you don't magically know what that something is, well then you're just a fucking **nerd...** and richly deserving of endless scorn from all of your buddies (who are equally as clueless as you, but need an easy target to keep the bullets away from themselves). To make matters even worse, everyone knows that **one dude** growing up who seems to have figured all this stuff out on his own (by sheer accident usually) and is making time with every girl in the neighborhood!

Dare you admit that this joker has some secret power to charm women that you don't possess? *"I could be just like him and get girls too... **if only I wanted to.**"* Sure thing Doc. But we were just kids then... stupid kids, so what? Well of course, it begins to matter *a lot* several years down the road when most every one of your friends finally fumbles his way into some kind of relationship, but you're still left out in the cold. Soon panic begins to set in...w*hat the hell is wrong with me?* Why is it that everyone else I know figured out how this 'hooking up' stuff works, but I can't even muster up the courage to ask a girl out on a date?

> *And like a man with a tiger outside his gate,*
> *Not only couldn't relax but he couldn't relate...*

After a while your social ineptitude starts to become a real stone in your shoe, *an obsession.* There must be a way to overcome this **fear of being rejected** so that you can "become normal" like everyone else, but the answer isn't obvious. Like quicksand, your fears draw you down ever deeper the more you struggle against them. Why? Because it isn't just fear of women that you have – something which could be overcome with a courageous burst of willpower every now and then. What is really suffocating your social life is more akin to a *phobia* that finds its source in a complex network of **shame** and shaming events that may have either happened to you suddenly in a single traumatic accident, or (more insidiously) built-up in a very gradual fashion over a long time and in a way that was so far beneath your radar that you never even knew what happened.

Bit by bit you were made to understand that *certain natural emotions* which were beginning to express themselves in you were *evil or bad...* that they were to be ***repressed*** and hidden away and never acted upon. And the tool used by society, your teachers, parents and other authority figures to control your behavior (and ultimately your thoughts as well) was the powerful psychological hammer known as ***shame.*** The integration of shame into your young and highly vulnerable psyche served to provoke painful thoughts that eventually needed to be flushed from your consciousness (probably with the help of various mood-altering agents and substances) or they would've driven you insane... *that's* how powerful they were. **All addictive behaviors find their source in hidden or repressed feelings of Shame.** But it's the warped thinking process and especially the unconscious behaviors that are even more dangerous to our healthy development as well balanced individuals, as you'll soon see.

In men, one of the places where this terrible shame can create problems is in our self-concept of what it means to be a man, and by extension, of how we handle the most critical aspect of our "manness" – our romantic-sexual interactions with women. Did you ever say to a girl, *"something about you makes me feel young again..."* just because it was true? What I'm trying to show you is how critical it is to be able to operate in a psychological environment side-by-side *along with the complete freedom to fail*. But if you're held fast in the grip of paralyzing shame, merely trying to speak such words can feel like rolling a huge boulder up a steep hill. A big part of Life has been made inaccessible to you.

I'm no scientist and I don't claim to have all the answers, but I know that **females will not mate with non-aggressive males.** This is a fact of life all across nature from rats to pigs, dogs, monkeys *and* humans. And while on the surface it may seem as if humans have civilized the mating dance so much that it bears little resemblance to the actions of lower animals anyway, you'll soon see that so very much of what goes on between men and women is spoken only in the language of *movements and looks and attitudes* just like what happens in the barnyard. So much so, in fact, that it's a wonder we even bother to weave words into the process at all!

But, alas, we do... and so you must know how to manage your words very precisely as well. I'll present you with a template for using words and actions that will insure the best possible chance to impress women... as a *Man* – no matter how much "wimp time" you may've logged so far. I will offer you a bit of my humble knowledge, and you will **provide yourself** with the training.

> *And like a man with a tiger outside his gate,*
> *Not only couldn't relax but he couldn't relate...*
> *Now he can,*
> *family man, tried my brand...*

You may have heard of the ancient, pre-Roman greco society of *Sparta* if you stayed awake during history class. This was the famous warrior race of supreme fighting men whose amazing combat skills were featured in the recent movie *300*, which recounts the Greek "Battle of the Alamo" that was fought brilliantly against the Persians at *Thermopylae*. Sparta was an incredibly fierce society where male children were removed from their parents at a young age by the State and placed through a brutal training ritual that lasted until the age of 18, where *the survivors* were then elevated into the army to seek glory and honor in military combat. These were the finest and toughest soldiers in Greece, analogous to our special-ops Delta Forces, Green Berets and Rangers of today.

Savagery permeated all levels of this strange society, to include the women as well. They too were natural fighters in their own right. Spartan "seduction" back then consisted of a man physically attempting to wrestle a woman to the ground and literally raping her, *an act which made her into his wife!* Nice wedding, eh? If the woman took a liking to the man, she simply wouldn't put up much of a fight and would eventually submit to him. However, if she *didn't* like the guy then there could be hell to pay because Spartan women were no slouches when it came to scraping and fighting. Many an unfortunate Spartan "suitor" ended up having his balls kicked in if he were lucky, or feeling a knife blade slide in-between his ribs if he were having a particularly bad day.

Talk about Rejection... yikes!

Can you imagine such a brutal courting ritual? And we worry about a little emotional pain and humiliation? Of course, since we don't play like savages anymore, mental blocks can *still* be a formidable barrier to us in the psychic mind-space which we must operate in today. Still, I believe it helps to have some perspective on how crazy things *used* to be. The point is that on every level in all human societies throughout time, capturing the sexual favors of a woman has been made into a chore of some kind. Sex is something that the women *possess* and which the men must *fight for* in some manner and on whatever playing field their culture deems acceptable. Ours may be a strictly psychological battlefield nowadays – but you will see vestiges of our dark ancestry continuing to lurk in the shadows of the roles that men were once *expected* to play – and which still hold a surprising amount of sway over the **unconscious clues and triggers** that women employ in their search for suitable mates. These laws of romance have been shaped in the crucible of fire and passions that were born of far more desperate times than our own.

Once you begin to understand the legacy of these events in the workings of the female consciousness, it will start to become clear to you how seduction *must* go down. And when you begin to employ this knowledge to re-imagine a new way to present yourself... your chances of having your advances rejected by women become diminished. When you reach elevated skill levels in your understanding (but there's no perfect 100% score in *this* game) you can begin to act pretty much with impunity, and then set your sights wherever you'd like.

Oh sure there will still be a few land mines out there waiting to trip you up if you're not careful – but it's nothing like the mountain of psychological boulders that probably stand between yourself and a fulfilling social life at the moment. Our job together will be to start rolling these babies out of the way so you can get a clear view of the possibilities that lie ahead of you. Perhaps then the only time you will encounter any difficulty is whenever you get so over-confident and arrogant with your new found seduction powers that you venture outside the system and try to force a play when none seems possible. This is ***good*** – I encourage you to step beyond any limits that I might suggest for you and **charge forward** with as much risk-taking action as you can stand – *and then push yourself still farther!* This will accelerate your development greatly and is ultimately how you will learn to ***crush*** your demons one-by-one... driving them back into the pit of poor parenting and lousy social breaks from which they came.

Let's get started.

Without Embarrassment

Chapter 1: Is Your Ego Roadkill Yet?

Stop Trying to Get Lucky, Get Informed

Okay I admit it... I stole that subheading from the radio promo of some gambling outfit that advocates its "stone-cold-lock" football handicapping service with this cute little moto. ***Stop trying to get lucky... get informed.*** I liked it because it pretty much describes the approach that men have been taking with women since we were no longer allowed to club them over the head or buy them from their fathers for two pigs and a bale of grain. *Getting lucky.* The whole notion of "getting lucky" sums up what little control most men have over the course of events when it comes to the game of seduction. Try some desperate gambit, roll the dice, and see if it works. And if you do actually "get lucky", it's altogether unclear just what the hell you did that was so wonderful... therefore you can't repeat it! Next time you try the exact same approach, you get rejected flat out.

Oh, I get it... I guess this time you were "unlucky".

Well, forget all that bullshit. *Without Embarrassment* is going to give you the techniques, knowledge and confidence that you need to overcome your life-damaging fear of rejection. You will learn some of the classiest methods imaginable to influence and seduce the kind of great looking girls that you've always fantasized about having. ***It will do this by teaching you precisely how to act – in both look, attitude and moves – like a High Status, Dominant Male.***

Dominant male? Absolutely. You will soon come to appreciate how *this* type of behavior is what women truly want to see in a man who has romantic desires on them.

Trained by biology and social convention to ruthlessly reject men who are perceived as occupying a low rung on the Male Dominance Scale, women control a contest where they set all the rules and understand with fine precision exactly how the game of seduction should be played. Any man who can hold his own in this highly charged arena of combat will have captured her interest regardless of what he may lack in classically handsome physical attributes. Seduction is a game requiring masterful wits and an effortless sense of timing. You must learn to wield powerful psychological weapons with the delicacy of skating across the fragile surface of a soap bubble. One misstep, one clumsy comment, one impatient forced play and – pop – the chance for a successful seduction vanishes and is lost forever (at least with *that* particular woman).

Getting 90% of the way there is a total fuck up. You need to have a better edge than that. Now you have one.

BloodSport... Seducing Women

BloodSport? Roadkill? Sheesh...are you telling me that trying to meet and seduce women really all that dire? Isn't the grand game of wooing women supposed to be a light-hearted adventure taken on with playful humor and an air of restless good spirit?

Sure... but only if you don't suffer from **Severe Rejection Hyper-Sensitivity** like I used to. **SRHS** is a life-damaging psychological millstone around your neck which I had the sheer luck to discover has a very concrete underpinning in the way that you were treated by your primary caretakers (parents) as an adolescent. I'll discuss this problem in depth in Chapter 4 when I introduce you to the eye-opening concept of ***toxic shame***... a malady that lies at the heart of a constellation of various neuroses and thought distortions – not just this double-damned "shyness".

Look, if you can suffer all the various "kicks to the teeth" that this maddening game of approaching and seducing women often creates – and just let it all slide off your back like water from a duck – then you might as well stop reading right now. This book isn't for you. You can probably make some headway with women here and there, now and again. *Without Embarrassment* is for the guy who is stopped dead in his tracks by the thought of having his advances rejected... who stands helpless at the moment of opportunity when a beautiful, available girl is nearby with his feet rooted to the floor in anxiety... his mouth paralyzed to utter a single word or his body produce a stray movement that might be judged ridiculous or somehow diminishing – whose mind has gone white-hot blank in a haze of staggering **fear**.

> You and I are kindred spirits. I'll bet you've been to the place that I just described. Maybe you've lived there all your life. I know the agony of this kind of self-imposed isolation, and the frustration of trying to overcome it, or even just understand it. The key to freedom, as you will soon see, is **knowledge**.

Face it, on a most fundamental level, the reason why you are afraid to open your mouth and say something to a woman in a social situation is that you simply don't know **exactly what** to say. You understand that you have to say something that deviates from the ordinary run-of-the-mill type of small talk BS that we all engage in with friends and co-workers... but *what*? You know that the basis for seduction is *speech* – that you have to talk to a woman in a certain precise sort of way in order to get her to feel or reciprocate some kind of attraction towards you, but just *what* are these magic words? What topics do they focus on? How are they presented? Does the delivery matter more than the actual content of what you say? And if it does, then what does the unspoken nature of that delivery say?

I wrestled with these question endlessly in my forsaken youth, as I suspect you might have too (and might still be doing). One of the characteristics of us thoughtful, withdrawn (sexy) guys is that, besides being way too judgmental and hard on ourselves, we tend to ***think too much***. Intellectualizing and ruminating are **thought addictions** that give us a shield behind which to hide our true selves. You'll see that once I show you exactly how the mental, physical and gamesmanship aspects of seduction are developed and deployed, your powers of the mind can then be turned to the more productive task of applying these technologies for each individual women that you encounter, *instead of trying to invent* the whole damn technology right on the spot!

That's where paralysis comes in. How can you be expected to suddenly invent a seduction routine when the opportunity sneaks up and presents itself to you when you're least expecting it? Who could possibly operate under that kind of pressure other than a professional actor who's skilled in improvisational techniques? Hell, even if you're in a bar or a nightclub and have the time to stand around and daydream as all the pretty women swirl around you, you still can't think of what to say! Your overly-critical mind just keeps rejecting one thing after another until you run out of ideas and go home frustrated again.

That's because you understand intuitively that you just can't say any old thing... you have to say the perfect thing or you'll just get rejected and laughed at as a hopeless idiot. And rejection must be avoided at all costs right?

So how do you avoid all this pain and agony? **Knowledge**. When you have a specific plan of action all worked out in your mind beforehand, which includes an idea of what exactly you should be saying in order to make the best impression possible (and thus diminish your likelihood of being rejected), your ability to **take action** skyrockets. That's because you can approach the task with the confidence of someone who knows what they're doing. ***Knowledge and training breeds confidence in any kind of human endeavor.*** Seducing women is no different than any other task in that respect. (And remember I'm all about avoiding rejection at all costs, so my training has to be extensive in order to cover all or most eventualities).

Romantic Ratings

We accept or reject people for their romantic potential based upon an internal criteria that we carry around with us deep in our brains. We have categories where we place people of the opposite sex and then grade them accordingly. In order to avoid rejection, we have to do, say, or be something that fits us into the *Acceptance* category and keeps us out of the other person's *Reject* category. We can't do this until we understand the major basis upon which the sexes grade, and they are vastly different for men and women :

1) Men grade visually based on physical appearance. This, of course, is universally understood... no big mystery here. There is some degree of personal variation on what every man finds precisely most attractive, but the majority of men will fall into a tolerance range that's centered around our culturally defined image of female beauty or prettiness. The better she looks (young, sexually mature, healthy enough for child bearing, etc. etc.) the more desirable she is. Very straightforward. *Personality* figures into the relationship quagmire later... for now I'm talking about the kind of initial attractions that are based solely upon snap first impressions.

Women understand all this of course and work diligently with make-up, hair styling and clothes to present an enticing visual appearance for men to admire (most of them, anyway). What's **less** well understood however is the criteria that *women* use to grade men...

2) Women grade men by gathering a sense of their position on the grand scale of male pecking order, known as the Male Dominance Scale. And the higher up you are perceived to be on this scale, the more attractive you will seem... often in spite of a surprising assortment of physical shortcomings. This principle is understood in a peripheral sort of way by most men, but it doesn't seem to make the same kind of powerful impression on us the way that most women intuitively understand the need to keep their visual appearance as good as they possible can in order to remain attractive to men. We all know how this principle works in the extreme... that a Congressman, a Rock Star and a Rich Guy are more attractive to women (despite how they may look physically) than a janitor and a homeless bum. **But men for the most part don't perceive to what fine degree women can sense the subtleties of where men grade out on this all important "Male Scale".** Nor do they understand just how decisive their position is to a woman when she's trying to decide (even unconsciously) if a man is attractive to her in a romantic sense. I'll bet that most men probably think that their physical appearance is central to their attractiveness to women, when in fact their *attitude* is vastly more important. Why?...

Because attitude exposes your rating on that all important Dominant Male Scale!

This grading process takes into consideration your appearance (actually, your *packaging* in the form of how you dress and groom is most critical here) but is filled in primarily by how a woman senses your dominant behavior patterns. **This stuff is absolutely critical to know and understand!** I'll be delving into the topic of male dominance in great detail in Chapter 3, but for now just understand that if you think your situation is hopeless because you don't look like George Clooney or Ricky Martin, you're wrong. Dead wrong. **You can actually modify your attractiveness to women by how you behave and present yourself to her.**

Without Embarrassment is a structured program of deliberate actions that allow you to interact with women in a seductive-romantic fashion while protecting your rejection sensitive ego at all costs. This is how my system is *designed* to function.

Four Types of Rejection Sensitivity

First I'd like to discuss the structure of the physical-psychological makeup of most men from which their success or lack thereof with women can often be traced. This is really pretty common-sensical but I like to articulate the obvious in order to make sure that concepts later on have a clear basis for understanding:

Category 1... **Attractive – In-sensitive to Rejection**
The Best! This guy gets too much action...we hate him

Category 2...   **Attractive – Sensitive to Rejection**
Still gets laid because women drag him out of his shell

Category 3...   **Unattractive – In-sensitive to Rejection**
Can push through rejection to find his 5%er

Category 4...   **Unattractive – Sensitive to Rejection**
Worst situation possible! Hermits Club Charter Member

The first three categorizes I've described here probably don't include you, otherwise you wouldn't be bothering to read this book. So let's go through them quickly...

Category 1 is the best situation to be in – a guy who's *physically attractive* to women and *insensitive* to what little rejection he might pick up along the way. What can you say about a guy like this, except that he's got it too fuckin' easy? His experience with women is pretty much incomprehensible to the rest of us mortals. Bastard.

Category 2 describes a guy who's good looking and *attractive* to women, but has been handicapped by a shy nature for whatever reason and is highly *sensitive to being rejected* by them. He still makes out okay though because he can play the game of seduction *passively*. So long as he doesn't act too withdrawn or weird, women will push themselves at him because of his physical attractiveness... the women he knows as friends will set him up with their girlfriends, etc. This guy probably doesn't need any help, but *could* actually move up closer to the first category by studying the methods in *Without Embarrassment* and putting them to good use.

Category 3 is getting closer to home. Here's a guy who *doesn't have the great looks* to attract women, but he *shucks off rejection* like a duck sheds water. So he can at least get laid now and then, if only because he knows how to bull his way through loads of rejection until he finally scores. She probably won't be the prom queen, but that's alright. A Cat 3 guy can definitely make his life easier and start getting more decent looking women by following the advice in *Without Embarrassment*. At the very least, he won't have to make himself suffer through so much rejection between scores. In fact, combined with his natural insensitivity to rejection, he may find himself with too many women on his hands! Why? Because his **boldness** happens to be a *very powerful dominant male signal* that goes light-years in canceling out the fact that he won't be mistaken for Brad Pitt anytime soon.

Which brings me to the **Category 4 man...** ***unattractive*** **to women and highly *sensitive to rejection*.** Yeesh! This is by far the **worst** way to find yourself after you've already gone through the agony of a nerdy adolescence, only to arrive at what you'd hoped would be a more enlightened adulthood. **Not so, because you carry the roots of your problems buried deep within your unconscious mind.** I know because your humble author here was a Cat 4 schlep all his life until he finally figured it all out.

This situation is the absolute *pits* because -- besides the fact that you have no natural physical attractiveness to give you any sort of edge -- your crippling fear of rejection makes it impossible for you to interact in a positive manner. Your too-keen perception of how others may be regarding you only serves to drive you deeper into a cycle of withdrawal that tightens your social noose ever more securely. You are on a glideslope to becoming isolated, alone and increasingly seen as *strange*. **Deadly!**

I can show you how to slip this trap before it's too late. At times it may seem like more training than you can handle... but that's too bad. You've got a lot of catching up to do, so let's get started.

My Sad and Pathetic Story

I'm 5'6", unathletic, and have a nasty lisp to my voice. Women find me unattractive and unacceptable as a potential mate. They laugh at guys like me...

This is basically how I thought about myself for **years** – from adolescence to adulthood -- in the deepest core of my being. I'm talking about my unconscious mind, where fundamental statements such as these which describe your sense of identity (or at least, certain aspects of it) are held **un-critically as the truth**, and are then used by your conscious mind to form the basis of a set of internal rules that guide all of your essential behaviors and reactions to other people. Holding this specific sort of woe-is-me belief in the very core of your unconscious mind where it's *accepted as absolute truth* is particularly life-damaging because it **lays down the stench of the weak, rejected male all over you.** Even before you've ever actually been rejected by the very first girl you may've approached in high school for a date or a dance, you've already been rejected. The first person to have already rejected you, is YOU. And boy, does it show!

> *At all costs you must remove this stink of rejection from your being or women will smell it a mile away and happily join in on the social embargo which you yourself have already begun.*

If there's one concept that I'm going to pound relentlessly into your skull at every opportunity all throughout this book, it's the notion of **male dominant status**. If this sounds like some S&M shit that you'd find in one of your sick Mr. SpankyTime porno videos, I assure you it isn't. I never fully understood just how absolutely monumental the whole male dominant status thing was to women when it comes to the process they use in their minds to sort out men. With surprising speed, women will categorize men into *three* distinct groups:

> A) men from whom they would *accept* romantic overtures, and ultimately consider falling in love with, or at least fucking...
>
> B) men who, no matter what, could *never* be regarded as anything more than mere friends, and...
>
> C) men who completely *repulse* them for some reason (physical, social, character factor, biological, etc.)

The key issue here is **speed**... women can make this judgement about your romantic potential in a highly temperamental, almost capricious way. They seem to know within mere moments of meeting you which "pile" you belong in. That's why it's essential that you immediately make the **correct first impression** or you are forever banished to non-romantic "FriendsLand" where you simply cannot recover. Okay, *sometimes* you can recover, but it takes a Herculean effort. Why not learn to do things right the first time and save yourself the hassle of always trying to heal a blown opportunity? As you will discover, this notion of having to always remain light on your feet in an emotional-intellectual sense cannot be over-emphasized.

Anyway, now for some more of my stupid fuck-ups **as teaching tools**...

One of the worse ways to act around women is in a way that attempts to make them feel *sorry for you* so that they'll take you home and nurture your poor lonely little self back to emotional health with love and kisses and lots of wonderful, exhausting sex. Unfortunately, this trick only works if you happen to be a kitten, puppy or some other breed of cute furry animal (love and kisses only, no sex for Sparky...). If you're a human male however, you will soon find that attempting to appeal to a woman's natural instinct to love and nourish the downtrodden in such a pathetic way will only make you the object of her merciless and never-ending *contempt.*

All the so-called "nice guys" of the world learn this simple fact of life, or others like it, in the hardest possible way. They are way too needy (we'll go into all the reasons why later on), but for now understand that **acting needy and desperate is a signal of Low Male Status which is always a HUGE romantic turn off to women!**

You see, women all have an instinctive attraction to males who demonstrate specific behaviors which suggest that they have attained some kind of fairly high "pecking order" status over other men. It's similar to the way in which men are universally attracted to the visual appeal of a sexy figure and a pretty face. These subjective cues are genetically hard-wired into the "old" primitive brains of both sexes and resist being altered by social conditioning. In a similar fashion, women are drawn almost magnetically to males who exhibit high status demeanors and attitudes, and are driven away from males who display low status behaviors... personality traits that suggest he's been *made to submit to the will of other men in some way.*

Read that last sentence again and study it until sinks all the way to the bottom of your skull. Men who act in a way that denotes a low pecking order status did not get that way by being "pussywhupped" by women... *they got that way by being subjugated to the will other men.* What do I mean by that? Well, men compete for status against each other in all manner of subtle and overt ways in life, sports, school, the military, the workplace and even in families. There is a sorting and grading process that takes into account physical power, looks, intelligence, popularity, a willingness to take risks and economic status, in the earlier part of our lives. It graduates into a display of financial wealth and position in the workplace, achievements, accolades, community prominence and possibly career or political fame as we move into middle age and beyond. I'm sure you know what I'm talking about.

Different levels of male status produce different types of distinctive behaviors and attitudes that are commonly recognized... i.e., the high status male will typically display confidence, strength of character, generosity, likability, charisma and so forth. Meanwhile, the low status male is typically very angry due to being stepped on all his life and ordered around everywhere he goes. He will lack confidence, avoid eye contact, seem either desperate and needy (or aloof and bitter), can be controlling and obnoxious, and will have generally developed some kind of an annoying personality. The important thing to realize is that all these attitudes are formed in **response** to a lifetime of conditioning (either positive or negative) by the actions of other *men*, **not** women.

So women have learned to "read" these attitudes and personality quirks in order to understand just where a man fits on the male dominance scale, possibly in order to help them determine what kind of potential provider he might be for her children. And they're damn good at it! Conversely, men get a sense of a woman's potential to bear healthy children by looking for signs of physical attractiveness, which are primarily signs of youthfulness and fertility... 70% hip-to-waist ratio, big eyes plus small chin (childlike face), smooth skin (youth), ample breasts (post-puberty), slim figure (more childlike indicators), etc. So we make the exact same kind of judgements about women, but using a different criteria that plays into our different *strategy for reproduction*.

Which is all that "maleness" and "femaleness" really represents in nature, you know... two diverse yet complimentary strategies for reproduction. You see, men have plenty of sperm to spread around so our strategy involves attempting to inseminate as many females as we possibly can until we drop dead. Sheer chance will then assure that some of them will survive and prosper and become world leaders or major league baseball pitchers, and the more and varied the females that we can inseminate the greater our chances of successfully spreading our genes around become. Society doesn't like our biological strategy any more. They feel it's corrupt and have instituted something called *marriage* to put a stop to it.

Women on the other hand, faced with the daunting task of actually rearing the children produced in their bodies, need to find a male of some character who is willing to provide resources and protection for her brood over a long period of time. And, unlike most other mammals, women don't know exactly when they go into heat (estrus) either, so they need to *husband* a male to inseminate them on a regular basis in order to stand a good chance of becoming pregnant. Society admires and honors the female reproductive strategy. They feel it's righteous and have instituted something called *marriage* to promote it.

These differences in biological imperatives are the source of much of the "Venus and Mars"-type conflicts that occur between men and women, but here we're only concerned with the way in which females look for the appropriate signs and signals in a male's behavior that tell her if this **particular** man has any mating potential. *Seduction* of an enticing female is our goal here, and so our mission is to understand just exactly how the game of psychological persuasion is played, and how to play it in a way that harnesses our energies in a positive way instead of letting them run loose in the form of a paralyzing fear of rejection.

We'll get into this topic is greater detail later on as we study how to project those behaviors women find most attractive, and how to disguise those that give off the kind of repulsive signal that assures rejection. Key to this understanding is an actual *definition* of these behaviors and what they seem to be communicating to women on an unconscious level. **Seduction is really nothing more than learning how to avoid adverse behaviors, while adopting the attractive ones into your demeanor.**

In some ways men really have a much easier time of it – for while women must struggle mightily to put on a physically attractive appearance in order to appeal to men (sometimes in the face of overwhelming genetic misfortune), *we* only have to change our behaviors and attitudes in order to step into the arena and compete at a high level. Our actual physical appearance plays little into the calculus of female attraction (within reason, or course, Swarski...). Even this can be a cosmic revelation for some men, as many of you probably think you have to possess great natural looks to score with women, or else compensate for the lack of it with extraordinary wealth or fame. Not so. As you will soon discover, seduction is a game fought and won strictly with **attitude**.

Becoming Fearless is a Learned Skill

Believe it or not, you *can* become fearless... no matter how pitiful a coward you may be at present. There are many ways to approach the elimination of a personal, deeply-rooted fear that's been interfering with your life... desensitization, re-framing, anchoring, positive self-talk, or other forms of self-confidence training. **But the best type of confidence is always a natural one that flows from simply knowing what the hell you're doing!** The military can take a bunch of pimple-faced kids fresh out of high school and turn them into competent, battle-ready soldiers in just a few short weeks. They come in fearful and uncertain and come out confident and full of pride by being forced into situations where they discover deep reservoirs of inner strength that they didn't know they possessed.

The truly sad thing about fear is that we contain the potential to exhibit a lot more personal power than we often think, but the fear blocks our discovery of it... thus preserving its "imperial" status as unchallenged manipulator of all our behaviors. If we can somehow get beyond these paralyzing aspects of fear, whole new worlds will open up to us. Acceleration in our growth as individuals can be turned loose to develop an unstoppable momentum all its own. Institutions that train people to perform extraordinary tasks facilitate the unleashing of this anti-cowardly energy.

I can get you to destroy the rejection blocks that are making it impossible to enter into the first stages of the seduction process. The knowledge of what to say and, more importantly, *how to act* are the lonely beacons out of this rat maze.

Using Your Physical Flaws Like a Stun Gun

I showed you how those **Category 1** guys with all great looks have it pretty easy in life when it comes to making out with women. But *not* having great looks can also be an advantage too. Huh? Once again, the critical element is **attitude** and how you handle your perceived physical imperfections. Guys who aren't anything special to look at often carry around a kind of "woe-is-me" hang dog attitude about themselves when it comes to flirting with women. And because this attitude is so pervasive, women have for the most part come to expect it. In Chapter 5, when we dissect those distinctive male behaviors that communicate the kind of high pecking order status women are drawn to, you'll see that a boldness in taking the initiative to open a dialog and make first contact is viewed by most women as an unmistakable sign of high male status.

Of course, I'm not talking about being super-pushy which suggests a disconnect with reality, but the simple willingness to accept your role in the social convention that dictates men take the opening risk in a man/woman meeting opportunity is a big turn-on to them. This kind of risk is not **expected** from a man who doesn't have lady killer good looks. This particular "element of surprise" is something that no good looking guy can possess, and that gives us a weapon he can never have.

Again, the precise details of making a classy, successful approach will be hammered out for you later, but I just wanted you to understand how stepping out of character can work heavily in your advantage. Women think they know pretty much how guys will act based on their appearance and dress, so they find it pleasantly confusing to encounter a guy who acts out of character by displaying dominant male behavior (boldness) despite the fact that he doesn't look the 'hot guy' part. When a good-looking dude is in the area, women sense his presence and have their guard up for a possible approach by him – thinking that the stud's been emboldened by his previous successes with women. But they don't expect it from an "ordinary" guy and that leaves them open to our sneak attack of seduction! Women **do** grade status ahead of looks per se, and to encounter a man who signals high status "out of character" intrigues them tremendously.

I'm sure you know that a lot of great looking women end up with guys whose physical looks leave you scratching your head wondering what the hell's going on (he must have a massive tool, you think to yourself...). Hey, if he *did* have a king-sized wang, how did she know this at first glance? Did he whip it out and show it to her at the supermarket? No, he used his lack of looks in conjunction with behaviors that were more likely to be exhibited by someone with a lot of wealth and/or power to **stun her** during their initial encounter. Remember, no one can possibly know yourself as good as you... so your own self assessment – as projected by and communicated to others by your **critical first actions** – must be taken at its face value by someone else... at least until they get to know you better and can begin to form their own judgements about you. So get ready to set your phazer on **STUN** for whenever she pops up!

The combination of your being comfortable with yourself, "flaws and all", along with knowing the proper things to say on a first encounter can be an awesome weapon that you carry around with you always ready to use on a moment's notice. Our goal is to get you to this level of competency.

The Female Mating Call

Think you're the only guy who locks up in the presence of a cute chick? The problem seems to be as much cultural as it is personal. Here's some anecdotal evidence about how far ahead of the game you are if you can just manage to open your mouth and say something even remotely pleasing or enticing when you see a woman in a situation that could be defined as a "meeting opportunity".

I was reading an article in one of those women's magazines like *Cosmo* or something similar (don't worry, I always keep these psycho-babble rags hidden inside my copy of *Hustler* while reading at the library)... Anyway, it was all about how these really hot looking babes were having so much trouble getting a rise out of American men. This story was written by some super hot model-type chick, and all she did was lament about the fact that anytime she sees some cute guy and tries to lay the heavy flirt on him non-verbally (with long, pouty looks from across the room, that sort of thing) he gives her the aloof treatment and doesn't respond. Are all these guys scared of good looking girls or what?

She goes on to contrast the *European* male with his American counterpart. Miss Model and her foxy friend are sitting in some outdoor café in the Greek Isles somewhere (don't you just love the tough life these chicks lead?) Sampling the local drinks. Seems that it's Miss Foxy Friend's birthday, so Miss Model tells her to pick out any one of the handsome men scattered about the patio that she would like to fuck that afternoon as a kind of "present". Foxy chooses one, and all Miss Model has to do is meet eyes with the guy and hold his gaze for a few seconds. The Euro dude gets the message right away, walks straight over to introduce himself, and the seduction is off and running! Foxy is blown away at how easy it is for Miss Model to lure a man over, but Miss Model tells her later that "... this technique works everywhere I go all throughout the world, *except in America*". An American man will typically look away and act cool and aloof, pretending that he doesn't see my signal of interest in him. How sad." Poor Miss Model is discouraged by the way in which men everywhere seem willing to play the game of seduction except here in the good ol' USA.

Moral of the Story: The typical "Euro dude" understands what his role in the seduction game is, and has been culturally indoctrinated on how to respond to flirtatious women properly. He's a natural. You and I are clueless lunkheads. I know, I know... you just want to smack the snooty, jet-setting Miss Model upside her head. Nevertheless, her gripe is valid. Few men seem to realize what the deal is when it comes to flirting with women. Our training in this field really sucks **because it's pretty much no training at all.** Either that or a culturally-induced aversion to the whole topic exists because it doesn't fit in with our macho, Clint Eastwood-style of behaving around women.

Apparently European men don't labor under this stupid and confining self-image. They understand that when a woman summons them with a signal of curious interest they respond appropriately by promptly introducing themselves. The point is that *women always initiate a seduction* with some kind of non-verbal signal. **This is the female Mating Call.** *Non-verbal* is the key here – they will not (by most every social convention) usually be the first ones to utter a word. The "rules" of the game then state that it is the man's next move to acknowledge this signal and initial some kind of verbal greeting. It's our job to say something first. This is the moment where most of us rejection-adverse dimwits fall down and go boom. **Make no mistake about it though, women are the ones who choose the male, AND set the mating dance into motion.**

Just knowing this fact can put you light years ahead of all your competition, because many other guys have chosen to take themselves out of the game and stand on the sidelines and snivel that they never get laid. They've thinned the field for you. After reading *Without Embarrassment,* however, you'll be one of the rare guys who'll know how to recognize the female mating call in all its various articulations, and – most importantly – have the **precise** knowledge of what to do next jumping up and down inside your head!

You see, the game of seduction is all about knowing when to escalate and move forward to the next level. You must believe that women want you to win the game and steal their heart – but they will not throw the match and let you win without a contest.

You must play hard and smart, and you will be rewarded at every successful step along the way. *But, you must be willing to play.*

There are dozens of crucial decision points to breech along the way from the first trembling glance to the moment when you can finally slide your cock into her and make her crawl the walls. But *BEWARE*... the entire mating dance is as delicate as that soap bubble I talked about before. If you fail to "up the ante" at the proper moment... *POP* goes the seduction and you lose. There is rarely a second chance handed out along the way. Women tend to lose interest in a man with breathtaking whimsy if he misses an important signal that it's time to escalate to the next level of intimacy. Nice guys fall into the trap of being too timid to raise the stakes on her cue. This is why their lame attempts at seduction usually end up somewhere on the dead end avenue called... **FRIEND STREET!**

Knowing how to recognize and respond to a woman's mating cues will limit your rejection chances because you're not just charging headlong into her world uninvited. This gives you a huge edge. **Remember, women choose, men respond.** Will you score easily every time? No. Because her call only indicates that your visual appeal and your attitude suggests a high dominant male status which has placed you into the category of possible mating material. I say *possible*... she won't know for sure where you stand in her heart until much farther on down the road as the seduction unfolds, and you amaze her by clearing every hurdle along the way ('cause you read this book... that's why!).

"...but women never look at me and send me any 'come hither' signals, I'm too ugly..."

No, you're just ill-informed and probably untrained in this arena of life, but I'm going to change all that right now.

Without Embarrassment

Chapter 2: Seduction: How the Game is Played

Establishing Yourself as a Player

One of the damndest principles in all of life is that wretched one which insists that the rich get richer while the poor simply get poorer. You only have to look around at nearly every aspect of how society operates in order to observe its effects in action. For those already doing well financially, there seems always an anxious banker or drooling businessman standing ready to push still another opportunity at them so they can make more money (that they hardly need), while some joker slaving away for minimum wage works himself to the bone for every single dollar he can wring out of his miserable job without anyone ever giving him a shot at some easy money. An actor who already has more movie offers than he can handle will have directors and studios pestering him relentlessly to take on their pet project, while the struggling actor can't scare up a walk-through bit part in a B movie to save his life. And so it goes.

Well, as one of life's major losers in the arena of love, sex and romance, I don't have to tell you that this principle operates with remarkable precision in the dating and mating game. The "Rich" (i.e. guys who are already getting more action than they can handle) always seem to be encountering a constant stream of opportunities to become romantically entangled with new women, while the "Poor" (guys who couldn't buy a date with a woman) never so much as catch a hint of interest from any chick. Sound familiar? Did you ever notice how women always seem to want to flirt with any guy who appears to be hanging out with his girlfriend, or maybe just talking to some other girl in a bar? Meanwhile, the schlep who's standing around by himself looking for anyone to talk to may as well have the goddamn Bubonic Plague!

While there may be a variety of reasons for this near universal state of affairs – some of which have to do with only wanting to eat from someone else's plate like a spoiled little brat (which describes the character of many women, incidentally) – I personally believe that the major motivation for this catty female behavior is simply that women look to *other women* for clues about the acceptability of men as mating partners. One of the most important of these clues is merely **the romantic interest that another women expresses in a man.** In other words, the more women seem to be interested in a guy, the more interesting he becomes to the other women surrounding him. To a certain degree, women want to steal each other's men!

Can you see how this "me too" behavior assures that the rich just keep getting richer? It's like our friends the Rock Stars who have to beat the groupies off with a stick (while you just get to beat off... period). The adoration of a group of deranged women catches hold and spreads like wildfire throughout legions of girls, almost as if they're hypnotized (actually, they are... *self-hypnotized*). This phenomenon has displayed itself from Elvis to Michael Jackson to Ricky Martin and will probably continue to do so until we're all dead and gone.

Men typically don't act this way around women rock stars because their status as successful performers is not impressive to men. In fact, female fame and success can be downright intimidating. Only the *physical attractiveness and sex appeal* of a females is enticing to the male. This points out in crystal clear fashion something that you will come to understand about women or that I will die trying to teach you: **Women are *not* impressed with male appearance (so long as you maintain good hygiene and style) nearly as much as they are impressed with your perceived *status* on that mysterious male dominance scale that I referred to before, and that we'll discuss at length in Chapter 3.**

Therefore, one of your primary goals in moving up the ladder from loser to chooser is to be viewed by the women around you as a "player". All sorts of good things will begin to fall your way once you establish this impression of yourself in their minds. Did you ever wonder why none of your female friends ever fix you up with their cute cousins when they're available? Probably because they don't see you as being a player. You've got to work on changing that perception of yourself if you would like to see a galaxy of romantic opportunities open up in your life.

You see, one of the strange, inverted rules of life (that people who complain they never get a break don't seem to grasp) is that the universe will always strive to *help people who try to help themselves.* When people sense that you are genuinely struggling with some kind of problem in your life, they will come out of the woodwork with all sorts of offers to lend a hand. "The Lord Helps Those that Help Themselves"... goes the old saying, and the truth of this wisdom extends to all areas of life, not just the subject of this book. Once your friends and associates get the notion that you're a **player** and working the dating field aggressively, you suddenly become "thought of" in that sense when people are considering hook-ups for their single friends, or women spread the word of your availability along through the female gossip grapevine. Now you become the center of attention whenever opportunities present themselves!

In order to reach this high point in your social development, you're going to have to bootstrap yourself up from shy loner to "Mr. Popular" and you'll have only yourself to rely on in the beginning. Your task is to practice what you learn in a step-by-step fashion and just try to keep making steady progress as you study the techniques in this book. At some point when you least expect it, people will come to see that you have become "for real", and they will quite suddenly *throw their weight behind your cause.* You must have faith that the process will gain momentum and take on a life of its own after a while.

This was actually one of the most pleasant of surprises of my own personal transformation when I finally got wise to the ways of seduction, and I'm sure that it will be one of yours too.

It's All Subconscious With Her

Many of the impulses and 'prime directives' for finding a suitable mating partner are hardwired deep within the primitive parts of the human brain. Some women can just knock you right out the moment you first set eyes on them, while others barely move the needle on your peter meter. Why? Because an unconscious image exists within you of what your ideal female looks like. When you happen to stumble across someone who matches this internal portrait walking down the street or standing in line at the supermarket, you are assaulted with all sorts of alarms and whistles going off in your brain. You instantly launch into all sorts of uncontrollable sexual fantasies.

Since spreading his seed far and wide is the male's most elementary biological imperative, it takes only seconds for him to determine if any particular woman is someone he'd like to mate with, since obvious signs of health and youth (adequate breeding potential) is really all he needs. In that sense it's fairly easy for the male. For us the calculus of attraction is relatively straightforward. For women it's more complex... *and therein lies the challenge of seduction.*

The female must make a determination about the suitability of a man not just in terms of his visual attractiveness, (which only partly reveals his genetic stock) but also his character. Since it will be necessary for him to contribute his time and resources in order to successfully raise any offspring resulting from their union, this takes more than just a quick visual once over, but interestingly enough, the female brain is also wired with mental shortcuts that allow her to promptly size up a potential mate. **Playing to these *subconscious shortcuts* can powerfully affect the way in which you are perceived and categorized in her mind.**

In other words, **First Impressions are critical!**

You see, a woman's interest in mating always begins deep within the limbic portion of her brain where her most basic instincts for procreation reside. All your efforts to seduce her must take into account *an essential duality of her psychology* so that you are simultaneously stimulating two divergent parts of her consciousness in order to lead her along towards that coveted moment of sexual surrender. 1) You petition her **higher conscious mind** with your words and the intriguing content of your speech. At the same time, 2) you must quickly begin to signal your desirability as a sexual partner to her **unconscious limbic brain** with your attitude and subliminal behavior patterns. You must get both aspects of this mojo working correctly or any budding seduction will fizzle with stunning dispatch. And unfortunately, *you* will likely be the one being dispatched!

The mistake that you're probably making right now is being focused too much on what you're saying (your content) while completely ignoring the critical messages that you need to be conveying with your attitude (your intent). This could be why you are consigned to "just friends" hell with many of the girls you already know and may've had passionate designs on. While being friendly or even interesting might impress her *conscious* mind, you'll never engage any romantic interest in yourself without calling out to her primal instincts with compelling communications to her lower brain – statements about your male sexual self that can only be transmitted **non-verbally through specific actions and attitudes.** For any seduction to succeed, you must relentlessly convey your desirability as a mating partner *to her subconscious mind* with the goal of stimulating her primeval instincts into awakening. This is where thoughts of love, lust, sex and all that other good stuff flow from.

> The supreme trick to seduction is lighting up all those captivating thoughts of mating and breeding in her unconscious mind (where they manifest themselves as intuitions rather than actual well-formed thoughts) and getting them focused in *your* direction!

NOTE: whatever you do, don't try to communicate your

"desirability" by directly proclaiming it and telling her what a sexy guy you are. This comes off as totally ridiculous! Your sex appeal has to be self-evident through your *actions and attitudes* or it simply doesn't exist for her. It's the same way as if some unattractive chick came up and told you how beautiful she is... but she was actually just fat and dumpy. Would her delusional self-assessment have any chance of changing your mind? I don't think so. And neither will yours. So don't go off trying to short circuit the seduction process by just flat out stating what must be communicated subtly to her subconscious mind. You must have patience to become a seducer. Your approach and style must ooze patience and therefore, *confidence*.

Why patience? Because dominant males are in no hurry to score with any particular woman, no matter how foxy and enticing she might be. They have plenty of women in their universe, right? Desperate nerds are impatient because their blue balls are giving them fits. If you need it so bad that it shows, you won't get any. It's the guy who *already* has more than he needs who remains knee deep in new opportunities. For love, money, whatever. You have to act "rich" even while you're still poor until the riches finally give in and start flowing in your direction. That's the secret.

As for the secret to seduction, understanding how to balance the verbal and non-verbal aspects of communication with the intent of getting her to see you as a potential mate forms the essential difference between a classy seducer and a clueless loser.

The Nice Guy Blues Explained

Just friends? Again? *Aaaarrghhh!* That's the most hated of all things to hear from any woman that you'd like to bang. When you finally get up the balls to show how you really feel about her she just wants to be your buddy. This seems to be the bane of many intelligent, but passive, men. In their eagerness to demonstrate how well they can connect with women and understand them, they end up "solving the mystery" that forms the basis of the dynamic sexual tension between men and women. As a result, all the passion goes out of any potential relationship between the two of you. You've engaged her conscious mind – but have failed to affect her limbic, primitive mind where all her lust triggers are hidden. Guess what...

You've just become her new GIRLFRIEND!

One of the major gripes of passive men is that great looking women always reject them for jerks who mistreat them. Despite the best efforts of these wonderful, passionless men to adore every girl they meet and raise them high up on a pedestal, the best women always seem to gravitate to this hated town jerk instead. Since Mr. Bad Ass Jerk fails to grasp the magnitude of his good fortune, he eventually ends up abusing his goddess. What a tragedy. Blind to the power of her own great beauty, of course, goddess runs around kissing his ass and taking all the crap he can dish out... until he finally dumps her, beats her up or ends up on extended holiday at the local state prison. If only she could have opened her eyes and seen fit to choose Mr. Passive instead -- her world could have been a paradise of love and happiness. She just doesn't get it though. But don't worry... we still love her – no, *adore* her – anyway. We're **nice** after all.

The never-ending saga of the scorned nice guy is a pattern of perceived injustice that begins in high school and trails these losers all around everywhere they go. You yourself might even be in a situation where you've befriended one of these great looking girls (who refuse to see you as a *man*), and you actually spend your vacant hours sympathetically listening to her piss and moan about all the various low life dickbrains she gets involved with. Typically she ignores your good advice to forget about these jerks and immediately goes back for more punishment anyway. Then she calls you up and tells you all about it.

Who do you think is the real jerk here?

My prose drips with sarcasm instead of sympathy for you.

Why? Because if you're a nice guy you've established a residence at the very **bottom** of the male dominance scale and you deserve everything that you get (or, more precisely, don't get). Do you know what the male equivalent of the nice guy is? **Fat girls.** Yes that's right, *fat girls*. Most men won't even consider dating them unless they are desperate bottom feeders themselves who've long since given up any hope of catching a decent looking girlfriend. How come? *Because they don't turn us on sexually.* Therefore we don't bother with them. This works the same for both men and women. We cannot force ourselves to become romantically involved with people who don't speak to our most primitive sense of lust and desire. Love is not a conscious act. It is a **primal** one.

But wait a minute, how could a woman not have some romantic feelings for a guy who only wants to love her, worship the ground she walks on, drink her bathwater and generally make her every wish come true?

Two reasons... first the obvious: *undeserving adoration* gives people the creeps! It's a sign of mental instability that involves deep issues of control, most likely forged in the crucible of a lousy childhood. Hey, wanna know a secret?... **Nice guys aren't really all that nice.** It's a front. In reality, they're passive-aggressive controllers. They've learned how to use "niceness" as a manipulative weapon to regulate the actions and responses of people around them. *Their goal is the inflation of their own ego at the expense of others.* In doing so, the nice guy avoids intimacy and any true emotional involvement because his actions involve the subtle transfer of shame to the target of his fake generosity, often in a subliminally hostile fashion. He tends to inhibit the emotional growth of both himself and his partner because no one can ever get any honest feedback of their actions from him... everything always gets absorbed into his smothering, unrealistic, 'nice' behavior. No one can get angry at him without feeling guilty of course, another powerful weapon of control in his toolbag.

That was the quick psychoanalysis of the situation – something we'll dig into in far greater depth when we explore your fucked-up head in Chapter 4. But for now it's critically important to understand the *second* reason why women dislike nice guys...

It's a sign of low male status! And low status guys are nothing more than "fat chicks" to women. How is this so? Simple... any psychologist will tell you that people will attempt to control the actions of others around them to the degree that they themselves secretly feel that they are not in control. In other words, controlling behavior (which is all that "niceness" really is) sends a clear signal that a person has no genuine, recognized position of power or social/economic status in society. A person caught in this situation will often try to compensate for his social deficiency by trying to control others around him as much as he possibly can. However, since he possesses little or no actual authority to exercise a controlling influence *directly*, he must resort to various forms of trickery or employ some kind of psychological coercion in order to get the job done.

Passive aggressive-behavior (withholding the full expression of your effort or personality as a way to punish someone until they relent and let you have your way), flying into violent rages, and being aggressively "nice" are all attempts to exert control. This type of conduct stems from the deeply-rooted sense of insecurity that (for men) comes from having very little real authority... i.e., being *dominated* by other males in the world as opposed to being dominant over others.

It's your status on this male pecking order totem that ultimately makes you attractive to women... or <u>un</u>attractive.

If you've been red flagged as being far down the male status totem pole, then women will have little interest in you as a mate, and the more beautiful the female (*high* status for her) the more this is likely to be true. So guys who try real hard to please and smother women with their promises of ridiculous love and devotion are seen as meek and therefore undesirable. Fat chicks. They're trying to compensate for not having any power or authority in life, and it's pathetically obvious. Get it?

Don't be a "nice" guy. I know... you can't help it. We'll examine and work on the reasons *why* you've been behaving this way in Chapter 4.

Anyway, you're telling me that some bad-boy jackass who mistreats women is actually preferable to Mr. Nice Guy? In a sense, the jerk's status is often no better than the nice guy. That's why he's a jerk... i.e., because he's a low life who's never really accomplished anything, is marginally educated, probably works some low class job, etc. But it can take a woman longer to discover this because his tough guy persona is a more acceptable psychological mask to her than the niceness cover-up. At least the jerk can wield the power of physical intimidation now and then. Some men are scared of him (probably all the nice guy pussies) and this tends to brandish some fake status, albeit of a very savage sort. (Threats don't get you very far in the modern world, money does.) Any female who is attracted to the jerk eventually finds this out.

But look at how long and difficult a process it is for her to disengage with this guy. This only goes to show how – once properly seduced by having her most basic mating instincts switched on – a woman can remain thoroughly captivated by a man's aura, even one that doesn't serve her true interests. It remains so even after it's long since become obvious to everyone else around her (including you, her good ol' gossip buddy) that he's using her and playing her for the complete fool.

Nice Guys on Parade

Here's 4 examples of what I mean by the type of nice guys that women will keep as a friend, but show absolutely no sexual interest in:

The Easy-going Pleaser. He tries too hard to be pleasant and thoughtful at every turn, but there's something about him that suggests he's really very self-centered. There's the sense that all his attempts to "act nice" are really based in insincerity and are *manipulative* in a very sly sort of way...

The Geisha Boy. Acts servile or submissive by always *apologizing for his actions,* especially those that might suggest he harbors any sexual desires or motives. One of the worst things that you can do around women is to act apologetic for your desires as a man. **This completely emasculates you in the eyes of any woman.** Women expect men who are interested in them (sexually) to show it in some way. Geisha Boy may as well be wearing a sign on his ass that says "Kick Me".

The Turning Worm. After doing so much terrific stuff for a woman while absolutely insisting that he wants nothing in return for his all his wonderful generosity, he suddenly gets all pissed off (usually by becoming pouty) when she finally gives him what he claims he wants and comes to take all his good deeds for granted and shows him no appreciation whatsoever. *That's because Mr. Nice Guy is really very **selfish** at heart.* Remember, he's trying to use his niceness in the same way that a bully uses physical intimidation to get his way. Down deep, he expects a result that's more in line with his true desires (i.e., getting the woman to "love" him). When he doesn't get what he wants, he sinks into standoffishness. But, since he's careful to keep his true motives hidden and unspoken, others don't understand why he's always being so "moody". This frustrates him even further, and a descending spiral of nastiness ensues.

The Know-it-All. The more aggressive breed of nice guy is also something of a *meddler*, constantly making "suggestions" or telling you how you "should" be doing everything. This one doesn't have the patience for a passive approach, and instead seeks to control by pushing people to do things the way he wants them done (by "suggesting"). This kind of subtle attempt to manipulate is very annoying once a person catches on to what's really happening.

If you saw yourself in there somewhere, then I hope you'll take all this in the spirit of how it's presented... as an attempt to help you. Someone has to tell you how screwed up you are, so it may as well be me... a guy you'll probably never meet and get a chance to scream at in person (or punch in the face). Your buddies are probably too uncomfortable to broach the subject or are simply embarrassed by your self-defeating behavior.

The last word on the nice guy friend is this: **friends don't get laid.** You must strive to establish and maintain a man-woman tension in your relationships at all times. Remember it's the intense emotional states that women crave from their relationships with men, not just sex. They are consummate romantics – and for them romance is not just some ideal that would be nice to have if they can manage it... they want to feel romantic with a *special* man always... and for life!

You should understand that a woman's lover cannot be a converted "buddy" – it has to be someone who stirred up her deepest instincts to mate and copulate with actions that spoke to her identity as a woman right from the very start. *Only a few people in her life will ever be considered in this special way by her.* You don't earn that special place in a woman's heart by going through the usual channels of friendship and common experience, you have to slip in through the back door of her subconscious mind by immediately provoking feelings of lust and passion in her from the very first few moments of contact... or the opportunity is lost forever.

Words as Power Tools vs. Pointless Chatter

One of the major foul-ups guys make with women is that their conversations often tend to be unfocused and pointless. When we get into the nuts and bolts of how to negotiate your seductive conversations with women, you'll see that you'll need to be careful to manage both the content and the intent of your words if you have any desire to eventually direct the relationship along towards the bedroom. Things have to occur in a certain order. If you try to skip over an important step, the seduction will explode in your face like one of those trick cigars in a Bugs Bunny cartoon. You must **read and react** to her cues to escalate the nature of your relationship at the proper time, or you're dead meat.

This means you must keep the *goal* of what you're attempting to accomplish always somewhere in the forefront of your mind. Make sure that your actions remain natural and appropriate to the situation... don't just focus in all laser-like on your mission and buzz through the steps like some kind of robot. You have to stay light on your feet and respond correctly to what is happening around you. No two encounters will ever go off exactly the same in real life, no matter how much you rehearse for them in your mind beforehand.

Seduction is a little like *fishing*... when you hook a big one you have to let her run for a bit to tire her out, right? Slowly you reel in some slack, then the fish fights back and runs and you let her do so... then you reel her in a bit closer. Keep this up and pretty soon she's in your net! Don't try to turn a seduction into a lot of frantic reeling and pulling and tugging... you've got to let her run free or she'll only slip the hook and swim away. Remember, people only want what they can't have. You make yourself seem like the prize catch by being confident (*attitude!*), by not coming off as too anxious or desperate, and by allowing the entire seduction to unfold at it's own relaxed pace.

Be careful, however, that you don't get too damn relaxed about everything to the point where you fail to actively advance the seduction towards its ultimate goal. Being passive is cool, but don't get carried away. It degrades into simple inaction after a while and then random forces take over. These forces can never be counted on to act in your favor unless you're incredibly lucky and we already know that your luck sucks. **Balance!!!**

Words are everything in the arena of seduction. You must use words as power tools to rachet a man-woman relationship along to its next logical level... gradually building a womans' intrigue in yourself and leading her along towards the idea of becoming your lover. This is what the concept of **escalation** is all about, and it's an absolutely vital one. We'll get deeper into the mechanics of escalation in Chapter 5. For now though, I only want to caution you about the pitfalls of falling into a pattern of pointless chatter in your conversations with women. Some of what you say can be lighthearted B.S. of course, but it's important to always keep your eye on the prize and be on the lookout for her signals to escalate to the next level. *Then be ready to act!*

You're on a mission, never forget.

Instant Charisma and Classy Courage

One of the best ways to elicit a positive response from any woman is to have a presentation about yourself that appears **charismatic**. Your prospects for acceptance go way up (and, conversely, your chances of rejection go way down) if you can aspire to come across with charisma and a stylish flair. What is charisma? Webster's defines it as "**a.** the power or quality of winning the devotion of large numbers of people   **b.** Great personal magnetism: charm." Now, for our purposes we won't consider the religious co-definitions or the fact that you're probably not interested in taking over a country and ruling it with an iron fist a la Adolph Hitler (then again, maybe you are?). In any case, we only care about how to use the concept of charisma on a personal basis, one-to-one with some hot little fox that we're trying to impress. Incidentally, charm or finesse or even *style* might be a good way to think of it too, but these terms are equally vague. What I mean by charisma is this... **it's the ability to make someone feel BETTER about themselves as a direct result of having encountered you!**

If you walk around all day like some miserable bastard with a scowl plastered to your ugly mug, or if you always endeavor to put someone down in a clever way with a subtle sarcasm whenever you see them, then you're a skilled practitioner of *anti*-charisma. A person feels psychologically diminished as a direct result of having encountered you, having sensed your value judgement of them in some way as being worthless.

Humans are simple creatures on a surprisingly fundamental level: we seek pleasure, and (more forcefully) avoid pain.

If an encounter with you is distasteful in that it causes some degree of put down or rejection, what happens when that person has an opportunity to encounter you next time? They cross the street. They avoid you. You suck. But hey, can't they take a joke? What's the matter with them, are they super sensitive or something? Shit, if they think I'm bad they ought to try being me for a day, and see how much garbage I have to eat from other people...

Nobody cares. They don't. *Your rotten life is a direct result of your own actions and attitudes.* Other people only reflect back to you what they see. Don't tell me all about your sick childhood and all the other misfortune that may've caused your sorry outlook because I'm telling you right now that you can stick the whole load of it straight up your ass. I don't care. If that sort of thing is the source of you problems then it's just a lot of crap that you'll have to overcome on you way to becoming a master seducer.

Your mission from this moment on is to trash bag your internal pain and begin acting in a way that leaves people with a good feeling about themselves after they've been in your presence. In theory, it's that simple. In practice, it'll take some real determination. You'll have to keep in mind that a seducer is a manipulator, but a benevolent one. The idea is to leave any woman that you encounter feeling better about herself after having met you than before your paths crossed. Flattery is the primary tool that you'll employ, but in a very specific way that I'll show you later.

Once you practice this and start to become good at it, *your personal courage in such situations will begin to go up steadily.*

That's because once you know you have the power to elicit a positive response from someone your fear of being rejected by them diminishes to nothing. Remember that the rejection you fear so much is partly a reflection of your own miserable character and attitude. Change this and your "rejectability" changes with it. And anything that we can do to reduce your fear of rejection is a major step forward, right?

It's easy to have courage when you have little or no fear. Moreover, your brand of courage will be **classy** because it's based on your own personal style of charisma that makes people feel good about themselves. I once read in a magazine somewhere that if you can be flattering, funny and fearless most any woman can be yours, (and this article was written by a woman). Two out of these three are possible simply by making a commitment to being charismatic in your approach towards women, and by taking a relaxed, lighthearted approach to things the third one is easily in reach as well. It's as easy as having the right tone of voice, remembering to stay on message, and keeping in mind the goal of having her *associate good feelings with being around you.* You're the honey, and she's the bee. You're too cool to try, you *attract*.

Never forget how magnificently you score points by **demonstrating courage** to women... this more than anything else instantly ranks you way up high on the Male Dominance Scale, and it does so as a first impression. That's why all those dummies who couldn't hold a candle to your brilliance get the girls while you get to go home and pound your meat... because the one thing they do have is the courage to open their mouths and say *something*. What they actually say can often be lame or even juvenile, but once again it's the non-verbal **communication of their status by way of their attitude** that's given more weight than the actual words they say anyway. It gets the little wheels of lust turning in the woman's subconscious mind. That keeps the jerk in the dating and mating category and makes sure that he stays out of the despised "just-friends zone". So, while you're agonizing over just the perfect thing to say, jerk-o's already said it with his **willingness to take a social risk** and is now waltzing away with your woman.

Don't worry, you'll be in this fight soon.

How Does Your Blood Smell?

Say what? *My blood?...* are we hoping to score with Elvira Mistress of the Dark now or what? No, but get this: there's a curious aspect to the man-woman seduction and mating dance that plays itself out on a strictly biochemical level. This is going to sound wacky but I wanted to make you aware of it before we move on to the meat and potatoes of my system just to show you that not every factor in seduction is controllable no matter how good you get with women.

It's been documented with hard medical evidence that a woman responds to the body odor of a man in such a way that it effects her decision about whether or not a *particular* man holds any mating potential for her! It turns out there are olfactory clues present in your sweat – (sweat is derived from your blood) – that acts as a very crude but effective marker of your genetic make up. Specifically, women have an ability to detect the character of a man's MHC genes, which have something to do with the expression of certain properties in your immune system. This talent is not limited to human females, many other animals display a similar ability (you know how dogs like to stick their noses up each other's asses to say hello), but it's somewhat surprising because people don't typically rely on their sense of smell to make choices about things.

What's the significance of a woman being sensitive to a man's smell? Well, it actually seems to give them a better chance of locating a mating partner who has a high probability of fathering a healthy baby for them. The research on all this is quite fascinating. It turns out that women are drawn to the *natural* (unperfumed) scent of any man whose MHC genes turn out to be completely **dissimilar** to her own. We're talking actual Body Odor here – this has nothing to do with any type of cologne or that funky 'pheromone spray' that you bought from some website. The women in the study were all genetically typed from blood samples before the experiment was conducted to determine what their DNA classification was so as to contrast them with the men.

It seems that men with **mismatched** MHC genes were reported to exhibit a pleasant, sexy, almost intoxicating smell to the women who participated in the research study (performed by sniffing the soiled t-shirts of men they'd never met before, I kid you not!). On the other hand, men whose MHC genes were a **match** produced a body odor the women reported as being foul, repulsive and sometimes even nauseating. Different women had strikingly different opinions of the 'scent of a man', but the patterns always showed that mismatched DNA was *pleasant* while matched DNA smelled disgusting. What's amazing about all of this is that the women's reaction was visceral and occurred on a profoundly unconscious level.

It appears that the female brain has built into it a primitive, deep-seated means of finding a mate who has a high chance of giving her strong, healthy babies... while rejecting those males whose DNA might actually be dangerous to the health and viability of her future offspring. ***How's that for complicating matters of seduction?***

The curious thing is that there doesn't seem to be any similar capability among males. We're programmed primarily to look for the *visual* signs of healthy child-bearing capability in the women we find attractive... i.e., youthfulness, 0.7 hip-to-waist ratio, large breasts, etc. However, it's interesting to note that women, too, are programmed just like men to seek out the perfect partner for procreation, it's just that their sensory apparatus makes their detection methodology different. Since men use vision we can stand back and make all the assessments we need to make remotely from a distance. Women, though, need to get in close and actually get a whiff of a man. Imagine that! This whole thing becomes especially complicated in modern life because clothing and deodorant soaps and colognes can interfere with her olfactory assessment, in effect *masking* our true genetic nature from her.

This is why it might take several dates, and probably a casual encounter where she can get a sniff of your BO somehow (like right after a workout), before a woman knows for sure if a guy has any real hope of becoming her sexual partner.

This creates the possibility that an otherwise friendly girl might go very suddenly cold on you if she gets a sniff of the "real" you on a third date! This whole situation is further confused by the fact that most women probably don't understand what's happening to them when it comes to male scenting. At least not on a direct scientific level the way that you now do. They're just reacting to instinctual urges and puzzling "feelings" about a guy. *"I don't know why I didn't like him, he was real nice and we were having fun together... there was just **something** about him I didn't like after a while. I can't explain it!"* she might lament to her girlfriends later on. And she will be tormented by her crazy feminine frivolity for weeks to come. Too bad.

So what's the point of telling you all this? Only to make you aware that there are aspects to the game of mate selection that lie completely beyond your control because they are most likely *genetically hardwired into us.* Especially so with women, who have a much greater biological and sociological stake in the act of reproduction than do men (who only provide the starting fluid, after all...).

What this means is that there is no way to guarantee absolute 100% success with every woman out there – no matter what amazing system for meeting women that you are trying to take advantage of... mine or anyone else's. The dance of seduction invokes such deeply primordial sensations that it can't be completely manipulated with clever words and perfect attitudes alone. In other words, you could do everything I show you in this book absolutely perfectly to the letter and you could *still* get rejected once she catches a good sniff of your DNA... and it turns out to be a mismatch!

Bottom line: *There's just no way to drain all the risk out of meeting women, no matter how good you ever become at it.* Certain aspects of biology that are simply out of your control. Perhaps this is why women value the demonstration of the characteristic of **risk taking** so much. The more a man seems willing to risk harm to his ego (since he can never be sure how a woman will respond to his advances), the more flat-out impressive he appears to her.

I just wanted you to appreciate this plain and simple fact of life as a kind of final punctuation mark to the discussion we've been having in this chapter about the nature of seduction. I don't suspect this'll pose too much of a problem with many of you guys, because I feel your problem is more about fearing being rejected *immediately* when you try to approach a woman rather than later on after you've dated for awhile. For some reason, that doesn't seem to be such a devastating event as does the snap negative judgement of a perfect stranger (especially a really cute one!). **Instant rejection creates a cascade of negative self-defeatist thought patterns that can corrode away your confidence real fast.** Well the knowledge and techniques in this book will get you past that very frightening initial meeting phase... the part of being with women that's been giving you nothing but grief all your life.

Just be sure to wear a touch of good cologne so that, when you're on the hunt, you can confuse her sensitive sniffer long enough to at least buy yourself some time to bag her!

Chapter 3: The Male Dominance Scale Exposed

Are You a 2.5 or a 9.5?

The notion that men are ranked by women for their attractiveness as sexual partners is something that a lot of guys either ignore, reject or are frightened of so badly that they refuse to even think about. You do so at your peril however, because the fact of the matter is that this ranking process goes on all the time and is just as important to women in their decision making process as it is for men. We know what we like when we check out a pair of killer legs or gaze deep into some awesome cleavage. Well it's time to fess up to the fact that women have a similar calculus they use to grade men.

Similar, but definitely not the same.

This is where a lot of guys screw up, thinking that women probably rate men in the same general way that we do... namely, *by physical attractiveness.* While these factors do come into play, they are not nearly as important to women as they are to men. Guys casually walk around with a system in their heads for ranking women that ranges anywhere from the lowly, ugly "1's" all the way up to that rare creature... the perfect "10". This ranking process is for the most part unconscious – that's to say it runs far below our level of ordinary awareness. But did you ever notice how it seems to be constantly ON? You are always making judgements of all the women that you encounter. In fact, you're probably so skilled at it that it happens within seconds without your even being aware of it! I doubt you actually go around assigning numerical values to the women you see during the course of the day like a complete geek, but these ratings make themselves felt in the back of your mind as a kind of impression or "intuition" nonetheless. Admit it... it affects how you relate to women, from cold and indifferent to stupidly fawning like a silly dumb ass.

Well, don't think for a moment that they're not doing it right back at you!

It's **how** they're doing it that most men are clueless about. Both sexes weigh several common factors like physical look, body style, personality, etc. into the equation of love. Here's the critical difference though: men incorporate physical attractiveness into 90% of that equation and cram most of the other factors (like, oh I don't know... personality...) into the other 10%. Women also take physical attractiveness into consideration, but typically give it only a 20% or 30% consideration when sizing up a man. Other aspects of our personality are far more important. The mistake men make is focusing most of their effort trying to attract a woman based on their own physical appeal. They waste time goofing around with their hairstyle or collecting the latest piercings or by working on a set of totally ripped abs at the gym, etc. While I certainly won't say that none of this matters, it doesn't matter as much as you probably think it does. Don't get me wrong, being as much of a hunk as your genetics will allow certainly helps your cause – but it merely gets *integrated* into an overall picture of you that tends to define your style... and that's mainly about attitude and the way in which you carry yourself as a man.

She doesn't just see a great looking guy and think he's automatically "the bomb" or her "type" because of the way he looks. That's only the beginning, there has to be a lot more. Why? **Because women rank men by how far up they perceive them to be on the Male Dominance Scale.** The higher up you seem to be on this invisible Male Scale the sexier and more enticing women will find you, all women. High status males are good potential mates, husbands and fathers. Even if the women you're after seem like air-headed party girls who want nothing more than a momentary good time with some stud, they still think the stud is more sexy and desirable if he's a high status stud. More than just hot to look at, but the entire package.

Before you can become skilled at seducing women, you must have a thorough understanding of just what that package is. You must become familiarized in all aspects of the grading system that women use to place the label SEXY on a man. After all, you can't begin to seduce them until you first capture their attention. And... there's no better way to reduce the likelihood of being rejected than by getting a positive GO signal before you decide to attempt an of opening gambit. My goal is to reduce your odds of being rejected so that you can operate with confidence. And since confidence is one of those critical qualities that women always grade highly anyway, we want as much of it as we can stand because... **Confidence comes from Knowledge!**

Ok, school's in and here's your first assignment... *go take The Test!*

That's right, I want you to skip ahead right now to **Appendix C** in the back of the book and take **The Dominant Male Test.** This is a fun, multiple-choice test that should give you a pretty accurate idea of how your 'male status' appears to the eyes of most women. I want you to take this test **now** before reading any further, because I'm afraid you'll be tempted to give "the correct" answer based on what you're about to learn in the rest of this chapter instead of a genuine answer that reflects your true personality characteristics. This is no joke... you need to know this kind of information about yourself in order to be able to contrast your improvement as you study the techniques in this book. Don't cheat yourself – go take the test now, then pop over to Appendix D to see how you scored and then come back here to get a better understanding of what the hell it all means!

High Status Males vs. Low Status Males

Jockeying for pecking order among males is something that goes on constantly in all species of animal on Earth. It takes place in every human culture too, probably dating back to the very beginnings of Time itself. Men compete against each other every day and in all manner of ways, some subtle and others painfully obvious. From the high stakes power plays that define the bitterness and intrigues of office (or governmental) politics, to deciding who goes first at a 4-way stop sign, the struggle to demonstrate yourself better, smarter, faster *more powerful* than the other guy derives itself from an instinct that is submerged deep within the very oldest parts of the male brain.

> ***All this happens because women take note of the results of this never-ending struggle – quietly noticing who the apparent winners and losers are, and just how well they seem to be holding up under the pressure of battle.***

Understand that women don't witness most of these little fights that go on (some are so subtle they can hardly be noticed) but they are extremely interested in the results. You are continually being sized-up for signs of the all-important winner or loser *mentality*... have you gotten the better of most of your opponents and risen to the top of the heap?... or are you a defeated and cowered wimp? At the heart of this particular question lies the answer as to whether or not you are a sexy, attractive man.

And so the never-ending hunt is on for signs of a victor... the confident air, the appearance of wealth, the look of athletic stock, and the worldliness that shows you either have the time to engage in great leisure, or an inquisitive mind that can't be held down. You have a thirst for new experiences and risky adventures. All these things speak to her about a man who has excelled in the struggle for supremacy among his peers, and *this factor* more than anything else (including physical attractiveness to a great extent) is what weighs most heavily in her calculation of what makes a captivating guy. Remember, the consequences of sexual activity are vastly different for a woman than they are for a man, and so the factors that serve to turn her on sexually are different too. These factors are hardwired into her brain by Nature just as yours are, and really, they make a lot of sense when you stop and think about them. It's been said that maleness and femaleness are simply two different strategies for reproduction – each simultaneously complimenting and in competition with the other.

With that in mind, let's see if we can't define what some of these characteristics might be so that you can begin to integrate them into your own style...

The appearance of Wealth must be a priority. Certainly you don't need to be "millionaire" wealthy – but you do need to project some kind of non-verbal evidence that you've done alright for yourself, or (even better) that you are ***still going places...*** either with your company, in the business world, the universe of arts and entertainment, etc. Just the appearance of being economically competent is enough to attract the attention of most women. You see, in order to achieve their personal level of highest fulfillment, women are faced with the urgency of someday having to raise children. For this they need to find a man who will help out with the money, not just the sperm donation. I'm simply talking about the normal desire to find a man who can bring home the bacon, not big time golddigging or anything. *Two areas of high visibility are your apartment and your car.* Your car doesn't have to be a Mercedes but it should be about 2-6 years old and rust free and at least somewhat stylish (no old-fart tan Buicks, please!). And your apartment should have a certain *seductive* style to it, however you define that for yourself. This particular subject will be expanded upon further in Chapter 7 because it's important.

Clothes are an important signal of your Male Display. I realize that for many of you this notion will be a tough pill to swallow, especially for all you nerds whose wardrobe consists strictly of sneakers, jeans and t-shirts (some of which breathlessly proclaim the imperative need to rid the Federation of Romulans). ***Clothes speak to your socio-economic status nonetheless,*** and women read them like secret visual code for an insight into your character. You don't need to go suit-and-tie and fancy Rolodex watch, but you should at least be aware of some fashion trends (checkout *Playboy or Maxim*) and try not to look so totally fuckin' clueless all the time! If you're an aggregate fashion slob and steadfastly reject anything that takes you away from your effortless comfort-wear, it only indicates to women that you're not a real "player" and that either you've given up all hope of attracting them, or that your self-image is so firmly cemented into a low status mind-set that you don't even realize how sad an image you are projecting.

Low self-esteem is particularly bad because it signals a *beaten-down character* that red-flags you as a loser. Just keep an eye on the latest magazines in order to get a sense for how to accessorize (yeah, I know...). At the very least you should own a leather jacket and a pair of dress boots for going out. Two things to remember about clothes is 1) use them to **enhance the good aspects** of your physique while disguising your flaws (i.e. flab) as much as possible, and 2) try to develop **your own sense of style** as much as you can. This intrigues women and draws their attention to you. It signals that you're a player. Finally, don't worry too much about what you'll look like when all those clothes come off. Women understand the fantasy aspect of clothing and know full well that much of it is illusion. They love it anyway! *A man who's willing to play their game is what excites them.*

Learn how to Smile and make solid Eye Contact. Why do men find it so hard to make eye contact?... because tits don't have eyes. Ha ha! (Sorry, I'm going to sit in the corner for the rest of class...) Seriously, you know that a High Status Male is a confident man who is not afraid to look someone in the eye. On the other hand, a subjugated little piss-boy who has been cowered by all the other men in the world averts his gaze when encountering other people, lest it might be taken as a challenge. He knows his 'place', so he surrenders and says "I am beneath you, I will not meet your eye, you win..." That's bullshit. You always want to **take the initiative in smiling, saying hello, and introducing yourself.** Even shaking hands when it seems appropriate to do so, such as in a business or formal situation.

Don't forget to stand tall and project a confident air. Not to sound like your mother, but this seemingly insignificant attention to posture goes a long way towards making a subliminal positive impression on women. Again it all goes back to your attitude – you stand proud and tall because you're one of Life's winners... you conquer all before you! Be careful here... this is the sort of message that must be communicated to women **non-verbally**, you don't dare come right out and say something like "I'm one of life's big winners, baby..." in even a semi-joking fashion or you will be pegged an instant asshole. *Try not to diminish with put-downs or jokes any of these important aspects of your character and attitude that I'm outlining here.* This is all profound stuff to women... this dance of seduction. One of the big secrets of guys who are successful with women is that they have **total respect** for her view of its significance. If you act like the idea of flirting, seduction and romance is all a bunch of horseshit, you can expect to be limited to making it strictly with 3's and below... since they'll take anything they can get. Even a lame-brain like you.

Strike the delicate balance between being cool and coming on too strong. If you're going to be seeing her on a regular basis (at work, as a waitress in a restaurant you frequent, etc.) then your best move is to advance the seduction just a little bit at a time. We'll talk about the actual techniques later, but you should understand that the delivery is just as important. *Be playful and flirtatious, don't take things too seriously, stay light and amusing, always make them laugh.* **Important:** keep your humor of the *clever* sort, never sarcastic or as an attempt to take a subtle shot at someone (women are very sensitive to this), and don't go overboard with the funny stuff or you'll come off as a clownish boy instead of a seductive man. Men are *humorous* – boys are foolish jokers who don't know when to quit. It's painfully obvious when you're so happy to have someone finally cracking up at your stupid jokes that you don't know when to slide off the stage. Because you're confident that your well-timed quips are funny, you don't need to spray them all around the room. Just relax and have the patience to pick your spots carefully. *That's* how you get the reputation of being a guy with a great sense of humor.

If it's appropriate, take a little risk. I know the whole thing about risking your ego is the central challenge to your being able to do anything effective with women, but it's important for you to understand that the act of risking helps to bootstrap your confidence and projects a very high status image. What's the big deal about risk-taking anyway? Because if you're a "winner" at the game of Life, then you expect to continue winning at whatever you try to do. Therefore, what looks scary to a "loser" is not really a risk, for you. **The ability to accept a risk with apparent ease is an activity reserved for the High Status Male.** This *expectation* is the signal... get it? Trust me, she does. It immediately tags you as being intriguing to women. You want the label of the "risk-taker" at any cost, so seek it wherever you can.

To wrap this up, just keep in mind that **perception is reality** when it comes to seduction... it doesn't matter if you aren't some "Thadius Rich Boy" in real life -- you only have to *approximate his attitude* in order to do amazingly well with women. They understand that it's all just a game and are willing to suspend disbelief in order to make the whole thing work, the same way that you accept the utterly fantastic premise of a way-out science fiction movie like *Alien* and simply enjoy it for what it is... great entertainment. It doesn't matter that you're a man of modest means or if your belly sticks out a little once you slip out of your stylish Euro shirt... by then the killer first impressions will have been made *and trust me, it lasts.* Heck, she's not perfect either... you'll both begin to discover each other's warts once you become more intimate, but by then the seduction will have matured beyond the flirting dance and moved onto something else entirely (like determining just how much of your emotional needs you are able to fill for each other, but that's another topic for Chapter 7).

> The higher your perceived socio-economic status, your ranking "number" on that invisible but all pervasive Male Dominance Scale, the more interesting, sexy and desirable you will seem to women. It's just that simple. In terms of getting your foot in the door of seduction, that's really all

there is to it. *Fishing*, not hunting.

Remember to always look your best when you're out and about, as the opportunities to meet women always seem to occur when you least expect it. You can dress casual but try to show some style. Lose the sweat pants and the reversed baseball cap, especially if you're over 30 (you're just making an ass of yourself). **Not being afraid to act appropriate for one's age is a clear sign of higher male status.** You have no time for immaturity... a man who's climbing the socio-economic ladder finds the journey exhilarating and can't wait to get where he's going! He revels in the changes brought about by the march of years... realizing that men can get sexier as they get older due to the accumulation of experience, expertise, power and money. **Status typically rises with age.** If you've got the world by the tail, why bother to cling to the past? So don't be afraid to give yourself the advantage of reveling in your current level of maturity. Just don't shuffle around looking like a sullen, vanquished bum. Be aware of the visual you project -- and the absolute power that an "I've-got-the-world by-the-balls" image conveys.

Dominant males have characteristics which are easily identifiable to women everywhere... they are confident first and foremost, have a likable quality about them, listen well and focus on the woman totally and completely while she's talking. The ability to pay attention to others without fretting or seeming self-conscious demonstrates that you have you shit together. You are not imprisoned by anxieties due to the fact that your life situation is out of control, or that you're desperate for someone to listen to your problems. Other qualities flow from your magnanimous nature... integrity, strength of character, genuineness and compassion. All this adds up to a sexy package... *give this guy a 7 or 8!*

The weak (*dominated*) male, by contrast, has a personality that has been forged from the opposite end of the human spectrum. It is marked by bitterness and rampant insecurities, jealousy, pettiness, and an inability to accept even the slightest criticism. Flying off into hair-triggered rages released by pent-up anger from being pushed around all his life, sarcasm and stupidity are the hallmarks of his nature. The whupped and wussie side of him emerges with a despondent, groveling edge... constantly apologizing for himself and his male sex drives.

He makes poor eye contact (a sign of submission), fawns over any woman who shows even the slightest interest in him (demonstrating how rare such interest is), talks about himself and his own problems and reveals way too much about himself in casual conversation ...signaling how desperate he is for someone to listen to his lonely self. He's usually very boring too. This is not a guy with all his ducks in a row and it shows. His low score on the Male Dominant Scale assures that he's doomed to flounder around with unattractive women. This notion doesn't suit his highly self-delusional ego however, tending to increase his hostility even further. **Unsexy** is the word... a 2.5 rank or less.

Let's change all that for you right now.

The Way Women Want Men to Act

If you're the kind of guy who's been getting rejected by women all his life, you may've come to the conclusion that most or even all of them absolutely delight in shutting guys down. They relish the opportunity to bait some nerd into asking them out for a date so they can humiliate him, preferably in public, by viciously crushing his ego flat as a pancake with as much malice as they can possibly summon. They'll teach you to dare try and ask them out for a date. They're going to make you pay for the way Johnny Bad Boy broke their heart in sixth grade. They will show you who is really the more powerful sex by whipping your skinny ass into total submission!

But stop and think about it for a second, how would it serve women to have all the men in the world walking around with their tails tucked between their legs? What for? So they can bitch to their girlfriends about how all men are a bunch of useless pussies who don't even have the courage to say hello to them any more? Not only wouldn't this state of affairs make any sense – since women are generally more interested in playing the game of romance than men are and need someone to play with – *it simply isn't reality.* I don't care what part of the world you're in... women long for love and affection, and for that they require the men out there to be interested in the sport of romance. It's quite possible that your bitterness over the long string of rejections you've gathered up has blinded you to this reality. The generalizing that all women love to reject and put down men (unless they happen to be rich or rock stars) is just a defense mechanism created to protect your ego. At least that's how it probably started out. The danger is that it may have grown into a full blown philosophy of life by now and, if so, then it's been slowly poisoning your personality right through to the core.

I'm warning you about this because I've "been dere done dat" with this sort of twisted psychology. Your biggest adversary in all this is located within your own brain. That means the enemy (**fear**) is already inside your armor and doing damage. The grandest battle of all will be fought with yourself, even though you probably hate to hear that. Much of the attitude change that you'll need to undergo has to do with short circuiting the hardened ideas you have developed about the motives of women. It's possible that much of your resentment stems from the fact that women seem to establish the rules of seduction... but then *neglect to publish what the hell they are!* It's left up to us guys (who have better things to think about, like football) to figure out how we're supposed to behave in order to make any headway with them!

The problem is that this discovery process involves trial and error and necessitates *a painful rejection for punishment of every false move.* If you have a low tolerance for rejection to begin with, then the need to avoid it becomes more important than perfecting your flirting-seducing-mating skills. You may give up on the process long before your training is complete and can begin to reap the rewards of your efforts. You stop learning, and your stunted development precludes any further success... insuring a high probability of continued rejection. Since the rejection pain now overwhelms whatever drive you might have to meet women, you withdraw completely. Withdrawal is the worst thing you can do because as your skills atrophy your attitude follows along with it. Now you're beginning to take on all the characteristics of the low level submissive male, and women will show less and less interest in you. See how this damn thing slowly spirals out of control?

One of the ways in which guys get totally fouled up with women is by failing to understand that seduction is really a very elaborate sales process, and, rather than concentrate on selling the product, **they focus instead on how badly they need to make the sale.** Here's an analogy... imagine you're wasting a perfectly good Saturday morning gabbing with a car salesman, but instead of filling you in on all the wonderful benefits of owning the shiny new Nissan you happen to be checking out, he's wining on about how much he needs you to buy this car so he can pay his rent and feed his kids. You would expect the guy to be belching out statistics and features and appealing to your emotions by painting a picture of you behind the wheel... cruising down an open country road with the convertible top down. He should be trying to get you jazzed up about making a buying decision by unleashing a flood of reasons why your life would be greatly improved if you purchase this car today. Any good salesman knows that he sells most effectively by demonstrating *what's in it for you,* the customer. Instead, by pissing and moaning about how they're going to fire his ass if he doesn't move a few more cars to make quota, so could you please buy this car, boo-hoo-hoo... this goofball is focusing on what's in it for *him*.

So tell me, which approach seems better? What's in it for you... or what's in it for him? Yeah I thought so. You honestly couldn't give a shit about him making quota or paying his rent. What's in it for him is of no interest to you – you're only going to part with your hard earned loot if he can convince you that new Nissan is something that you can't live without. Something that puts stars in your eyes! A way for you to look cool behind a new set of wheels! Would you buy a car from some chump who only appealed to your sympathy to help him out? No way! You'd essentially tell him to go fuck himself. *If there's nothing in this deal for me, I'm not interested.*

Hey guess what... you would *reject* him.

This is how all people think, no matter what they tell you differently. Everybody is in it for Number #1. They are always asking themselves the question "what's in it for me?" dozens of times a day whether they know it or not. Everyone is fundamentally selfish in this way. **Self interest** is the proper term for it... and there is absolutely nothing wrong with being self-interested – it's human nature. The economic system called Capitalism works because it harnesses the incredible power of individual self-interest. Communism fails precisely because it tries to deny it's existence. Humans are not worker bees in a hive laboring only for the good of the community. People work to reap the rewards of their own efforts in a very *personal* way... not for the common cause of "mankind". Sorry, that's not how it works. **People have hopes, dreams, aspirations and goals.** They fantasize about their future and will leap at anything that looks like it will help to advance their life situation, and reject or avoid whatever threatens to diminish the value of their own private universe.

When you engage in seduction, you are really embarked on a sales process whereby *you are the product being sold*. **You have to sell yourself by demonstrating the benefits that you will bring into her life.** You have to give her reasons why accepting you into her heart is going to enhance her life. What's in it for her?... you have to answer this question!

If instead you come off as being whiny and desperate, it only exposes the fact that your focus is mainly on what's in it for *you*... i.e., sex, love, a feeling of being normal, an end to your loneliness and isolation, a trophy to show off to your friends, etc. In other words, you see her only as a means for an advancement of your own selfish goals. *This is dehumanizing.* Why? Because anyone could theoretically serve this purpose, there's nothing to make the particular women whom you've come to focus your interest on feel special in any way. You're acting exactly like the callus, crooked car salesman who's begging you to buy some jalopy just so he can get his hands on a fucking commission. Guess what? *She* will do to you precisely what you would do to the slimy salesman... *she rejects you!*

Before this gets any worse, let me show you how you can skip a lot of these fearful trial-and-error learning processes and do the best things possible to aid your cause. Here's **seven ways** that women wish that men would act. If guys would only be and behave like this, women would be more than willing to drop all pretenses of aloofness and take up the dance of seduction with all of us at every opportunity we gave them.

The Seven Attributes Women Love to See

The great fear that you have when it comes to approaching women undoubtedly grows from the fact that you have a gnawing uncertainty of exactly what to say and how to act in a way that a great looking woman would find charming, clever and intriguing, as opposed to stupid, laughable and humiliating. Right? The need to avoid these negative emotions overrides whatever horniness that you have. Simply put, ignorance begets fear.

Well then get set to burn these next seven ideas into your brain forever. If you can adopt these manners, you'll be light-years ahead of your clueless competition.

ONE – Always Dress Stylishly and Appropriately. I know we covered this already but I need to ring your bell on this issue one more time just to make sure you get it. Clothes are super important to attracting women, just like big breasts are to men. (Hey I know it's perverse, but I didn't make up these rules!). No, you do not have to walk around like some 70's disco asshole with lots of fancy gold chains hanging off your neck. In fact this is the worst thing that you can do. That's trying way too hard and is ridiculously obvious. All you need to do is make sure that you **stay abreast of the latest casual fashions** and keep 90% of your wardrobe safely within these bounds. I'm not going to tell you exactly how to dress because fashions change and that sort of information gets dated fast.

Go take a peek at the GQ or Playboy websites (www.GQ.com or www.playboy.com) for an idea of what the latest styles are looking like. The key thought here is to always endeavor to look good... the problem with most guys is that they tend to dress up only when they know they're going out somewhere and there's likely to be some single women hanging around. Otherwise they dress like they do on the job at the steel mill. (Note: and if you're a white collar guy, lose the suit when you're not at work... they're only to be worn at appropriate formal events like weddings and funerals or while on the job. Otherwise they mark you as either a mobster or a Secret Service agent).

Unfortunately, Murphy's Law states that the best opportunities to meet women will only show up when you least expect it, like when you're out at the store buying a six pack. There's that hot chick standing in line next to you and you're doing your imitation of a stinking, unshaven bum today. Wonderful. Always seems to happen that way, doesn't it? But when you go out to the clubs looking fine the good chances never seem to come along, do they? Plus the competition in bars is absurd... if you're not one of the big strong "pretty boys" you don't so much as get a second look from most of the women there. Your best chances tend to pop up in every day life. That means that you must *always* dress in a stylish, but casual manner. Don't let it look like you're trying too hard, but try not to be caught looking like a rag john all the time either. Stay somewhere in between... **balance!**

As a final nail in this particular coffin, did you ever notice how a lot of married guys end up looking like overgrown 10 year old boys because of the way they're dressed? Yes, I said *dressed*. After two kids and thirty extra pounds, their wives have gradually taken to buying most of their clothes for them via Christmas &

birthday gifts. Don't think there isn't a method to their madness... they make a point of keeping their men sealed in cheap k-mart shirts with goofy patterns and mismatched pants. They do this in order to send very deliberate "stay away" signals to other women – knowing just how put-off any potential competitors will be to their husbands' doofus wardrobes. The clever and crafty wives know that – just as the proper clothes make the man – the wrong clothes will completely drag him out of contention. Probably without the dumb ass even knowing it. Nuff said.

TWO – Show that You're Normal, Harmless and Creative. One of the major worries that women have when being advanced upon by a man they've never met before is determining whether or not he's a psycho. I mean a seriously dangerous bastard. Signs of a twisted personality include things like a complete lack of any sense of humor, disheveled hair and clothes, or any kind of incoherent mumblings. A guy who seems too slick and polished (a phoney liar) is a warning flag too. This is a qualifying test that you have to pass right away or you will not be given a chance to work any of your seductive magic. I trust that you've managed to stay out of mental wards for most of your life or at the very least are attentively taking your medication every day, so this shouldn't be too much of a problem for you, right?

Showing a bit of imagination and whimsy in your light-hearted approach is a good way to score points too. Again, there's nothing specific I can tell you to do here, you just have to learn how to react to the situation you find yourself in with a touch of resourcefulness. *Think...* assume the dominant male attitude you wish to convey before you speak. Also, try not to use the opportunity of meeting a woman as a launching pad for one of your dissertations on how the government is secretly test-flying captured UFO's in Nevada – at least not until around the third date when she knows you're just kidding around. You are, aren't you?

Here's something I call the **Handshake Trick** that make's a subliminally cool first impression on any woman. In situations where you're being formally introduced by a third party (like in a business setting) you may have an opportunity to shake a woman's hand. There's a right and wrong way to do this. Assuming she's foxy and worth playing for, here's the right way: First, make sure that your hand fully engages hers until the webs between your thumbs and index fingers touch (no wimpy, submissive male-style limp wrist handshakes... ee-gad!). Grasp firmly but don't squeeze hard (like you would do with a man in the old "I'll-crush-your puny-fuckin-hand" power handshake competition).

Then (this is the best part)... very subtly, while maintaining eye contact and smiling, **turn your hand very slowly and slightly in a clockwise direction to the right so that her hand is above yours with your palm turned upwards** (instead of side-by-side vertically the way they started out). Hold on gently for a few seconds, then release her hand and let it slide out of yours while you remain perfectly still. Why women get all turned on by this I don't know, I suspect that it has to do with the way in which the shining Knight takes hold of the maiden's hand before kissing it (her hand above his, knuckles up). Chivalry... a fantasy! It's vaguely intriguing and suggestive, and puts you in an *immediate positive light* that separates you from all the other clueless schmucks she's met today who either gave her the 'squishy fishy' or 'bone-crusher' greeting.

See how you've got to be *thinking all the time* in order to play the seduction game like a pro? Stay frosty and remember to do the little things properly. You have to build a seduction brick by brick... and think of the first brick that you lay (your first impression) as your all-important cornerstone. Remember, first impressions have nuclear importance when it comes to meeting and seducing women – if you start out wrong, you are almost never able to recover without a huge effort. So save yourself the agony of frustration and do it right from the start. This will set up your next play.

THREE – Be a cool, relaxed flirt. A dominant male is calm and in control, right? So a passive, "got-my-shit-together" approach is always better than a frantic, nervous one. Of course, you can't act completely aloof unless you're an famous athlete or celebrity of some kind, in which case your reputation has preceded you and done all the preliminary work of seduction in advance. However, "normal" guys like us have to walk a fine line between showing complete disinterest in a woman and behaving like a silly lapdog. Advertise your delight in meeting her with crisp eye contact and a gentle smile, but keep your flirting *subtle*. Act friendly and show that your intrigued by her feminine charm, but communicate most of it **non-verbally** through the use of open body language and a mischievous gleam in your eye. As your confidence rises with the techniques you'll be learning about throughout this book, I'm sure you won't even have to think about stuff like this consciously for very much longer.

FOUR – Show that you can Listen as well as talk. In your charged-up state it's easy to start running off at the mouth and begin blathering along about nothing of any real importance... so happy are you to be getting any kind of hopeful response from her. One of the basic emotional needs that woman have, however, is a need to be heard by men. They find this to be validating in some way, probably since it's still a man's world to a large extent and being taken seriously by any man is very energizing and endearing. **Listening is a powerful and effective way to build rapport.** You should become skilled at *actively* listening... i.e., making little supportive comments here and there to demonstrate that you're comprehending what she's telling you (even if you don't agree with her, or think the topic itself is trivial), and not just letting it run through your skull unprocessed. Then, **mirror** her thoughts back to her using a different set of words. I swear to God it's true... people think you're brilliant if you endorse their own ideas back to them in an improved form! All you have to do is add an idea or two of your own into the mix here and there so that you don't seem like a patronizing suck-up. This is a trick that politicians and slick salesmen utilize to get people to admire them so they'll either buy something or vote for them.

Listening also sets you apart from the average guy since just about no one does it anymore. It also lends an air of mystery because you won't have a chance to blab too much about yourself. This is a key issue. You should aspire to reveal only bits and pieces of yourself to a woman during any given encounter with her – never spill your guts and talk about your personal problems, medical abnormalities or past history, etc. Always hold something back in reserve. Make her want to see you again to find out more. Otherwise you become just another unremarkable story in the big city, nothing to distinguish you from the teeming crowd. It's your *distinctiveness* that intrigues women, not the fact that you're just an everyday, fart-blowing Joe. Women don't want generic, they want something unique and interesting. Why do you think she fantasizes about actors and rock stars and secret agents. Speaking of secret agents...

FIVE – Speak in a Relaxed, Low, Mysterious Voice. The voice is your primary instrument of seduction, so you must be certain to use it wisely. We concentrate a lot on the content of what you say in this book, but don't forget that the delivery is incredibly important too, especially at the appropriate moments when the two of you can share a flirtatious moment alone. For the purposes of seduction you'll want to park your usual 'nails-on-a-chalkboard' screech and coax your voice into sounding more full-bodied and deep. A good way to accomplish this is to stretch out your vocal chords before you speak by pretending to yawn before speaking (but keep your mouth closed!). Try it right now. Open the back of your throat by doing a "yawn stretch" for a few seconds. Notice how much more deeper and sexier your voice sounds? If not, keep practicing until it does. Your voice should feel like it's originating from deep down in your lower chest instead of from your neck area. **A throaty voice is highly erotic.** This is a simple trick and probably the hardest part is remembering to do it when you're actually chatting up some fox and your mind is twirling away in a dead panic.

Avoid any sort of weary drone, impatient staccato or especially a judgmental scolding tone. These types of articulations belong to guys who are all bone-stroking assholes. Think *conspiratorial* instead... lean in close to her like you're revealing a secret, like your exchange is private and for her ears only, and watch how she's drawn in to you. Women love this sort of thing. Remember, most of what you're doing is **listening actively** anyway... so use your voice like a rudder to steer the conversation along with occasional comments delivered in a deep rich tone. Use the yawning technique only, don't try to cheat by booming your voice because that's obviously fake and sounds stupid and you'll make a complete fool of yourself. This trick takes some skill and an ability to think reasonably on your feet.

SIX – Match Her Mood. One of the cleverest ways to effect a sense of rapport with anyone is to mirror them. If they glimpse a reflection of themselves in you it somehow validates their own thoughts and feelings. It's intoxicating to the human spirit... so make certain to exploit this tool early and often. I mentioned reflecting back a woman's ideas, but it's just as important to mirror back her mood too. If you meet a girl who's in an "up" mood because of some goings on around you like a wild party or whatever, your mood should be similarly upbeat. Park your slow, dark and soft-spoken sexy demeanor for another more appropriate time. Now is the time to be bright and loud in your approach and interaction with her. If you run across her in a quiet library somewhere, that's where the slow, soft and mellow "you" makes it's appearance.

Otherwise you're attempting to pull her out of her present mood and into yours. That means she has to make an effort to mentally switch gears in order to match your mood, and why should she? You're a perfect stranger – there's no reason for her to make that kind of mental effort on behalf of someone she doesn't even know yet. You double your chances of rejection by failing to match her mood. There'll be plenty of time to explore different emotions with her on future dates. For now, you are the "salesman" trying to make the sale. Therefore it is *you* who must entice the customer.

SEVEN – Focus is Flattering. One sure way to knock any woman out of her defensive mode is to keep your attention *absolutely focused on her.* It's not advisable to be constantly breaking eye contact and looking around while you're out together, especially when she's talking. And checking out other women with a roving eye is tantamount to complete social suicide. If she so much as picks up a sniff that you're just another horn dog who thinks that "all tail is the same", and that checking out the other trim in the room is no big deal, you're dead meat. Period. Your introductory conversations with her on first dates are all about her getting a sense of who you are and ***IF YOU CAN BE TRUSTED.*** As I stated before, trust is a huge deal with women... their biology compels them to seek out males of some character who will stick around long enough to help them raise their children. This is a test you simply *must* pass.

One of the smoothest ways to keep your attention focused is to use a visualization technique that imagines you and the woman that you're interested in huddled together beneath one of those droopy old 70's-style umbrellas. Remember those? They were shaped like the helmets those old English constables used to wear, or the Keystone Cops. Visualize yourselves trapped together inside this little pod – separated from the rest of the world as if caught in your own private rainstorm. Try it next time you're chatting with any girl, it's a mental trick that you play inside your own head so no one will know. But the effect it will have on your manner can be profound.

You'll discover that keeping your attention focused on her becomes effortless. *She'll be enthralled by the intimacy of the conversation!* Crowd her personal space a bit and she how she responds. Play with her... hold solid eye contact. Of course, be sure to break eye contact from time to time so that you're not boring straight into her like some crazy.

But None of this Works for You...

I know, this all sounds good on paper and when you read it you're resolved to remember lots of this stuff and use it next time the opportunity to impress some cute chick presents itself, but then when you finally get that chance you freeze up and forget everything you learned and just fall back on your same old destructive behaviors. What's up with that? Well, some of what you're doing wrong is learned behavior that's become so familiar you tend to act it out almost unconsciously -- messing up and making key mistakes before you can even think to stop and change what you're doing. But what we're interested in is the *why* behind it all. Why do you act in a shy, bumbling way that proclaims your low male status while some other smooth dude happens to know all the right things to say? He never got any training at this stuff either, so why's he so good at it?

The answer lies in our *critical early experiences with women* – either negative or positive – and the resulting kind of thoughts that occur in our heads automatically whenever we meet them again. Those thoughts are reinforced over and over until they become rooted in our consciousness. Negative experiences in particular have a tendency to create feelings of **shame and humiliation** that become associated with those early bad encounters that first created them. When the future brings you back into a similar situation, it dredges up those old feelings of shame, which can result in unstable thought patterns and lead to some highly self-destructive social behaviors. Alright, psycho-analysis meat-n'-potatoes time. Let's get going and explore this intriguing subject of *toxic shame* right now without further delay.

Without Embarrassment
Chapter 4: Comfortable Wimps, Tough Men

Toxic Shame Keeps You in a Straitjacket

Little Bobby is 2 years old. He likes to run around the house naked -- laughing and screaming with joy as his parents chase him from room to room with the camcorder. They tell him to "quit showing everybody that silly poo-poo bottom....", but they think it's hysterical and do nothing to stop it. Why should they? Dashing around butt naked is appropriate, healthy behavior for a 2 year old who's just discovered the most delightful means of coordinating the rapid movement of his legs in such a way that he can now *run* (a transcendent advancement over mere walking, which was last month's big achievement). Being without clothing is no big deal either, of course, as long as it's not too cold in the house. Life is good. Life is magical.

A year later Bobby is 3, and grandma is visiting. Bobby decides to run out of the bathroom after his bath and surprise grandma... make her laugh and be silly. But today it's Bobby who's in for the surprise. When grandma sees him running towards her *au naturel* with his ding dong happily bouncing around, she gets an angry look on her face which stops him cold. She scolds him, "Shame on you Bobby, go put some clothes on!". Bobby is confused. Mom and dad never told him anything like that. They never yelled at him for being a silly poo-poo head. As far as he knew, there was no real difference between wearing clothes and not wearing them (except for going outside when it was cold, *yikes*!).

So what's wrong with grandma? Why is she making Bobby feel so **bad** all of a sudden? "You shouldn't run around like that," grandma scolds. Bobby looks to his parents, messing around in the kitchen getting dinner ready, for some support. "Mom?" he asks quizzically. But now both his parents have funny looks on their faces, adding to Bobby's dismay, and what... fear? Mom quickly grabs Bobby by the hand and takes him upstairs and gets him into his PJ's. Now when he comes back, grandma is happy again. But why? What was the big deal? What's so important about having clothes on?

In the future, anytime Bobby thinks about running around the house naked, he gets a funny, uncomfortable feeling inside him that he doesn't like. The feeling goes away if he puts his clothes back on. And he would never, *ever* dream of running around the house naked in front of grandma again! Soon, he won't be comfortable doing it in front of his parents either, and they seem to be okay with that. They never seem to want to play chase my poo-poo bottom with the camcorder any more. Oh well...

Welcome to Behavioral Modification 101.

Bobby has learned to associate the emotion of shame with being naked in front of other people. In the coming years he will learn that it's also shameful to touch himself down there in public (even though it's been feeling pretty good to do so lately...) and to not let anyone watch him when he's in the bathroom on the toilet, and then in the tub either. Things sure are becoming different than when he was younger.

Shame – The Master Controller Emotion

The development of a sense of shame is normal and healthy when it serves to set appropriate boundaries for our actions at various stages in our evolution from toddler to adult. Shame endows our flowering sense of identity with a certain **humility** that guides our interactions with other individuals in the world around us. Childhood is characterized by a self-centeredness that must yield to a sense of empathy for others as we grow older. We learn to take on more and more responsibility for our actions, slowly becoming aware of how they affect everyone else around us. We need to learn that the Universe doesn't rotate around us as the pivot point.

It's important to understand that the mechanism of shame is mostly one of association, that is, we learn to associate the unpleasant emotional sensations of being ashamed with behaviors that society wishes for us to control or suppress.

Bobby's little sister Betty will also learn to be ashamed to show off her pee pee in public, especially when visitors are over. She will also be taught to cover up her *chest* in time, even though it looks exactly the same as her brother's at this age. How come? Bobby doesn't get taught to associate shame with his exposed nipples; he feels no shame whatsoever when he walks around with his shirt off. So why does Betty feel so uncomfortable if she lets people see her without a shirt? The world sure becomes weird as we get older...

Shame occurs when we are exposed – either physically or emotionally – in a way that diminishes us in the presence of others, and in a situation where we are not prepared to experience such exposure.

This negative emotion called shame is very painful and thus very powerful. Shame is commonly wielded by parents and those in authority to modify and control the behavior of people, especially children and adolescents. Morals and values and the boundaries of acceptable public and private behavior are all "taught" to us by way of inducing shameful experiences at some point in our lives. We gradually learn to swerve away from actions and behaviors that threaten to provoke this highly uncomfortable feeling.

To a certain extent this is okay, but the grip that shame can take on our soul increases with repeated exposures, and this gives this strange, uniquely human emotion the potential to run out of control and become **toxic**.

It's when shame begins to exceed its normal function within our minds, i.e. to provide us with a sense of humility and ground our identity somewhere between God and the lower beasts, that it begins to create problems for us. Humiliation is an extreme form of shame that is so awful men will put their lives in jeopardy in order to avoid experiencing it, especially in combat or even athletic competition. Physical violence and murders routinely are committed because of shame. Emotionally rigid cultures like the Japanese partake of a form of ritual suicide called *hara-kiri* in order to absolve themselves of extreme shame or "loss of face"... killing oneself to restore honor to their family name.

How pervasive are the effects of toxic shame? Well, in almost every model of human society, there is no greater punishment than being forcibly ostracized by your peers by having to wear a scourge of shame and humiliation. The Scarlet Letter, so to speak. Almost every form of addictive behavior has its roots in the desperate need of the afflicted individual to escape from an overwhelming sense of shame that he or she feels has become trapped deep within himself.

We all carry some dysfunctional shame within us since no one experiences a perfect childhood or adolescence, but this emotion-state can get twisted and distorted way beyond what was intended if we are forced to experience it in major doses. Usually this happens either through a low-volume but unrelenting source (harassment by parent or peers), or by way of an isolated or repeated traumatic event (abuse). A person concealing a great deal of toxic shame within himself will demonstrate increasingly extreme expressions of addictive behavior in an effort to cover them up and make the painful feelings go away.

Addictions Galore

Let's talk about addictive behavior for a moment, since it's likely your failures with women have found an escape route from the resultant pain via some form of addiction. There are three distinct categories in which addictions manifest themselves:

1) Ingestive addictions... these are the most well known forms, characterized by individuals putting something directly into their body (ingesting) by drinking, eating, snorting, smoking or injecting it, in order to modify their mood in a way that makes it impossible for them to engage in too much painful self-introspection. *Drugs, alcohol and food* are the usual suspects here. You know how out of control some poor bastards can get with these substances. Hopefully you're not one of them. Next are...

2) Activity addictions... sexual preoccupations (fetishes) and *gambling* are commonly recognized activity addictions, but the list is long and includes such seemingly innocuous things like being a *workaholic or a compulsive clean freak*. Some people distort the true value of religion and become *religious addicts,* obsessing endlessly over Biblical passages or seeking evidence of miracles. This form of addiction includes any sort of activity that a person engages in excessively (like golf !!!) to the detriment and neglect of other more important aspects of his life (i.e., family and primary relationships). Finally, there are the less well recognized but very common...

3) Emotional addictions... where a person's character becomes defined by a particular kind of emotion which they've become addicted to expressing over and over again. Some people are so angry they can get addicted to the power of their *rage* and become "rageaholics" -- whereas a depressed person finds himself addicted to his *sadness*, a serial philanderer is addicted to being *in love*, etc.

So what the hell does any of this have to do with seducing women?

I'm trying to shine a bit of light on the reasons why you may have acquired many of the social difficulties that you are burdened with. **Understanding** is one of the first steps along the road to permanent change because it cuts through the fog of emotion that prevents you from seeing yourself and your own thought patterns – and by extension, your problems – in an objective light. *Knowledge allows you to step outside of yourself and become your own therapist.* The mind has an interesting way of calming itself by adapting to whatever sort of behaviors it has created and declaring them to be "normal". This is a self-delusional (probably protective) mechanism that everyone exhibits and is in itself not bad -- but it can become a problem if it grows too elaborate and transforms into what's known as a shame cover-up.

Cover-ups occur when a person chooses to completely immerse himself in his favorite addiction in order to keep his mental demons from causing him pain.

Sometimes the more violent among us direct the product of our shame outwards at a world we feel has wronged us. Men of this breed can become very dangerous. Ted Bundy killed over 40 women by viciously bludgeoning them to death with a club. *Every one of them resembled a girl who'd rejected him in high school!* Shame... never forgotten, festering, growing highly toxic. Serial killers commonly become addicted to the actual thrill of killing.

I mention this monster Bundy only to demonstrate the frightening power of shamed emotions. His madness ostensibly grew from a *single* rejection that became so reinforced by repeated replaying within his tortured mind that it drove him to commit gruesome crimes borne of a need to exact a kind of twisted vengeance over and over and over again. Each killing only gave him temporary relief from his agony and so it needed to be cloned many times. I doubt his rage subsided until they finally gave him the gas.

Although Bundy is an extreme example, it demonstrates just how potentially devastating the act of being rejected by a woman can become for any man. Why?... Because **rejection**

equals shame. Being romantically accepted by a woman validates a man's sense of self. Likewise, rejecting him causes him to question his sense of manliness -- threatening to consume his identity as a person and leave him somehow less human. Sub-human garbage. I know you've had these searingly painful thoughts when you've been rejected.

Women don't seem to understand the depth of damage they do to men by rejecting them. They think men are basically brainless lugs being led around by their dicks and that they'll just bounce away from rebuffs like a pinball and keep working on other women until they finally "get lucky" with some other slut who lives further down the food chain. No harm, no foul... they *think*. But they're wrong.

Rejection is painful because it's humiliating and thus toxically shaming by nature. Encountering too much of this mental poison threatens to destroy us, paralyzing us to take further chances with women. Many men are sensitive to rejection because they hold a very dark and pervasive foreboding within their hearts that the *next* rejection might just send them over the edge. Too Bundy-like to contemplate. Better to just watch our pornos and whack off and keep our distance. And our sanity.

What a huge price to pay... a dehumanizing lifestyle of loneliness and isolation that takes us on a prolonged journey to a place we always feared we would end up anyway. **As long as you are a prisoner of shame you will manifest behaviors that will continue to flag you as a low status male,** especially if it's your *affection needs* that have become shame-bound. Study the following section with an open mind and a little courage – it might just be the first time you encounter some insight into why your fear of being rejected goes beyond normal nervousness and into the realm of social paralysis.

Your Secretly Shamed Affection Needs

The need to secure affection from others is a basic, natural, *normal* human need that begins to form within most of us at a very early age, probably as a continuation of infanthood. The key issue here is **normal and natural.** The human animal has an index of developmental needs that seek to find expression and validation as we undertake the maturation process, a process that begins in early childhood and winds a twisted path all the way through young adulthood. The major players in this journey are the primary caretakers, i.e. usually our parents (or whomever plays their role in our lives). They must *encourage, guide and support* the various emotional needs that begin to emerge in us as we grow through early childhood. At the very least, they must allow them to occur or manage their expression **without associating them with shameful feelings or humiliation.** Unfortunately, this is exactly what happens much of the time -- and in some cases quite severely. This is where the roots of many neurotic inhibitions that torture us later in life are to be found.

Shame-binding, the process is called.

Consider this: one of those basic human needs I mentioned concerns our natural curiosity. Our urge to question the goings on within our environment must be supported and encouraged. It's through this process of wondering about the hows and whys of the physical world (and later, the non-physical world) that our intellects and ability to reason unfold. As we grow and ask questions, our curiosity about things should be supported as something good, not shamed as something bad. Now, you might be thinking, what kind of parent wouldn't want their kids to grow up smart? Well, many backwards-thinking parents often (perhaps inadvertently, but nonetheless) act to suppress intellectual urges in girls because of the misguided belief that "smart girls" are intimidating to men and therefore not attractive to them.

"...Don't want my daughters growing up to be uppity bitches that don't know to defer to their husbands..." This is a cultural

phenomenon that, sadly, still exists in many places. Parents engage in this kind of psychological suffocation by shaming or reacting in disapproving ways to every attempt this girl makes to express any kind of intellectual ability that goes beyond what her misguided parents feel is "proper". *"You'll never make anything of yourself",* they'll tell her repeatedly, or *"I'll do that for you, you don't know how it works..."* the implication being that "you're too stupid... let a **man** do it".

Decades of this sort of negative conditioning, especially drawn out over the course of one's critical formative years, can have a devastating and long-lasting effect on a person's personality. In this example, what happens is that the **need to be curious** and express any advanced rational thinking becomes shame bound. Every manifestation of that "curiosity urge" has been met (associated) with a shaming experience, usually verbal, that produces a painful emotional state in the recipient. In the future, anytime the desire to be insightful or creative arises, it pulls an unconscious sense of shame up from the depths along with it -- causing this poor girl to feel vaguely distressed in some way. So she never volunteers an answer in math class, because she's been trained to feel "stupid". Whenever she has a eloquent thought, she remains silent. Her intellectual powers cannot manifest themselves without causing a related emotional discomfort which is both very powerful and detrimental to her mental development. She has become crippled by her own shame, almost as if an auto-immune disease has turned against the very host organism that it was designed to protect.

Humans are simple psychological reactors in that we all tend to gravitate towards feelings and sensations that are pleasurable in some way, *but we are even more strongly repelled by the opposite sensations of pain and discomfort.* In other words, people will go through all manner of twists and turns in order to avoid pain, even at the expense of denying themselves something they would love to possess (like, for instance, a girlfriend).

Pain blocks our growth into complete emotional maturity by acting as an obstruction to the actions that are needed to accomplish any meaningful personal goals that we may have for ourselves.

Here's the point insofar as being cursed with an unreasonable fear of rejection is concerned. Fundamental emotional needs like the desire for affection can also become shamed by an ill-intentioned or clueless parent. When this happens, it becomes impossible to experience this particular urge without simultaneously feeling deeply ashamed of it! It took me years of study and introspection to understand that this is what had happened to me, and to see this psychological anomaly as being the source of my rejection sensitivity problem. I was so hypersensitive to rejection that I became paralyzed to act when an opportunity to meet and flirt with a girl presented itself. I would simply withdraw and clam up. No one could see that I was consumed by silent shame at the merest thought of what I would *like* to do in that situation... i.e., attempt to strike up a conversation with her.

Now here's the really important thing to understand about this particular form of toxic shame... it wouldn't matter whether or not my advances had actually been rejected by the girl, **because it was the very act of flirting with her that was shameful.** By attempting to talk with this girl in a way that was obviously within a man-woman context, I was *revealing* to her that I had a need for affection... a normal, human emotional need. However, since my sense of this emotion got shamed as a little kid, "declaring" that I possessed this desire was extremely painful for me. I was exposing myself in public, and it was humiliating!

After a time I began to understand that I didn't fear being rejected so much as I feared exposing the fact that I had a desire to have a woman in my life. This communicated that I had a need for the *affections* of a woman, and of course I was horribly ashamed to demonstrate this "character flaw". Remember, it's not the rejection that's shameful, it's what the action of attempting to meet a woman reveals about yourself... that you're not a "powerful" loner. In effect, you're screaming out loud that you're not a man who can go it alone and tend to his own emotional needs. Instead, you're a weakling who needs someone to love and to take care of you... trading a girlfriend and eventually a wife for your mommy.

See how totally fucked up this stuff is! Eventually you begin to rationalize and intellectualize your twisted view of the shame-bound emotion to the point where it becomes a kind of personal ideology that you live by. It can go so far that you actually begin to feel superior to other people who go around exposing their shameful emotional needs in public like weaklings and fools. Didn't their mommas ever teach them not to act like that?

I don't know to what degree, if at all, any of this resonates with you. Everybody has their own unique upbringing and story that goes with it. One clue as to whether or not the way you were raised might've had anything to do with developing a hyper-sensitivity to rejection later on as an adult, would be to recall if any **openly allowed expressions of affection** were commonly encouraged or even tolerated in your family. In my case, while my parents were always supportive and never abusive to me and my brother, there was always an unspoken rule of maintaining an aloofness with one another and a respect for everyone's privacy. There was no hugging or kissing in my family, and certainly no one ever uttered the words "I love you" to anyone else. Even to this day I rarely act this way around my mother. It makes me feel guilty, but I just can't bring myself to do it -- so powerful are the deeply ingrained feelings of shame at the thought of such "silly" expressions of affection. Everyone just "knew" how we all felt about each other. We didn't have to say it or demonstrate it out loud. Such displays were considered horribly... *embarrassing*.

Today I marvel whenever I see a young child when I'm out someplace like a restaurant, lamenting for their mom to hug them or pay attention to them. Even at the age of about 4 or 5 I would have *never* so candidly sought to be embraced or sweet-talked by my mom or dad... that's how young I was when I had already come to understand that I should be ashamed of such feelings. I don't tell you this to gain your sympathy, only to illustrate just how insidious toxic shame can be. It's really a stealth form of abuse, so subtle that I suspect neither the abuser or "abusee" often know that it's even happening!

How could I have understood at the age of 4 that I was being programmed to feel ashamed of one of my most basic human emotional needs?

Of course, there's no way to be certain how any of this really happened since the beginnings of anyone's shame are lost in the faded memories of early childhood, but I was always very perceptive and it could be that I sensed either my mom or dads' discomfort with my affection-longing behavior and came to feel that there was something wrong with it. From then on I began to feel "funny" (shamed) whenever I acted that way. Naturally I suppressed the behavior to avoid provoking the shame and *ta-da*... a nicely shame-bound emotion to torture me for the next 30 or so years. Why did my parents do this to me? I suppose they felt that hankering for love wasn't a proper way for a boy to act, and wished to discourage such "sissy-like" behavior. Fortunately, I think parents are more enlightened nowadays and aren't so worried about forcing strict gender roles on kids at a very young age. There's plenty of time for character to blossom in later adolescence.

You can see the problems created when shame is introduced into our consciousness at a time when we are psychologically wide open and lacking the defensive boundaries of a well-formed identity to protect ourselves. Our immature egos make us profoundly hypno-suggestive and vulnerable to this potent emotional abuse.

Anyway, here's the bottom line to all this amateur psychoanalysis: It's possible that you only *think* you have an unnatural fear of rejection. I'm suggesting that if you examine it more closely, what you might really be experiencing is a deeply felt sense of shame whenever you expose the fact that you desire affection. Therefore, the very act of trying to interact with women is an admission (and a disgraceful one at that...) that you desire to be loved! Think about it... this is a trap with no escape hatch because no matter what you do, *you can't win.* Even if your amorous advances are not openly rebuffed by a woman, it doesn't matter. Why? Because your shame is awakened by making any sort of move on her in the first place. Such action is nothing short of an open admission of your natural human desire for love and affection. *The problem is that, for you, it's neither natural nor human.*

A shamed emotion is experienced as alien and strange, and therefore must always be kept hidden from view... much the same way that we keep our genitals covered in public to avoid being embarrassed and humiliated.

How do you distinguish the difference between a simple fear of rejection and the more complicated dynamic of shamed affection needs? Well, do you find that it's still impossible for you to approach a woman even when she's sending you "GO" signals all over the place with body language cues and unmistakable flirtatious behavior? Or to "up the ante" and show your interest in dating her if you have managed to strike up a conversation? If she's making it clear that she's not going to reject you, then what's there to be afraid of? That's right... you're afraid to reveal your secret weakness... that you need love and affection just like everyone else. *Shameful!*

Because these two very dissimilar emotions (a desire for love plus shame) are **bound together** in the deepest recesses of your unconscious mind, you cannot experience one without the other. Think of the shame as a monkey clinging to the back of the normal emotion... it pops up whenever you try to experience that emotion whether you like it or not. Sometimes the gremlin of toxic shame can be temporarily suppressed with the use of drugs or alcohol. This is the reason people become addicted to chemicals, it allows them to become uninhibited... meaning that under the influence of mind altering drugs the shame becomes decoupled and they are free to experience the emotion *shamelessly*, at least for a while. Think of how you act when you get too drunk or high. Pawing every girl in sight at a party or the bar?

The emotion we most often seek to express when uninhibited by drugs is the one which is the most tightly imprisoned by shame when we are sober.

Alright, having beat this thing to death in theory, how about some practical advice on what to do about it. The first thing you must recognize is that knowledge is power. Simply having your eyes opened to the mechanics of toxic shame and how it was adversely affecting your life all these years can become a compelling tool for dismantling it. Knowing and understanding that your shame-bound emotions are something that was done *to you*, and is not really you (i.e. an unchangeable aspect of your personality) is an enormous revelation in itself that holds vast potential for jump starting your personal growth.

No longer are you doomed to identify with an emotional characteristic... i.e., you aren't shy – you were *programmed with an emotional flaw* that caused you to utilize shy behavior in order to correct the problem. You adopted shyness as a shield against your shame, to keep it boxed in where it couldn't torment you. It was a pretty ingenious solution really. The drawback to using one type of emotion to fight another one is that the cure we create for ourselves produces its own unique set of problems that limit your ability to live life to its fullest expression. The cure ends up robbing you of the complete human experience. Not to mention the addictive behaviors they can lead to in our efforts to suppress them

A second weapon in your arsenal against your shame is what psychologists call **desensitization**. This idea makes use of the natural tenancy of the mind to adapt to anything after a while and actually become bored with it. What bores us becomes invisible and eventually gets taken for granted, and when that happens it loses its potential to generate any kind of emotion within us, good or bad. An event or experience that provokes no emotion is the definition of boring, after all. So how do we turn *rejection* into something that bores us? I don't know precisely what your level of courage is concerning your rejection sensitivity, but if you can, try something like this: Next time you have an opportunity to talk to an attractive woman in some non-romantic situation (like work or school), begin to think about asking her out on a date. Try to really do this seriously and not just as a joke in your mind. *You're **really** going to ask her out and reveal your shameful need for affection...* Wow!

If you've been focusing and doing this mental exercise properly, you should begin to feel that familiar **fear** start to swell in your chest and begin to choke your throat shut. Ah, the protective mechanism at work! Now you're getting it. *Try to hold yourself in that uncomfortable state as long as you can before you excuse yourself and slip away.* Make your retreat with calm good humor and class... don't bolt away in a panic to the nearest john and start puking... (if that happens, then you went too far!) Just relax; no one knows what fantasies are running inside your mind except you. There's no need to create an embarrassing scene over this. You will have to work this desensitizing program several times before it kicks in, so you can't go around scaring all the women into totally avoiding you by acting like a hysterical Woody Allen clone. *This is an internal exercise designed to establish control over your own emotions and thoughts.* It's a secret – don't ever give away what you're doing!

You'll need to institute a regular program of doing this "near-shame approach" in order for the desensitization training to really take effect. You should push yourself a little closer to actually opening your mouth and speaking the words "...would you like to have dinner with me tomorrow night?..." in order to provoke the feelings of intense fear and complete paralysis that normally troubles you. By raising the psychological bar like this one notch at a time, you'll make it increasingly difficult for the negative emotional-shame response to take command of your physiological state and trigger all those humiliating physical reactions that you hate so much... like sweating, nervousness, the squeaky little-kid voice, etc.

In essence what you're doing is *playing with your shame*... prodding and teasing it by deliberately getting close to performing the activity that draws the shameful feelings up out of where they hide deep within your unconscious mind, and then forcing them to run their routine for you on demand. What happens is that the negative responses begin to exhaust themselves after a while -- especially if you stay determined to keep poking at them regularly. Every time there will be some degree of mental discomfort to suffer through. The magic becomes apparent when, after a while, you'll find that you have to get closer and closer to the edge of actually speaking the dreaded words before you can get the fear to present itself. **Now you're beginning to cripple the shame!**

Think of it like this... each time that you pull the shame up it's like you're using mental sandpaper to scratch away another layer of it. With repeated actions, the veneer of shame becomes thinner and less powerful in its hold over you. You will be able to fatigue these emotions so completely by doing this over and over again that one day you'll find you can go right through the whole routine and *actually ask her out for a real date* without hardly feeling any nervousness or humiliation at all! I know that it seems impossible to conceive right now as you're reading this... but the technique of desensitization works wonders and is used regularly by psychotherapists to cure people of some very serious phobias like a pathological fear of flying, open spaces, crossing tall bridges, etc. By slowly edging closer and closer to the stressful stimuli and teasing the fear a little bit at a time, it gradually loses its grip on you. The fear simply gives up and goes away... too tired to torment you any more!

Anchors Aweigh

I imagine the most difficult part for you will be generating the willpower to keep experiencing the shameful feelings over and over again -- especially at the beginning when they are strongest and seemingly impossible to overcome. This is where another simple NLP (Neuro Linguistic Programming) trick called **anchoring** can help. The basic premise of anchoring involves replacing a negative fearful emotion with an upbeat, positive one by linking the replacement emotion to a physical "trigger", like the touch of a specific part of the body, and then firing it off when needed to instantly pull the good feeling up on demand. This replacement feeling should be one of genuine strength and power. If it's strongly enough imagined, it will shove the negative emotion aside and take its place... instantly modifying your mood exactly when you need it the most.

Briefly, the anchoring process works like this: First you need to decide on what kind of physical stimulus to use as a trigger. It has to be something that you can do unobtrusively since in our particular case it will be used "in the field", when we're considering approaching a woman. NLP trainers suggest you squeeze your wrist or tug on the third finger of your left hand to set or fire off an anchor, but I never had much luck with those kinds of triggers since they seem too ordinary and tend to just get lost among all the normal daily actions that your hands go through.

What I do instead is use a very small **rubber band** as a trigger because the sensation forms a distinct memory in your nervous system. I loop the band around my wrist and keep it hidden behind my watchband where no one can see it. Pull the rubber band upwards and stretch it about an inch away from your skin, and then let it snap back. The small sting that it makes is your **trigger**. You can snap it either on the top or the bottom of your wrist, but once you make your choice be sure to stick with it consistently because you'll be teaching yourself to associate this specific jolt with a particular kind of emotional storm in your brain, so it's important that the feeling is *exactly the same every time*.

Otherwise the neurology gets confused and nothing happens.

Next you must find some block of time each day where you can be alone to practice for about ten or fifteen minutes in a quiet, private place. Try for total silence, but if it's impossible to find a spot where there's no background racket leaking in, you might want to use some gentle music to cover over it. Get one of those New Age CD's, *Sensual Massage or Winds in the Woods*, something like that. No lyrics, just soft elevator music or even nature sounds like birds, ocean waves... whatever. Lyrics are too distracting. Try to set aside a period of time each day for your training since this is a **conditioning exercise**. Brains aren't like computers... you can't just install the new software in one quick n' easy operation and watch the machine begin performing the new tasks flawlessly. Alas, brains must be taught new tasks by repeated exposure to the same stimuli over and over again until new neural pathways are formed.

All training of any kind is either a mental or psychomotor skill (like playing music or shooting foul shots) that is based on constant, boring repetition until the brain locks the actions into its deep memory somewhere and the task finally becomes "automatic". You have to be committed to seeing any type of training through to its completion. If you play with it a few times and give up, you won't experience any real results. Then you'll call me a crook and demand your money back (you're not getting it. fuck you).

Okay, here's the NLP drill: Get yourself into a relaxed state by listening to the music or the sound of your own breathing. Buy a book on yoga -- they have some fantastic relaxation/breathing techniques. Make sure you have the rubber band in place and have decided on how to snap it *every time*, (over or under). Once you're relaxed, you need to conjure up a very happy or powerful feeling from your past memories and re-live it within your mind. This should be some kind of event or moment when you were swept with feelings of competence and power, as if you'd just won the Stanley Cup and are skating it around the rink held over your head with thousands of people cheering and your team mates surrounding you! Not a hockey guy? How about a spacewalk in the Shuttle payload bay? Floating along and watching the Earth slip by... Whatever you decide to use, you'll have to really get into the fantasy until you can feel the chills running up and down your spine. For this to work, the imagery has to produce a pathway to the intensely powerful feelings.

It's those awesome *feelings* that you'll want zapping through your brain as you reach over and snap the band. Snap once or twice, always the same way. If you can't seem to think of an intensely upbeat personal experience, **then make one up.** Borrow something from one of your favorite movies. Put yourself in the role of Bruce Willis kicking some ass in *Die Hard*, or whatever. Take your time to replay the scene in great detail in your imagination, feeling the rush of emotions build as you do. When those emotions hit a chilling peak as the scene climaxes make sure that the action is surrounding you at its center (put yourself ***in the scene...*** not just standing back as an outside observer like you're watching it all happen on TV), then snap the band. Calm yourself down, then do it once more. Two experiences per training session every day for a month will do the trick.

I used to use the music from *2001: A Space Odyssey* and imagine myself whizzing through the Universe. Then when the music peaked I would trigger the band snap and let the flood of emotions rush through me. After a while I could feel the same powerful state just by snapping the band when I was out someplace!

You might think it's all bullshit but this really does work. **Unfortunately, you've got to stick with the training for several weeks.** Sorry. I didn't invent how slowly your brain works. Once we all switch over to CyberDyne micro-cranial CPU implants I'm sure this'll all get a lot easier. Today, this is the best we can do.

Now you can slowly bring yourself back to reality. This entire procedure shouldn't steal more than 10 minutes out of your day. If you commit yourself to doing it on a regular basis (5 days a week?), not so much the fantasy scene *but the emotions,* will become associated with the sting of the band snapping in your unconscious mind. You can use different fantasy scenes if you want to so you don't get bored with the same one. Just make sure that the passions you generate make you feel **powerful, omnipotent and confident** somehow before you let the band snap. Wait until you have the perfect "high" emotional state buzzing around inside your head before snapping the band. That's really all there is to it. Your unconscious mind is trained (brainwashed?) this way.

You make practical use of this anchoring trick whenever you find yourself in a situation where you could use some courage, or to cut off the negative, defeating self-talk in your head that starts up when the opportunity to chat up some foxy chick presents itself. This can be a great weapon to use against the shame that comes tagging along with those affection-bearing passions that you would like to be able to experience without feeling embarrassed. Now you can.

On Being Appropriate

Finally, a word about being appropriate. If you use the techniques for meeting women that I'm going to be outlining in the next chapter, you'll be faced with asking her out for a date at some logical point in your conversation. A logical (appropriate) moment. In other words, she'll be expecting you to ask the question, and thus will be far more receptive to your offer. I mention this only because guys who struggle with fear of rejection sometimes end up springing the "will-you-date-me" question on a women unexpectedly out of left field (when it's *not* appropriate), at that instant when they are able to briefly overcome their fear through sheer force of will. The problem with the "willpower method" is that the sudden burst of courage it produces will usually occur at a random awkward moment – and when blindsided in this way a woman's first reaction can be a *defensive* one. She'll turn you down almost as an unthinking reflex. (Stop and think about it, so might *you*.) Possibly she'll regret it later, but by then the moment is over and gone.

Needless to say this is not the smoothest way to go about seducing women. You must *guide* the conversation along to the point where she picks up a few advance signals of what you're about to ask her, allowing her time to prepare and decide what her response will be. Then, if the "question" occurs at the proper moment in your conversation with her (as an *escalation* of your dialog, see next chapter...) it will be welcomed as the next logical step, **then the question will seem natural and not embarrassing.** It's only when your asking her out is done at an inappropriate or unexpected time do both parties involved end up feeling awkward, uncomfortable, and even humiliated. Blurting it out will only secure you an embarrassing rejection which reinforces your shame, *making it even more potent in the future.*

The point is that brute force doesn't work when it comes to untangling the twisted neuroses of the mind. You must carefully *desensitize* yourself to the shame that binds you by using anchoring and training methods similar to what I described above. Once the volume on your fear is turned down, it should be possible to assume a natural relaxed attitude about everything that will quietly signal to her that you are a Dominant Male... and that you do this sort of stuff all the time.

Of course, the subjects of toxic shame, addiction, NLP and anchoring are far more complex than what I've described here. This was only meant to give you an introduction and a working knowledge of these subjects to demonstrate how they might be used to control the source of your neurotic fears. If you feel that you'd like to learn more about these topics, there are a wealth of books you can check out. Try searching around on Amazon.com or any of the other major book retailers on the net, or visit your local *Borders or Barnes & Noble* stores. On Amazon, I found a few books on Neuro Linguistic Programming that are probably good enough to help you become an absolute master of the subject. It's probably more than you need to know... but what the hell, I guess you can never know enough about anything:

> ***Advanced NLP Submodalities Interventions***
> by Connirae Andreas
>
> ***NLP and Relationships***
> by Joseph O'Connor, Robin Prior

And, as for the subject of toxic shame, I learned everything that I know about it from the consummate authority on this subject, *John Bradshaw.* Bradshaw is an ex-Catholic priest and a recovered alcoholic who has made an enormous contribution to the understanding of the dynamics of dysfunctional families – and the immense harm that they do to individuals – by passing along family secrets which saddle children with toxic shame. The book that virtually changed my entire life is his first one called *Healing the Shame that Binds You.* If you want to get into any of his other books about families etc., go ahead, but get this one first. **It is absolutely the most profound work on the subject of toxic shame and addiction that you will ever find:**

> ***Healing the Shame That Binds You***
> by John E. Bradshaw
> (Paperback, October 1988 ISBN# 0-932194-86-9)

The Zone of Discomfort

Billy and Pamela have a really outstanding relationship. They share a deep, genuine affection for one another that is the envy of many other friendships. They always have a great time together and have gathered lots of terrific memories of the fun times they have spent. Their relationship is marked by the pleasant trademark of being almost entirely conflict-free. Oh sure there's the occasional disagreement or hurt feeling from a mispoken word or thoughtless act, but nothing compared to most other couples they know. When Billy does something wrong he quickly apologizes or corrects his behavior before Pamela becomes too dismayed, and she does the same on those rare moments when it is she who is at fault.

These moments of disagreement are so few and far between, however, that it's hardly worth mentioning them. Most of the time, Billy and Pamela spend lots of warm and cozy time together... chatting away for hours or enjoying common activities that are fun and fulfilling for both of them. Pamela is quite a looker, and when they go out somewhere socially, Billy always enjoys the jealous looks he gets from other guys at the bar. They hug and kiss frequently, especially when they part company. *They have the most nearly perfect relationship that a man and woman can possibly have.* Never any serious controversy, always very... **comfortable**.

Question: Why do Billy and Pamela have such an incredible relationship with no conflict whatsoever... only loads of fun, quiet times and enjoyment?

Answer: Because Billy and Pamela are not having sex. They are platonic best friends.

That's right. By mutual agreement, they have drained all the sexual expectation out of their relationship. They have settled into a state of banal affinity that is very comfortable and stress-free. This is great, this is very noble and in many ways satisfying to the spirit. There's only one problem though, at the end of the day they get to go home to separate apartments and separate beds and whack off. Maybe they fantasize about each other, or maybe they can't bring themselves to think about each other in that way. Whatever.

One of the problems faced by guys who seem to end up "just friends" instead of lovers with the women they know has to do with something I call the **Zone of Discomfort.** Think for a moment about all the timeless love songs that have ever been written. What are some of the common themes? *Heartbreak, sadness, disillusionment, joy, giddiness, hope, desperation, ecstacy, passion,* *rage, jealousy... yada, yada.* Almost without exception they all describe the great roller coaster of **emotions** that flow from the relations between men and women, from the loftiest joys of ecstatic love to the blackest lows of depression and anger. See what's happening here? These are all powerful emotions; in their own way they are each uncomfortable, painful or distracting. Being possessed by these emotions precipitates a disruption in your life. You end up agonizing over silly things, ruminating over the same thoughts obsessively, or simply being so happy or giddy or sexually addicted that you can't focus and concentrate effectively on the other things you need to devote your attentions and energies to.

In other words, the ongoing gusher of emotions that are touched off between men and women are a royal pain in the ass to experience. That's just how it is in the reality of romance. Welcome to the Zone of Discomfort.

Comfortable Friends – Uncomfortable Lovers

Diving into this turbulent pool of feelings takes a steely willingness that not everyone possesses – especially if you're the kind of guy who likes to keep everything neat and orderly in his life, and especially your emotions. You would rather embrace boredom than find yourself awash by forces that you cannot regulate. You like routine and control... no surprises. You're probably a logical, left-thinking sort of fellow who despises disorder. The realm of weak minds, eh?

Well, eventually a relationship can settle into a nice comfortable routine marked by regular sex and mutual respect of each other's needs and boundaries, *but it never starts out that way.* It can't. Turmoil and disruption and great swings of passion are what characterize the early stages of any man-woman relationship... this is the dreaded zone of discomfort I speak of. Because you realize (maybe only instinctively if you haven't experienced it for yourself yet) that you will have to subject yourself to this unpleasant ordeal, you have chosen instead to steer all your relationships with women away from the zone and towards the more easy to navigate territory of friendship. Friends can relate in a more tolerant, less emotionally exhausting manner right from the get-go. You can effectively short circuit all the difficult stuff and move straight along to the comfortable part of the relationship.

There's only one major problem with this situation of course, that in order to have a sexual-intimate relationship with a woman **you must be committed to passing through and suffering in the zone of discomfort.** All those churning emotions that they write those songs about have to be given free reign to rattle through your brain for weeks and months on end before you can settle into that comfortable relationship that you seek. The primary dynamic between men and women is always described by sexual tension (Nature demands that this be so). Establishing a "friends only" relationship with a woman is un-natural, and therefore falls under a special category in her mind. In order for her to accept you as a friend, strict control of passion must be agreed upon right from the start. That kind of mental / emotional control immediately kills all future thought of passion. You become viewed as something akin to her brother.

Once it's been established that sexual tensions will be subverted in some way, for the woman there is no going back. She will not be open to having the agreement of suppressed passion reversed at some point in the future. So if you agree from the outset that there will be no sex between you, that's it... as far as she's concerned, there will never be any sex between the two of you. Believe this. It will save you years of heartache and wasted efforts.

Guys get themselves into all sorts of trouble thinking that they can "sneak in the back door" on a relationship by establishing a nice little comfortable friendship with a woman first, and then somehow recasting it into a sexually intimate relationship in the future... **THUS SKIPPING ALL THE NASTY, TURBULENT EMOTIONS WAITING FOR THEM IN THE ZONE OF DISCOMFORT!** I'm sorry to be the one to tell you that it's an impossible dream. You must establish in the beginning exactly which fork in the road you will be taking with her: *friend or lover.* There can be no changing your mind and going back down the other path at some later time. Once friends, you can never be lovers; once lovers, you can never become platonic friends again. It simply doesn't work that way.

Why, you may ask? Why wouldn't a woman want me to spare her all those nutty, uncomfortable emotions and just ease her into a nice comfortable relationship with a nice guy like me via the friends-first-then-hot-sex-lovers route? Very simple my friend... women are enthusiastically emotional creatures first and foremost. They actually enjoy the turmoil, frazzled nerves, and crying spells experienced in the zone of discomfort, *and they will NOT be cheated of it!*

Yes, I know, it sounds completely insane to sane, logical guys like us that anyone would actually enjoy feeling strong and sometimes unpleasant emotions. It's perverse. Isn't the goal in Life to duck as much of this stupid shit as possible? Not for women. When dealing with women, remember that for all intents and purposes we are dealing with a kind of alien lifeform. At least in the different ways that their brains operate from that of the average male.

Unfortunately, since they have what we want -- and it's our task to properly seduce it from them -- we have no choice but to play their game as they dictate it must be played. Therefore, in order to bring women and the deeply satisfying joy that only they can bring us into our nice orderly lives, we must steel ourselves to pass through the zone. There is seriously no other way to get to that place you want to be with a woman.

Wimps seek comfort and avoid conflict, whereas *men* are mentally tough and are willing to do what it takes to get the results they desire. That's the difference in a nutshell.

Why You End Up Friends and Not Lovers

Just think how much more nervous and apprehensive you are when going to pick a woman up for a date, as opposed to just getting together with her and hanging out as a pal. Can you relate to this image? Would you rather play it safe and stay away from the man-woman sexual stuff -- too much trouble... too much frustration and horniness? Just be friends for now, then I can put the moves on her later if I want to. Yeah... I can take my time and not have to deal with any of the uncertainty and jealousy and all that other ridiculous crap...

If you find that your thought process about "seducing" women tends to work like this -- and you don't like the results that you've been getting from it – then consider these next seven ideas carefully. They may not all apply to you, but you'll probably see a reflection of yourself here and there I'm sure. Any insight can be valuable when it comes to delivering you from a worthless mindset to one that's at least got a chance of improving your life.

1) No Pain, No Gain

The human consciousness follows the same physical principle as water and electricity: it flows along the path of least resistance. There's no need for me to repeat the litany of wild emotions that are unleashed by a love affair. You've been ducking them all your life, coasting along the twisted path that winds its way along and around – but never *through* – those frightening feelings. I know that it takes a firm commitment to allow yourself to become vulnerable to these emotional storms.

In the sport of bodybuilding, you literally have to work your muscles to the point of exhaustion and then *go beyond that to the point of failure* to do any good. Actual microscopic rips and tears appear in the muscle tissue and the body responds by manufacturing more cell mass. The next time, you must lift more, go faster or push yourself farther to re-create another small amount of damage. Do this enough times and you can build up huge amounts of muscle by adding them layer-by-layer, a little "bit-by-bit" at a time. Body builders have a name for the mindset you need to maintain in order to stay focused down this difficult path... **No Pain, No Gain.**

Well it's the same way with your emotions. If you're the kind of guy who likes to keep your feelings hidden away and never exercise any of them, they will atrophy just like unused muscle and shrivel up. But if you pull them out and test their limits to the point of failure now and again they will respond by becoming more powerful. You just have to trust me when I say this is for real. I've experienced it. You will gain a greater tolerance for negative, painful feelings, and *rejoice* in all the ecstatic ones in a way that you never knew possible before!

The anticipation, the uncertainty, the self-castigation (after a wrong word spoken in thoughtless haste), the worry, the longing and the hoping; the dancing on the ceiling with joy... the disappointment and the ecstacy. You have to decide that you **want** to bring these crazy, illogical disruptions flooding into your life... to decide that your standing around on the sidelines is just **not** going to cut it any more. You must look yourself in the mirror one morning and resolve to become a participant in Life instead of a watcher – and damn the emotional storms that may come rolling in. Career, schooling and obsessive hobbies will all have to take a back seat while you work to get that "special woman" entangled into your life. This kind of sober intellectual commitment is extremely important -- it lays the foundation that you'll need to fall back on whenever the sledding gets tough. And at some point it will get very tough.

But remember, what doesn't kill you *only makes you stronger.* So live!

2) You Are Unskilled

Ignorance creates a vacuum in your consciousness. In your ignorance of what exactly to do and to say to a woman in an approach-seduction situation, fear has slithered in to fill the void. In order to displace this fear, you'll need to load up on all the knowledge that you can seize from a book like this one and others like it. In the next chapter, we'll be delving into the nuts and bolts of the flirting and approaching procedure, but I'll tell you right now that it all pivots around the *central idea of acting like a dominant male.*

Two of the key ideas that will open up a whole new world of available women for you are: 1) learning how to seize opportunities as a reflex, and 2) understanding the critical art of non-verbal communication. Learn to use the power of steady, flirtatious eye contact.

3) What You Don't Believe, You Can't Conceive

I know this sounds like a lot of New Age psycho-babble fluff, but there is some genuine value in the idea that *self-talk and visualizations* establish the internal framework for the kinds of things that we think are possible for us. If the basic instinct that you could really have a loving relationship with a woman does not exist in your mind somewhere, then it's likely that you've absorbed your loneliness into your identity to some degree. What I mean is that you've very discreetly and without knowing it moved from the notion that you often *experience* loneliness, to the belief that you are a lonely person. Loneliness and isolation are not states that you happen to be experiencing – they have become a description of your actual identity! You can have a girl as a friend, but not a girlfriend. Why? *Because lonely guys don't have girlfriends!*

The solution is to re-frame the way you see yourself in your mind's eye. You need learn how to modify the content of your own personal internal dialog -- that "stream-of-consciousness" voice that we all hear inside our heads – in order to change your day-to-day thinking for the better. A complete course in cognitive therapy is beyond the scope of this book, but if you go to Amazon.com and run a search on the keywords "SELF TALK" or "SELF-TALK THERAPY" you should find a few good leads towards books that can help you get a handle on this problem.

4) You Control Your Horniness Instead of Letting it Control You

Let's face it, if you're the kind of guy who's been taking care of your own business for most of your life, then you've probably got the "art" of self-love down to a friggin' science by now! I suspect that you probably practice your craft often and with great enthusiasm also. This is all well and good, but sex drive happens to be one of Nature's great motivators for getting the species to perpetuate itself. Without sex drive, men and women really wouldn't give much of a shit about each other. So as much as you hate to hear it, short-circuiting this urge will eventually lead to some degree of social withdrawal and awkwardness.

One of the drawbacks to the single life is that it's easily embraced as a lifestyle if you're not careful. It's takes no effort at all to backslide into self-indulgence to the point where you no longer consider taking on the responsibility of caring about someone else. This becomes especially easy if you've become proficient at tending to your own sexual needs on a regular basis.

What happens is that you've gotten into the habit of keeping yourself in a very comfortable state of **low horniness** much of the time. Can't say that I blame you. If you've got zero prospects of relieving them, what's the sense of torturing yourself with a chronic case of blue balls? May as well keep your system turned down as low as it can go so that you can sleep at night. It's important to recognize, however, that this low-horniness works against you as much as it does for you by obliterating your motivation to pursue real women. Sure, you scope them out and fantasize about tons of them every day, but since fear controls your actions it remains impossible to break through the barriers that rejection sensitivity and shame have placed around you. ***The valuable thing about Horniness is that it's one of the few emotion-states that is powerful enough to challenge and overpower Fear.*** However, by keeping your horniness in a perpetually depressed state it remains weakened and useless against your fear. Thus you are depriving yourself of your foremost emotional motivator for pursuing women.

With your horniness mostly tamed, it's easy to find yourself interacting with girls as *friends* instead of pursing them as potential lovers. After all, it's the horniness that provides you with your natural male aggression... and if you're not at least somewhat horny then you lack this critical quality of determination. In mating, aggression in the male is vitally important. **In almost no known species of mammal will the females mate with non-aggressive males.** Wimps simply don't stand a chance – even in the world of dogs, cats and gophers! People aren't much different because the game of seduction and mating – while seemingly civilized and very intellectual in the human animal – is still primal at its core. It is propelled by instincts older than Time itself which lie barely hidden under our more civil personalities. Therefore, something as simple as mere aggression (shown in the human male as persistence and focused interest) is rated highly by women everywhere. Male dominance again... dominant males are aggressive and go after what they want. This turns women on. Primally. Sometimes even against their will.

Your brain experiences an inverse relationship between your horniness and your anxiety over approaching women. When one goes up the other goes down by about the same amount. If you're currently at an 80% fear and 20% horniness ratio for instance, try getting that down to 60-40 or even 50-50 and watch what an *effortless* improvement it will make in your ability to relate to women as a man, and not as some non-aggressive eunuch. **Try it as an experiment for a month!** You can always go back to your old "wackin' ways" if your rejection fear doesn't seem to diminish... but I bet that it will.

Therefore I challenge you to consider cutting back on the frequency of your self-pleasuring and porno-viewing, in an effort to recover some of your lost horniness. *Allow your horniness to manage you for a change instead of the other way around!*

Remember, sex drive defeats fear. Anything that helps to lower the volume of your fear will make you more aggressive and demonstrate to women that you will not accept a "buddy-buddy" relationship with them. You will be surprised when you discover how much of your natural male energy you have been wasting away.

5) You'd Rather Be Pitied Than Loved

This one is like an ugly tumor growing from the underbelly of your toxically shamed affection needs. You've managed to adopt some other type of emotion – like *pity* – and substitute it for feelings of love and affection. In other words, since you can't allow yourself to feel love or affection because you're ashamed of these sentiments, you've decided that some creepy substitute like pity is okay. I'm sure psychologists have a fancy name for it -- all I know is that this kind of emotion-swapping is common among people who weren't allowed to experience the full sweep of their emotional life while they were growing up. The result? *Toxic shame cover-up 101,* I suppose you might call it.

You might be using some other form of "swap" emotion besides getting a woman to feel sorry for you... and I'll bet you've gotten real good at hankering around for whatever it is. "Scoring" this emotion gives you the same kind of thrill that a normal guy would get from enjoying an exchange of authentic love and compassion with a real woman. Unable to express these crippled emotions however, you've figured out a way to go for the next best thing.

How can you find out if you've been practicing emotion-swapping as a shame cover-up? Easy, take a mental inventory right now of the pattern of interactions that you commonly have with women – typical exchanges that substitute for actually being *intimate* with them. There's something going on because these unexpressed affection desires will gnaw at your soul like a corrosive acid, and will have to find some alternate escape route. Especially think about your "friendly" relationships with women.

What kind of manipulations and psychological games go on between the two of you? What kind of gratification do you receive from them? You're actually being satisfied in some bizarre way by the extraction of this substitute emotion from her. **This is what you need from her more than sex!** That's why you can put up with being her platonic, sexless buddy, whereas a horny dominant male cannot. It's sick!

My cover-up somehow involved extracting feelings of pity or compassion. When I was a kid, this was the only way that I could get an indifferent mother to show any sort of affection towards me... i.e., by being sick or otherwise downtrodden. Pity did the trick. Possibly it's a different emotion for you. Maybe if you can get women to admire you or fear you or whatever, then *that's* what you really need to secure from them. **Getting a fix of this particular emotion is like a drug for you.** You've gotten yourself hooked and keep repeating the stimulus over and over again just like any other junkie. Your warped relations with women have become habituated like an addiction. You must open your eyes and slap yourself awake as a first step to destroying these addictions. Admit you are powerless and out of control, just like they do in those 12 Step AA programs. I'm serious... this is always the first step: *dispense with your delusions and fess up*.

This may be personally disturbing for you to contemplate I know, but at least you don't have to spill your guts about it in a book and try to sell it on the Internet like I'm doing here! I'm simply asking you to take some time out to meditate (find quiet time to become introspective) on your deeper motivations for the way that you behave, and see what you can find out about yourself. Step back and do some self-observation -- check the attic for old useless clutter, uncomfortable as it may be at first.

Then, when you recognize a disempowering behavior coming on, resolve to change it whenever possible. This process is called *"interrupting your pattern"*. Figure out what your "shame swaps" are for you, then stay alert and steer a new course whenever you find yourself slipping back into those same old crummy patterns!

6) You Are Afraid of Your Own Sexuality

It could be that after years of masturbatory perfection you have now become such a Zen master at the art of self-induced orgasmic ecstasy that you don't dare let anyone into your private playpen. Why? *Because you could easily be controlled as well!* A man with your intense internal pleasure mapping could be manipulated by a woman with ease once she found out just how to pull your strings, so to speak.

I'll admit this sounds rather farfetched, but if you stop and think about it, this is just the sort of basis of a deeply rooted, subconscious fear. A fear so strong that it acts on you *subliminally* to keep all those dangerous women at bay! Again, this is something that you'll have to go deep inside to determine if it's happening to you on some level. Be honest with yourself -- it's all just self-examination and you'll never have to reveal what you discover to anyone. But you can use it to help yourself by becoming aware of just what is really going on in your mind... maybe for the first time in your entire life.

If this type of fear does exist in you, it should be easy to debunk as unreasonable. Yet the mere thought of sexual surrender – thrilling to a woman – can be downright frightening to a man because it suggests complete emasculation. This is a stealthy fear that loses much of it's power over you if you can only drag it out of the dark place it hides and shine some light on it. You are too mentally strong to let any woman control you.

7) You Are Afraid of Becoming Addicted to Her

This is Part B to the idea that we just discussed above. If you've got some form of toxic shame brewing around inside of you, then you also have the basis for some kind of addictive behavior lurking within. Toxic shame is the root cause of all addictions... *period.* You're probably struggling with (or maybe even enjoying) some kind of addiction right now aren't you? If so, then you know how easily the focus of that behavior could be transferred over to some woman that you've really gotten yourself hooked on. Down deep you understand the power that any woman can wield over a man.

Women struggle with their emotional control. They know how delicate female emotions can be (because they are so compelling, thus barely containable), and they are very afraid of being hurt by them. In a similar fashion, men struggle with their *sexuality*... which for many men remains just barely under *their* daily control.

As men, we can easily develop a fear of being overwhelmed and manipulated by a malicious woman skilled in using our own male sexual responses as a weapon turned against us. This is a comparable fear to the one women have of being heartbroken by a two-timing user. Again, this kind of fear is very subliminal and could be sneaking around the edges of your consciousness without your even being aware of it. It could be another brick in the barrier you've erected between yourself and the possibility of becoming intimate with women. Challenge yourself and find out.

Your Failed Commitment to Suffering the Journey

So there you have it, my humble attempt to help you gain a deeper understanding behind the underlying causes of your anxieties about women... fears that are interfering with your natural ability to meet and seduce them from the posture of a dominant male. The things I've discussed here will not apply to every one of you guys, of course, but I'll bet that your own *particular* psychology is cobbled together from bits and pieces of the menu that I've presented here.

It's important to understand that all of this psychobabble is only a prelude to the nuts and bolts of meeting women -- because no amount of technical training will do any good if the subconscious basis for your aberrant behaviors are not searched out, hunted down and stomped into submission by way of your own determined personal self-analysis. The things I've shown you were mostly dug out of my own fucked-up skull and presented in a way that hopefully you can use to correct your own situation. I implore you to make an effort to do the "inner work" necessary to straighten out all the contorted thoughts that are blocking your growth as a man. Only then will you *really* be able to use the tools that I'm going to clue you in on next.

Otherwise those tools will just lay around "rusting in your toolbox" and nothing will ever get fixed in your sorry love life. Read the books I've suggested or search out your own. They will help.

Chapter 5: Essential Flirting

Seek Adventure, Not Outcome

One of the most profound personal leaps that you're going to have to make in order to move from the mindset of a fumbling, failing nerd to that of an easy-going, successful seducer, is to start looking at the entire process of flirting and seduction as a light hearted game instead of a desperate life-and-death test of your manhood.

Did you ever see a quarterback like Joe Montana at the peak of his career when he would get himself into the "zone"? Perfectly timed passes humming down the field like a fine-tuned machine... shredding defenses with a total command of the situation... an unfailing nerve on display? When your confidence is high and things are going good for you, this is how your life works. Everything just seems to fall into place like it should.

Now picture another quarterback who's *lost* his confidence because his team's been on a losing streak. He's coming under lots of criticism, much of it originating from within his own head. He goes out and can't seem to complete a crummy swing pass anymore. Poor throws, bad decisions, forcing the ball into double coverage. Finally he gets picked off for a touchdown by the opposing free safety, and the hometown fans boo him off the field. In football parlance he's "forcing the ball", i.e., *he's trying too hard.*

His desperation to succeed only attracts total failure.

If you've been a life long fuck-up when it comes to making out with women then by now you're probably forcing the ball really bad. You come on like a sweaty, desperate loser so badly in need of any sort of win to boost your non-existent confidence that you might as well be walking around with a block of fetid Limburger cheese hanging out of your ass. Your "trying-too-hard persona" signals every woman in sight that you are a low status male. It proclaims that most of the women you've ever attempted to seduce in the past have voted **NO!**... and by now their consensus opinion trails you everywhere like putrid chick repellant. Get the idea, amigo? Well, every journey begins with a first step. So says Confucius anyway. *Your* very first step up out of the gutter is to shake off this desperate "loser's stench" and get yourself free of the low status handcuffs that you've been shackled with. Let's go...

In this chapter, you will learn that a significant amount of communication passes between men and women **non-verbally.** So much in fact, that you'd think we're all actually telepathic when it comes to the subject of love and romance – and I'm not entirely sure that isn't so. **Even just understanding this one fact places you far ahead of about 70% of the rest of the male population – because most guys are absolutely clueless about the importance of non-verbal communication.** In fact, most of them don't even know it exists. They think that unless they have the balls to come right out and say something directly, then nothing of any importance has happened. You can't imagine how wrong this belief is. That's why women think we're all such brainless lugs even though we've just about invented and built everything of any consequence in the whole fuckin' world! Still, because most of us don't "get it" when it comes to this mysterious, silent communication that goes on between the sexes, we're considered just a bunch of hopeless dumb asses.

But the few guys who do get "it" also get laid like crazy... even if they happen to look like goddamn trolls!

I'm sure you can think of some examples of this "troll" phenomenon right now, either from your own real life experiences or from the world of TV and entertainment. Just look at some of the Hollyweird pukes who have hot women draped all over them. Courtney Cox (Monica from *Friends*) married to David Arquette?

Are you fuckin' kidding me? He looks like that dork we groomed as our spitball target in sophomore chemistry class. Billy Bob Thorton and any of those hot Hollywood babes he's always seen hanging out with (including Angelina Jollie, the one that he *married...*) *Huh?* The '10 Minute Mr. Lube' greaseball who changed my oil yesterday has more appeal than this guy.

Now you can see how being **accomplished** at something and using it to change your attitude in such a way that you give off Dominant Male vibes can completely overwhelm whatever flaws might otherwise exist in your physical appearance. The game of seduction is viewed through an entirely different prism by women don't forget. Nobody looks like Fabio, (thank God!) Nor does any guy need to. We spent all of Chapter 3 discussing how women are turned-on mostly by the non-verbal signals that a man sends which proclaims his lofty position high up on the dominant male scale. Guys only look for signs of attractiveness in women. Tits n' ass, what else is there... right? But women look for *attitude*, which is easier to fake until we make.

The only thing you have to keep in mind when it comes to looking good is simply to show that you are attempting to do the best you can with what you've got. In other words, **grooming, hygiene and dress** are more critical factors in your appearance than any natural handsomeness you might be lacking. Looking well kept demonstrates that you're a *player* because you're concerned about how you are being perceived by women. This awareness by itself broadcasts a powerful signal of its own, and it's all "free" in the sense that there's no need to learn any slick dialog in order to get some attention directed your way. It's all visual and silent.

In other words, you can begin any seduction merely by giving the appearance of being active in the game... of being on the field of play and ready to do battle. That you show yourself to be a *participant* instead of some
A) whupped married guy, or **B)** a defeated, withdrawn loner, sets the stage for the coming seduction by attracting interest from those women who think you might be their "type". Recognize that women

are fickle, they might not like you just because of the way you smell. Remember how I showed you they have a nose for sniffing out a chemical in your blood that tells them instinctively if you're a good genetic match for making babies with them? Crazy as it sounds...

The point is that you can't be attractive to everyone out there and we all have to learn to work our niche. So be careful of the all-or-nothing thinking malady that's a product of toxic shame. John Bradshaw calls this the **Disabled Will...** where you've fallen into the habit of thinking in unreasonable ways that seem more *godlike* than human, all because you've lost touch with your own natural humility. Your rage might also be directed inwardly, making it difficult or impossible to see yourself in an objective light.

How to change all this? You've got to stay on top of your thoughts and self-talk patterns *all the time,* or the twisted cognitive by-products of your repressed shame will slowly take over. Then you'll be just another unattractive, uninteresting wacko for every woman out there to ignore and reject.

The most significant mental readjustment concerns your view of the nature of seduction itself. You must begin to see all the interactions that you're going to have with women from now on as a *fun process*, not a dire contest that must be "won" or lost. Learn to stay focused on the mere enjoyment of flirting and yanking her chain a little (the same way she likes to cocktease men), and avoid getting your guts all knotted up worrying about the outcome of any particular encounter. **Process, not Outcome.** Remember that. Put yourself into a mindset where the act of flirting and joking around becomes an enjoyable end game in itself.

Now don't get me wrong, you still have to understand what your ultimate goal is and to carefully steer events towards that goal as much as you are able to, but you must stop making it all so life and death. As with everything else in Life, *balance* is the key. Remember how I talked about those two "yin and yang" qualities that make a top notch salesman? *Empathy and ego drive...*

consideration of the clients' feelings, but a steady push to close the sale and get your commission regardless? Right now you're probably all ego drive when it comes to seducing or picking up women – you put so much importance on the outcome, making the "sale", that the pressure to score is just enormous and frightening. Too frightening – to the point you can become paralyzed with fear.

If you can learn to think with a little more empathy instead, and forget about the need to score or get laid *that* night, you can take a more relaxed, playful approach to things. To develop some empathy, just remember to flirt for the mere sake of flirting and nothing more. Stop being so goal oriented -- at least initially. Once you've mellowed out your approach and gotten the empathy / playful thing down, then you can begin re-introducing a bit of ego drive into your temperament so that your flirting picks up more purpose and direction.

Of course, you can only carry on the flirting for so long before you reach "the wall"... a point where the woman expects you to **escalate** to the next logical phase of the seduction or get lost. You know what I'm talking about if you have shamed affection needs like I used to, because you'll find yourself so happy to be getting a rise out of her that you don't know when to quit and move forward. The problem is that you can't take it up a notch. Because you are so ashamed to escalate to the next level, you hold onto the flirting phase until you exhaust it. Notice how the woman suddenly goes cold and shuts you off? This happens because she feels like you were just teasing her to get your sick jollies. She accepts that flirting is how the man-woman thing gets started, but once it runs its course, its time to move on to the next step. *She* doesn't know that your shame prevents you from doing so... she thinks that you're just a prick who's been fucking with her. **Bam!** That sound is her slamming the door in your face. No mas. Get lost. Swift and certain rejection.

Learning when to escalate on cue is one of the most critical talents that you must possess in order to become a Master Seducer!

We'll get into all that in a moment. Right now I'd like to illustrate for you a few *Don'ts* to avoid when flirting with women. Doing these things will flag you as a low status male and shoot your chances all to hell with most every women out there (except maybe the lowliest "1's" or "2's"). Once we get these things out of the way, we can move forward to the more positive stuff...

Don't Be a Whiner or Complainer

The more powerless you are to affect things in your world, the more prone you are to complain about them because your frustration has no other outlet. Nothing tags you as a weak, marginalized male quicker than a non-stop barrage of pissing and moaning about anything and everything under the sun. Since you are a helpless, powerless victim of the tides of life, there's nothing left for you to do but bitch about it. And the more you complain, the more evident it is that your frustration has been ongoing and festering for a long time. You struggle under the burden of being one of lifes' chronic losers.

Do you think that dominant males gripe and complain about everything in sight? No? Why is that? **Maybe because they have the power to do the things necessary to make their problems disappear?** They fix the stuff that's wrong in their life instead of helplessly complaining about it.

Complaining = powerlessness = weak male

See? Winning brings with it an "easy-goingness" that is its own special reward. Women appreciate this like an intoxicating flagrance spilling out of your pores. Losers emit an contrasting stench that drives away the female of the species. So even if you're just a minimum wage bottom-of-the-barrel joker who gets pushed around all day, *don't take on the attitude of the defeated male that goes along with it!* Otherwise your love life will only parallel all the rest of the shit that you eat on a daily basis.

Remember... attitude, attitude, **AT-IT-TUDE!** If you must do so, *fake* your way up through the ranks of the male scale -- at least until you can get yourself on the scoreboard and start to achieve some success with women. Then your confidence will build naturally and some of it will translate into a better situation in other aspects of your life. Maybe you'll find the balls to punch you boss in the face or something and find a better career or move to another city and get a fresh start, who knows? Courage creates its own destiny.

**Don't Blab about Stuff that Interests You,
If it's of No Interest to *Her***

I'm amazed at, everywhere I go, how conversationally clueless most people are -- both men and women. Most people seem to have the social sense of the average sledgehammer. I can't tell you how many times, in a restaurant or something, if you dare to open your attention to anyone, they will seize the opportunity to bend your ear about all sorts of crazy shit that's all wrapped up in their own little universe (personal problems, some new gizmo they just bought, etc. etc.) with scant regard as to whether or not you have any idea as to **WHAT THE FUCK THEY'RE EVEN TALKING ABOUT!** Sometimes they launch right into it without even the slightest attempt to set up what they're talking about with some background first... it's like they're just picking up the conversation right where the two of you left off last time, except that there *was* no last time! Or like you're assumed to be telepathic or something and know what the hell they're talking about without being told. Sheesh!

I hope you're not a member of this club, but if you are then consider this your much-needed swift kick in the ass. Take a step back and try to see the entire picture. In order to establish a good rapport with someone there has to be some give and take, and a consideration of the other person's point of view. When you don't know someone, you have to chit-chat about obvious shallow things concerning your current surroundings or common knowledge subjects like sports and weather, or whatever. Then you very gently put out feelers and probe around for a topic that defines some **common interest or passion** that the both of you share – an interest in cars, politics, clothing fashions, movies... whatever – and explore that together. Don't just start hammering away at someone out of the clear blue about some bullshit that *you're* frantic to talk about!

Communication must always be a two-way street. There always has to be some degree of give and take involved to really spark a conversation, otherwise the person being verbally dominated feels like they're being lectured to. It's dehumanizing for an adult. Certainly it conveys the message that there's nothing special about the person you're trying to talk to, since any warm body with a pair of ears and a functioning brain will serve as your foil. People have no desire to play this role, especially for a person who happens to be perfect stranger whom they couldn't give a shit about in the first place. ***A woman likes to think that a man finds her special in some way... that's why he's making an effort to meet her in the first place!***

We'll talk lots more about *specific* kinds of man-woman communication, since seduction is really all about laying down the proper words on a woman. For now, just try to absorb the idea of how not to be a conversational boor and a bore. Oh and P.S., the best way to keep a woman interested in you is to get her talking about **herself**. You do the listening – speak only enough to guide the conversation along, always leading it back to her interests. If you're hitting it off, she'll be giving you cues as to what subjects to talk about *if you take the time to listen carefully*. We'll get into this when I show you a few simple tricks concerning how to establish a deep sense of rapport with anyone just like a professional (i.e., crooked) "used" car salesman. (Relax, all you wonderful used car salesmen out there who might be reading this, I'm just setting up the next segment on developing a sense of humor... *ha, ha, ha...*)

Know the Difference Between having a Sense of Humor and Being a Jokin' Asshole

Spewing out a non-stop stream of dumb jokes and other dreck designed to keep everyone in stitches is another pathetic cry for attention... at least that's how it's perceived by most people. It's alright to make women laugh – in fact it's one of the finest ways there is to create a sense of affinity -- but there's an art to it that involves two critical elements: 1) *cleverness* and 2) *timing*.

When it comes to humor, women are mostly impressed by a **clever wit.** An uncommon observation made from a twisted, funny perspective is sure to get them going. The timing aspect of it comes from knowing *when* to make the joke. You have to be patient and pick your spots carefully. Then, when you see the perfect moment, slip in your clever observation or cruelly funny take on things. Then shut the fuck up for a while! Don't overdo it and keeping stringing the joke along just because it was so good it got an initial laugh. This is what I mean by a "jokin' asshole"... a guy who doesn't know when to quit until he kills the source of the joke and everybody stops laughing. Yeah it feels good to make people laugh, but you have to be careful not to get addicted to the audience feedback and keep going back to the well too often because it will run dry. And it will do so very suddenly. *Bang*... now you've crossed over from clever guy with a sense of humor, to a pitiful jokin' asshole.

Humor is tough -- not everyone has a knack for it, but **less is always more**. Make a little clever joke here and there, then make your "exit" (give it a rest) before you wear out your welcome. Try to keep this cardinal rule in mind when developing your own personal sense of humor: humor is the product of a quick mind that can disassemble whatever's happening around it and put it back together in an absurdly enlightening way that tickles the funnybone. Run a lot of funny scenarios in your mind, but keep most of them to yourself. Cull out only the very best stuff to present to your "audience". You'll get better at knowing when to pick your spots with some practice.

In order to use humor most effectively, you only need to remember the Golden Axiom of the professional comedian... *always leave 'em wanting more!*

Don't Spill Your Guts, Reveal Yourself Slowly...

This is the poor, shoeless cousin to the jokin' asshole... the kind of guy who's telling you all about the size and shape of his fuckin' hemorrhoids after you've "known" him for all of about a minute. Why don't you just wear a sandwich board around your ass that proclaims: **Desperate Loser In Dire Need of Someone to Share His Pathetic Life** and just save us all the trouble? There's no better way to throw a bucket of cold water on a budding seduction than by spilling out all your secrets, fears, medical history, early childhood traumas and bathroom habits within the first half hour of meeting someone!

MYSTERY!... you've got to establish some goddamn mystery with a woman! Did you ever see James Bond telling the sweet young hottie he's lining up for a cue shot into his bedroom all about his latest mission and how many evil geniuses he killed last week? No! And it's not just because he's been trained to be secretive about his life... it's because Bond is a man who is careful to always maintain an air of mystery about himself, and the women lap it up like kittens at a dish of warm milk!

Being mysterious is **sexy**, it's one of the most intriguing qualities in any man. Women are curious about a man who doesn't let on everything about himself -- and their curiosity is a hook that you can use to lead them around by.

I play around with waitresses at the various eateries that I hang out at, and I'm always careful to dole out only little bits and pieces of myself whenever I talk to them. They'll hang around and chit-chat with me -- inevitably slipping in a personal question now and then *almost as if they can't help themselves*. Their curiosity about me must really nag them! I paint a picture of who I am layer by layer though, forcing them to wait and see the finished product.

But the product called "me" is never finished... I'm always mindful to toss them a curveball and show a different aspect of myself whenever they think they have me figured out or "pegged". This works to keep their interest piqued like a charm. It's a great method to use whenever you're in a situation where you frequently encounter girls that you'd like to seduce on a regular basis, like at work or school.

Always Have Your Antenna Out

As a review, just remember to stay focused on the process of flirting and kidding around with women, and release yourself from worrying about what the outcome should be. If you come to view the opportunity to flirt as a fun thing to do for it's own sake, instead of choking on the pressure of trying to score with her, you'll at least be able to function. The pressure of trying to score all the time is too much even for guys who are good at it, much less for the unskilled and the low confident. Being able to feel you have *no goal* in mind but to have a little verbal banter defuses the pressure cooker and re-frames what's happening in your mind so that it isn't so life and death. This allows you to: 1) open your mouth and not be afraid to at least say *something*... thus subduing your rejection sensitivity, and 2) assume a *relaxed attitude* that takes you light-years down the right track towards actually doing the thing that you're not really even trying to do, i.e., seduce her!

That's because a laid back attitude is the signature trademark of the High Status Male... exactly what women find most attractive!

Pretending You Don't Want It

If you really want something, the best way to get it (especially if it involves the cooperation of other people) is to pretend that you don't want it. This perverse but true phenomenon plays into the Universe's twisted desire to reward the nonchalant... and *torture* the desperate. Why this is so? Go figure. All I know is that this "law" seems to hold up under all aspects of life...

women, making money, getting killed in an accident (you ever notice how it's the safety conscious who always seem to invite disaster?), whatever. Since none of us can beat it, we may as well play along with it. Like the fighting art of *Judo*, you must learn to turn your opponent's weight and strength against him!

If you can place most of your focus on the act of flirting and little on the potential results – then you will find yourself in a position to look at the world in an entirely different light. Everywhere you turn "flirtable" women will be available for you to play with. I know that your relationship with the fear of rejection is very troublesome for you, but this new kind of attitude is a fantastic way to short-circuit away much of its power. When you flirt with a woman, you're just tickling around the edges of her psyche to determine if she has even the slightest amount of interest in you. If after a moment or two there doesn't seem to be any, then you simply move on... no harm, no foul.

If there is some interest however, then you pay attention to her subtle cues and escalate the conversation appropriately. I'll show you exactly how it's done step-by-step later in this chapter. *It simply can't get any more low pressure than this.* You have to take some kind of small chance in order to make contact with a woman... there just isn't any way to do it with absolute zero risk to your ego. It's like trying to dive into a pool naked without getting wet. It can't be done.

Women have a life long desire to experience intense emotions – she's always interested in a man who seems like he might be able to ignite forbidden passions in her. This is why it's of paramount importance that within minutes of first contact with any woman you establish the fact that you find her intriguing in a romantic / sexual way, or else you'll find yourself filed away into the "dud-bud" category very quickly.

The First Encounter is always a very perilous moment for her. It plays into every romantic fantasy she's ever had since childhood. She must feel at least some small spark of intimate possibility, or whatever potential seduction might be in the offing will fizzle out right on the spot. **Creating this spark of passion is your main task upon any initial meeting with a woman... NOTHING IS MORE IMPORTANT!**

I know this kind of advice may not be appropriate in situations where you will never get a chance to see her again – like a chance passing on the street or in a park. If that's the case you'll just have to make a bold move because you need to get some future contact information out of her *immediately*. Be warned however that this involves subjecting yourself to a higher degree of risk and an increased chance of rejection, so think of skipping any of the following steps as an advanced move to be attempted later on in your seduction career after you've gained a good deal of natural confidence and skill at this stuff. Stick with the program at first.

Your First Words are Always Non-Verbal

I like to consider what I teach as *seduction*, and having romantically meaningful conversations with women is the one big moat you will need to cross in order to gain membership. *Women require courting.* If you can't talk to 'em, you ain't gettin' nowhere!

However having said that, *talking* is not the first thing that you ever want to do when you are sniffing around with the thought of seducing a woman. This of course is the essence of your problem with rejection... i.e., your fear of saying the "wrong thing" and thus making a complete ass of yourself. Guys in general, and particularly guys like you and me (over-thinkers), get all bent out of shape trying to come up with the perfect opening line... the icebreaker, the stunningly clever witticism, that will make her swoon and tumble into a helpless love trance. I've been there, and so have you. You run through a scan of possible dialogs and ruthlessly reject each one as inappropriate, ignorant or stupid. There's nothing that seems to fit the situation or the girl in question. Unable to dream up the perfect line, we withdraw and fade away... our throats choked shut with fear.

But by focusing so much on the super-critical "pick-up line", we only place enormous pressure on ourselves to create something amazingly fluent on the spot – precise dialog that a screenwriter in Hollywood might labor over *for days* and re-write ten times over in order to get perfect for his fictitious characters. Listen, it can't be done. We will always wilt under this tremendous strain and simply clam up every time. Do you want to know what the real irony is concerning the dilemma of the perfect pick-up line though?

None of it matters.

Women hate dopey pick-up lines! They think they're stupid, contrived and for the most part completely ignore them. Her emotions get so spiked when she suddenly realizes that some guy is trying to make romantic contact with her that she usually doesn't even hear what the fuck he's saying anyway! How's that for a swift kick in the balls... all that pain and agony pulling up the courage to say something that we pray is even halfway clever or funny and the whole exercise is for nothing. Women shrug off our cleverest lines as stupid pick-up bullshit!

What they notice more than anything else is the intent of what we are trying to do... i.e., meet them. The intent communicated by our actions is a far bigger deal than the actual words we spit out!

Did you get what I just said? The *real* communication isn't to be found in the verbal part of our interaction with women (the goofy pick-up line), but in the non-verbal statement of our intent to meet them. Women tend to invariably "read between the lines" of whatever a man's actually saying and search for the hidden meaning behind his cloud of words. **It's the non-verbal signals coming from a man that are always assigned the most weight by women.** This seemingly academic little tidbit of information is something that I'll bet 95% of men don't completely understand or give any credence to. They think it's their clever "rap" that makes all the difference in either scoring with women or bombing out.

When instead, it's the silent intent that lies behind their babbling that's being read and deciphered by the women they are trying to impress!

This fact of mating life gives you an important clue as to the proper way to conduct yourself around the women you find attractive. This is why every book out there on the subject of meeting women – including this one – keeps relentlessly hammering away at the notion of attitude, attitude, ***ATTITUDE!*** Yes I know, you're fuckin' sick of it already. You don't have any natural confidence with women so you don't project this kind of sexy "he-man" attitude like all the tough guys, con artists and various other slick bastards out there. That's why they're out there scoring like crazy and you're home beating your meat. Well let's see if we can't begin to find an immediate work-around for this problem... a genuine solution that will suit a non-aggressive male like yourself.

The Rejection-Proof First Contact

It's important that you establish man-woman overtones right away when you first meet an attractive girl. Make sure she knows this will not be an exercise in polite pleasantries. At first she may get nervous, defensive or even cold, but once she senses that the man who is interested in her is a dominant one, she will pop off into a twilight zone of deeply programmed instinct. More on this so-called "Trance of Romance" later, but for now realize that if you create this state it is delicate and easily ruined. One of the worse things that you can do during the opening phases of a seduction is to try making a joke about what is happening to relieve the building tension... *"hey, relax baby I'm just trying to pick you up here, ha-ha... you love it when a guy does this don't you?... ha ha... It's okay, I'm available and ready for your love, ha, ha..."* Ha ha my ass... you broke the tension alright, all the man-woman dynamic tension that is the essence of moving her into the seductive trance.

The tension in your blue-balls will now continue to build until you 'hand' them over to good 'ol Rosie for further processing.

Step 1 : Don't surrender to your shame.

Remember, you are **deeply ashamed** to be displaying any sort of need for affection -- that's why meeting women is so difficult for you. But recall how I said that the only way to get beyond your shame is to go *straight through* it? You've been trying to zig-zag your way around it for your entire miserable life and look where it's gotten you. Nowhere. Now do it my way!

Make sure to use your NLP anchor to help get yourself into the proper frame of mind. Snap the rubber band you keep hidden behind your wristwatch a few times to get all those powerful and upbeat emotions flowing through your brain. This will act like novocaine for your shame (hey, I like that!...). Whatever you do, don't just passively give in to your shame and the terrible fear that it creates -- stay resolved to fight it whatever way you can. Use every dirty psychological trick you can dig up to reduce the volume of all your negative self-talk. Replace it with upbeat, courageous notions of yourself wherever possible.

Step 2 : Knock her off her Pedestal.

What the hell do I mean by that? Well, one of your problems is that you've built up great looking women to be *untouchable goddesses* in your mind. This stops you from approaching them because you are in awe of them. It's like when someone idolizes a celebrity then finally gets a chance to meet the object of their "reverence". What happens? They freeze up and can't speak a word! Why? Because the celebrity has been built up to such superhuman proportions in the mind of the adoring fan, that seeing him for real creates a paralyzing overload in his brain and he can't function in that person's presence.

Because attractive women have become nothing more than untouchable fantasy creatures which you only idolize and dream about you can't face them for real. When you encounter one it's like you've suddenly found yourself in the presence of God Almighty and all you can do is fall to the ground and tremble like some old Biblical prophet. This adoring attitude is a certain trademark of the low status submissive male, the guy that all women (except perhaps the most terrifying fatties) absolutely *despise*. If they even sense this as being your first non-verbal communication, you are dead before you open your mouth to utter that stupid pick-up line you've been working on all week. Read that again... **YOU ARE DEAD!** Death due to weak-male vibrations being emitted from your low status little body!

The first thing you absolutely **MUST** do is shed the suicidal attitude of subservient adoration like a gasoline-soaked jock strap that just caught fire. Use any kind of mental trick necessary to knock her out of the clouds and back down to reality in your mind. When you see a smokin' babe from now on, think of how crappy she must look in the morning disheveled and stinking of sour booze, hungover and make-upless. Imagine how she'll look when she's a 60 year old hag if you have to. The idea is not to totally turn yourself off to her, but to *snap yourself out of it* and realize that she's only human like you with warts and smelly farts and all the rest of it. The "look" she presents to the world is just her mask.

And don't forget that a lot of these great looking women turn out to be stupid asses, miserable nags or just plain psycho bitches once you get to know them. I met one that looked pretty cool but who turned out to have a medicine cabinet brimming with drugs from her psychiatrist. She was depressed and spent her afternoons lying around the house all day watching soap operas, didn't have a job, etc. etc. But she looked great when she went out bar-hopping, and always had guys sniffing around her... all long legs and pointy tits. Turns out that the attention of men was the only thing that got her out of her funk (the other 90% of her life). So don't think that just because she's a fox the whole package is complete. A woman who's lazy or crazy is a real boner shrinker after a while.

Take the attitude that, not only is she *not* some goddess that must be worshiped, she may not even be as sexy as she appears once you get to know her. Adopt the outlook that she has to *prove herself worthy to you.* Yeah she might be a hottie and you're just an ordinary joe, but that situation could turn right around once both your personalities are revealed to one another. Use whatever mental image you must to take her down a few pegs in your mind before you approach her. This tilts the balance of the "attitude teeter-totter" in your favor. Her status goes down in your mind, while your status as a man goes up in her mind. It works.

Step 3 : Demonstrate some Mystery.

Okay, now that you've executed this "inner game" to perfection (kind of like practicing a golf swing in your mind before actually taking your shot) you're ready to make first contact. *Remember, first meaningful contact between men and women is always non-verbal.* Guys go wrong by sneaking up to a woman uninvited and blurting out their carefully rehearsed pick-up line straight out of left field. The woman gets scared, jumps back in wide-eyed terror, and flames you with a cold glare. Now you become even more nervous, choke on your next words, fuck up some more, make a total ass of yourself, and end up taking a bath in your toxic shame. Afterwards, you pledge to never ever again try to pick up another woman because they all hate you!

What went wrong? *You opened verbally!* Only rock stars and celebrities can open verbally because their fame has preceded them and laid out all the groundwork in advance. A guy like you or me has to coerce some signal of interest from a woman *first.* This is why dress and clean grooming and smelling freshly showered are so important to your chances for success, it's the very first non-verbal signal of your availability. Forget the scum bum "grunge" look... that's for guys who have balls of brass and aren't afraid to impose themselves into a woman's personal space no matter what they look like. If you had balls of brass you wouldn't be reading this book, so *your* tack must be entirely different. You have to affect a sense of style that shows you have something more on the ball that the grunge-head doesn't. You have to do everything you can to draw a **GO** signal out of her to support your weak ego. Once your confidence goes up so will your attitude –

then you can have some fun pushing the envelope of rejection. For now though, go with the style "hook" and save yourself the agony. What you need most are a few notches in the WIN column... concentrate on getting some of those first.

Step 4 : Catch her eye.

I know this can a tough one. The socially-ingrained reflex to quickly look away if we get caught looking at someone is universally human. **But solid eye-contact is a bold signal of male status.** Therefore you must train yourself to defeat your 'averted gaze' reflex and begin to look people in the eye. It's sort of how I learned not to blink my eyes when putting in contact lenses. My blink reflex made it near impossible to insert them at first, but now my eyes lay open and relaxed as I plop the contacts onto my corneas and swirl them around. I defeated my natural born "blink reflex" with practice, and in a similar fashion, you can learn to defeat your "look away" reflex with practice too.

Simply become **conscious** of it wherever you are... at the store, in your car, whatever. Practice on old ladies and dogs if you have to, but keep doing it until you completely deaden the urge to look away when some cute chick catches you checking her out. Couple that with a quick, genuine smile and you're on your way to eye contact mastery in no time! Watch how it creates lots of opportunities with women out of thin air where normally you might've just passed like two ships in the night and never seen each other again.

I call this tactic *"Catching an Eye"*. This is one of the most effective skills you'll need to have in order to become really excellent at meeting and seducing women!

Timing is very important when it comes to communicating interest via eye contact. Try to hold eye contact with her *and smile* for about 5 seconds (the longest 5 seconds of your fucking life it will seem like!...), then break away for about two seconds to give her a psychological break, and then pick up the lingering eye contact again. ***Lingering eye contact is your very first "hello"... your initial greeting as a man greets a woman.*** It immediately sets the stage for 1) determining if she has any further interest in you, and 2) keeping you out of the "friends" rat-trap.

Don't get scared on me now... you have to learn how to make at least this little bit of effort. *You can do it!* An eye exchange is easy, straightforward and universally accepted as an initial man-woman mating communication.

Step 5 : Delete the Emotion and Save the Data.

Whatever you do, don't get caught up in the trap of **mentally berating yourself** for any kind of perceived rejection or failure, even a lowly "eye-to-eye" one. This will only trigger another shame episode and drive your courage down even further. And if you continue acting fearful and shy around women, you will be exhibiting a very loud, "non-mating call" that will send them running for the hills. View each opportunity that didn't pan out as another training or practice exercise. I know this is sounds hard to do because you love to wallow in your shame and sorrow like a pig in slop – but understand that winning the internal struggle that goes on within your head is THE entire game when it comes to seduction.

After any attempt to meet a woman that didn't go off as you would've liked, force yourself to observe what you did objectively – identify whatever mistakes you seemed to make, and try to get a feel for the kind of dominant male image you projected (or failed to project). And here's another radical idea: maybe it wasn't your fault... don't forget that it takes two to tango. Even if you do everything perfectly, the woman still has to want to play or any attempt to reach out and make contact with her will fail. She could not be in the mood that day, or not in the market... *or both.* How can you know this ahead of time?

Remember that in the best of circumstances you can only control *half* of this equation, so don't burden yourself with the phony (self-hating) idea that you're responsible for the outcome of the entire exchange with every woman you ever meet all the time and that she has nothing at all to say about what happens! That's nutty, god-like, Disabled Will thinking. We are not hypnotists who can place women under a spell and make them do as we command.

Anyway, the most effective mind-set to adopt for yourself is to 1) drain away all the emotion from these flubs, 2) calmly and methodically (like a scientist) extract the useful data, then 3) erase the file from memory and move on... applying what you learned to improve your chances next time. **It's all these damned negative emotions surrounding the task of seduction that makes the objective learning and improving your skills so difficult.**

Step 6 : Your Unbearable Lightness of Being.

Okay, once you've caught an eye, immediately shoot her a warm smile before she looks away. This should be what I call an **Old Friend Smile,** the sort of smile that you would burst across your face if you'd just spotted an old friend. Naturally you can't shout out *"hey how's it goin'?..."* or something like that because this would be inappropriate. But the warm smile communicates both your interest and your physical harmlessness to her in a split second, and lobs the ball onto her side of the court. Now you watch for her reaction. If she smiles back *and* holds your eye, you've just picked up a major **GO** signal!

If she smiles but then looks away quickly, she was probably just mirroring back your smile reflexively as most people will... but is displaying the fact that she isn't interested in pursuing any further contact with you. She's being polite but telling you to keep your distance. Not interested. *See how the two of you are talking without saying any words?* This is what I mean when I tell you that the first meaningful (i.e., man-woman) exchange between two potential mates is always non-verbal. They don't write songs about lingering looks across a crowded room for nothing!

"But no one ever looks at me, I never get any eye contact..." you're may be pissing and moaning right now. Two reasons for this: 1) you don't go looking for it and, 2) you don't present any sort of intriguing visual presentation to stir up her interest.

If you're dressed like a non-descript slob most of the time, you tend to become invisible – you melt into the background, disqualify yourself in advance. Couple that with the fact that you commonly avert most everyone's gaze because you're withdrawn and hateful as a result of stewing in your shame for so long, and well, you can see what's happening... *women are picking up powerful stay away signals from you!* That's right, you've been communicating non-verbally with women all your life and you don't even realize it! The problem is that you've been sending out the **completely wrong message**... *stay away, I'm a loser, I'm not worthy.* Inadvertent perhaps, but clear as a bell nonetheless.

You need to strike just the right balance between having the courage to say something, and coming on too strong. Either extreme leads to its own kind of failure -- either you reject yourself, or she likely rejects you. Some degree of nervousness on your part is perfectly fine and even expected. You are openly demonstrating the desire to take a risk *when the reward seems valuable enough (her!).* **This is a tremendous non-verbal shout of your high male status!** So don't feel like you have to be calm as a rock in order to move on a woman – a little bit of nervousness makes you seem honest and even sort of cute. Just keep your anchor band working to fight off any major shame outbreaks.

Okay, so you've done the opening non-verbal cha-cha, now it's time to "go verbal" and actually *say something...*

Step 7 : Get a Lifeline

First thing you should know about your opening words, *forget the stupid fuckin' pick-up lines!* They suck, women think they're dumb and don't even hear them through the fog of their own nervousness anyway. Yes, you heard that right, she's nervous too. I don't care how foxy she is... she could be right off the pages of Playboy for all I care and you might be nothing more than a skinny little geek, but when a man moves on a woman her instincts take over and force her into a state of arousal whether she likes it or not. It triggers a cascade of subconscious thought processes that run just like a software program. Now don't get me wrong here, I'm not talking about sexual arousal (that happens later) I mean having her man-woman-mating instincts getting all perked up despite herself.

The situation is just as stressful for her as it is for you. The difference is that, as the guy, you get to die the thousand deaths of the coward by running over and over what you're going to say to her *in advance*, whereas the woman gets sandbagged by the whole thing out of the clear blue. In a different way it's just as bad. Just think how you would feel if, after having caught some girls' eye you innocently smile back and return to your solitary thoughts, when suddenly she waltzes over and starts chatting you up in a way that suggests a romantic interest in you? Your first reaction would tend to be defensive, because being surprised startles us and our first reflex is to turtle-up into our shells until we figure out what's going on. So you too must allow for this brief moment of non-composure to let her emotions stabilize themselves before coming on too strong.

In fact, this is a great opportunity for you to make a classy first impression on her by demonstrating some *empathy* for her discomfort. In other words, you're not just wrapped up in your own little world, but have some sensitivity for the feelings other people. Ease her tension, provide a shield behind which she can hide her awkwardness by making a light, clever joke about something going on around the two of you... use laughter as your icebreaker.

Wait a few minutes to let the conversation pick up a bit of steam, and then shake her hand and exchange names. Remember the handshake trick I showed you before? Rotate your wrist very slightly (and slowly...) to your right (clockwise) until her hand is above yours, sort of like the knight in shining armor preparing to kiss the hand of the fair maiden. Now LISTEN to her say her name and REMEMBER IT! Then use her name within the next sentence or two *exactly as she gave it to you.* If she said 'Susan' then call her Susan, not Sue or especially Suzie. Never take the liberty of "cutesying up" someone's name when you first meet them as if you're an old pal or something. *This is insulting!* It shows that you have no respect for how a person wishes to present themself to others.

How would you like it if, after having introduced yourself to your new manager as 'John' he immediately began calling you Johnny or Jackie? Maybe you hate being called those names, how would he know? The point is that he *doesn't* know. So how rude is it of him to call you a by some goofy nickname that he makes up on the spot? It shows how little he respects you -- and that's why it's insulting. Do you think this joker would call the President of the company 'Johnny' even if he told him it was okay to call him John instead of Mr. President? No way. What's the difference?... **Fear and Respect!**

What? You say people do this to you all the time? So why not give them a taste of their own medicine for once? **Well they do it because you give off the fucking stench of the low status male!** People abuse the lowest part of the food chain without even thinking about it. Janitors, cabbies, bus boys, toll collectors... who cares about them? That's why it's important to start dressing and acting like you *expect other people to respect you!* If you do, they will!

But if instead you project the image of the lowly, poorly-dressed, eye-averting, minimum-wage-earning, rusty-car-driving scumbag whom life and society routinely trample on, then people will feel free to join in on the fun... including women! That's why you hate everybody! You are the only one who can turn this situation around for yourself. So smarten up and start demanding some respect for yourself even if you DO shovel shit for $5 bucks an hour. **Just don't act like it!**

Okay, sorry... I went nuts there for a second. Now, back to getting her to throw you a lifeline. Getting a lifeline means that -- if a woman is interested in talking with you -- she'll give you something to work with. She'll *signal* you concerning topics to talk about that are safe and interesting to her. This is a hint that she would be willing to talk to you "as an experiment" for a few minutes about this particular topic. She won't come right out and say "let's talk about x", but if she's even the slightest bit interested in you, she will offer you this subtle clue. That's why to have to listen... it's her first test (of many more in the future...) to see if you have something going on in your head other than trying to catch a glimpse of her boobs so you can run home and wack off. Here's an example:

"Hi, how are you doing? Looks like another Plumbers' Bong getting fobbed off as 'art'..." [says you, cleverly, to a cute girl looking over an incomprehensibly weird copper-tubing 'sculpture' at your towns' annual outdoor summer art festival]

"Yeah, I can't figure out what room in my new apartment this thing would look good in..." She smiles back.

"Maybe the bathroom, ha-ha! Speaking of bathrooms, you should see what I found living under my... [blah,blah... stupid, uninteresting bullshit about me... blah,blah... and here's some more...]"

WRONG!!!

She just told you what's all new and exciting about her life if you would just open up your shit-clogged ears and listen... *her new apartment!* Why would she drop such an obvious hint about something like that to a stranger if she wasn't excited to talk about it, to anybody? So go back and erase the part where you were going to tell her all about the alien face-hugger living under your bathroom sink, and instead say something like:

"Oh, you've got a new apartment? Cool. Are you out here

looking for some wall hangings? Did you see those goofy cartoon scenics the guy three booths back is selling?" says you.

"No! Where?" she replies, eyes wide and glowing.

"Back this way. Comon, I'll show you. Let's check them out..." you say as you lead the way into a spirited afternoon of junk-hunting with your new friend.

See? She wants to talk about her new apartment. It's interesting to her. But not to you, you say? Too bad. She's got what you want... and you must seduce it from her. So you must always be the one to defer to her wishes and interests.

Besides, you want to hold onto some mystery about yourself in the beginning anyway, so let her do most of the talking. You'll have plenty of time in the future to reveal things about yourself. Your job is to steer the conversation based on further clues as to what she wants to talk about. More testing. If you continue to gain her interest, you can be sure that more 'suggestions' will be forthcoming. In between, you demonstrate that you are safe and funny, flirtatious, and that you're interested in her *as a man*... not as her new buddy boy.

If she doesn't toss you any lifelines and you find that trying to have a conversation with her is like pulling teeth, then what's happening? *Right, you're being rejected!* Why? Who knows?... maybe she's married, or engaged, maybe she's just getting over a bad breakup, maybe your B.O. (And thus your blood, remember?) smells foul. It's impossible to say why people don't connect. But this shouldn't happen to you if you've been doing things in their correct sequence. Why? Because you got a non-verbal GO signal before you ever opened your mouth, right? So she's going to at least give you a chance to impress her based on your look, style and smile. There'll be at least one lifeline offered, and more to follow if you don't blow it and bore her to death. I know that sometimes you can't always catch her eye depending on the circumstance (it might have even been difficult in the fictitious scenario I just gave you), so you'll have to take more of a chance but hey... **snap your band, charge up and go for it!** You have to establish your own level of comfort at doing this stuff. It will surely improve with practice.

On Rejection Sensitivity

There's another aspect to shyness which might be giving you some distress, and that's the **flip side of shyness which is rage.** Rage, or even just a chronic, simmering anger that interferes with your ability to relate normally to others, is the dark twin of rejection sensitivity. Both these disempowering emotions have their source in a tendency to derive a major portion of your self-esteem from the judgement of others. Walking around all the time being psychologically vulnerable to what you perceive to be the silent appraisal of everyone around you will make you hypersensitive and fearful. That's where your shyness comes from. *But after a while, you will come to hate what you fear.* Your "tormentors" will eventually catch the focus of your hatred and it will express itself as a barely contained urge to fly into a rage when things don't immediately go your way. Check yourself for road rage for instance. Got any? I thought so. This is a nasty, powerful emotion that you must learn to deal with before it takes complete control of you and you either lash out at others or yourself.

A lingering, just-below-the-surface anger is one of the chief impediments to your pursuit of women. It blocks you from exhibiting the patience necessary to effect a calm, confident, easy going manner that women read as the signature of a high status male. A guy who learns to vent with sarcasm or a short temper is only showing off his low male status. Just a lowly grunt who gets kicked around all the time... ya know? Feeling like you're a full time **victim of life** will make it difficult for you to make an impression with women that puts you in a favorable light.

I want you to be aware that this is yet another momentous battle you'll be fighting inside your own head. The cycle of ***failure-desperation-rage-failure*** has to be broken somehow. You must be determined to destroy it by practicing these guidelines even if you have to perform them like a robot at first. At least until you start to get some success and can calm down a little. There will come a time when you fail to collect a positive GO signal, but decide to press forward into a conversation anyway. *Congratulations!* You have kicked your fear in the balls for once! A good, solid, personal victory that only you can really appreciate.

If, despite your best efforts, if you don't get any lifelines from the girl, then she obviously isn't interested in you. Disengage gracefully and move on. Fighting the good fight now is like struggling in quicksand -- you'll only sink deeper and make it more and more impossible to extricate yourself without massive humiliation. Don't make the mistake of getting into a righteous test of wills with her. Your obstinate manner only convinces her that you are the kind of asshole she wants no part of. Some chicks act cool at first precisely to smoke out the kind of short-tempered joker who's very insecure and blows up at the first sign of being rebuffed. *This is simply a test to determine your male status – don't fail it!* Here's where you really have to stand down your shame and refuse to let it produce the kind of delusional thinking about how everyone is out to get you.

Learn how to cut your losses and retreat with grace and dignity. Add the encounter to your experience base and learn something from it, then live to fight another day.

Instant Rapport?

Alright let's review a little. You've worked on your inner game, decided to **accept the process of flirting** for the lighthearted fun that it is, and not get all bend out of shape worrying about the high pressure notion of "...I must score at all costs!" You're a calm, high status dude now. Next you spotted a prospect, **got caught looking,** and held on for dear life. A **snap of the anchor** band brings up a tide of powerful emotions to keep the negative ones boxed up in a corner of your mind where they can do no harm for now. You **made non-verbal contact,** smiled and flirted with her silently. Your opening words are the next logical step... and therefore welcomed. They are friendly and show that you are harmless.

You've offered up a bit of **clever humor** about whatever's going on around the two of you wherever you happen to find yourselves. You've listened closely and **picked up a lifeline** from her about something she's willing and interested to talk about. You've **exchanged names** and you've **used her name** within a few seconds of discovering it as you offered her a **light, sincere compliment.** (Only compliment her on her "look"... hair, jewelry, tattoos, etc., never her body.)

If you couldn't think of a compliment right away, then skip it for now and pick up on your lifeline -- you can slip her a compliment as you part company later on. If you shook her hand you remembered to use the little **handshake trick** to give her a subtle subconscious thrill ride. You're also doing your best to maintain an open, inviting, harmless **body language posture** with your arms at your side and facing her square on... no crossed arms, scowls or James Dean-like sideways looks.

Well ain't we havin' some fun! Just remember to stay focused on *playing* with her and don't get all nervous thinking about how you're going to go about asking for her phone number or something equally terrifying. That would represent the moment when you would have to reveal your shame -- so it will be stressful for you to imagine and you're dreading it. Just make asking her out optional. That's right... if you get her number you get it, if you don't, you don't. Fuck it. The point to doing all of this flirting is totally pointless. *What?*... all this training a mere pointless exercise? That's right.... How's that for some heavy Zen?

Remember the nasty Law of the Universe that likes to give you just the opposite of what you want? The guy who wants it too badly comes off as desperate and gets nothing, while the "couldn't-give-a-shit" guy scores like crazy. Women all love a challenge – how come you're not after them all hot and heavy like the rest of the chumps they meet? Are you getting too much maybe? Hmmm?... *well then, here's some more!*

Isn't the life of the High Status Male grand?

Now it's time to work on creating an immediate connection – because women are generally into the fantasy of being swept off their feet by a man who suddenly appears in their life, just like all those sappy romance novels they read. This does not mean that you can act like some over the top asshole -- just keep a steady keel and work on establishing a good rapport.

Incidentally, don't discard your own feelings in the blind rush to get her to accept you. Consider how you feel about *her*. If during the course of getting to know her you decide that she looked better than she sounds once she starts yapping, then cut bait and graciously excuse yourself. That's right... *don't be afraid to reject her.* Never forget that rejection is a two way street. Try not to always feel that the gun is pointed only at you. Sure you're the one trying to do the seducing, but only because society places the onus on the man to play this role. If you don't like what you see in her character or manner once you make contact, you're under no obligation to keep grinding along just to honor some bullshit code of chivalry.

*   *   *

How do you achieve instant rapport with just about anyone? Is such a thing even possible? Not only is it possible, it's really just a matter of simple psychology, and it's all based on the fact that most people are in love with themselves and their own "brilliant" points of view. In order to get people to like you, the trick is to **reflect their own brilliance back to them** in such a way that it seems you are both on the same wavelength... i.e., *their* wavelength.

Once people discover to their great delight that you are the perfect foil for their opinions and ideas, they can't get enough of you! This is not always easy to do of course – especially if you're a miserable bastard who has his own strong opinions about everything and you're certain that you're right about every one of them. But remember, your goal here is to seduce a great looking girl... so submarine your nastiness for a little while and try to act like an interesting and intriguing character.

One of the great no-no's of seduce women is to come on like a strongly-opinionated, know-it-all jackass who's constantly telling everyone how they should do this and should do that. An attempt to verbally dominate another person, *especially when you first meet them*, is such a complete and total turn off that it's unlikely you have any friends at all. I believe some part of this problem stems from a deeply-seated intellectual insecurity. You secretly believe that you're stupid, so you try to ram all your ideas down someone's throat before they can get their bearings. However, knowledge is not a contest – you don't win anything by proving you know more than everybody else, except a lot of scorn and ostracization. Relax. It's no crime to learn something about life from other people, *in fact it endears them to you!*

For the sake of meeting women, you must learn how to become agreeable in a "non-kiss ass" way that will serve to create an immediate sense of rapport and likability. If you're succeeding, it should be easy to tell from the body language signals. In a few minutes I'll give you a list of what to watch out for, but let's have a look at the theory first.

You build rapport with someone a little bit at a time, using each previous success as a foundation upon which to smooth on the next level. What you want to do on an initial encounter is make that lasting good first impression. It's important that you understand how crucial this is. It's like the old adage that says, once you've acquired the reputation as an early riser, you can sleep in until noon and people will still regard you as a guy who "gets up with the roosters" every day. Why?... because once people tag you with their initial assessment, they rarely ever bother to update how they think of you. People are mentally lazy. That's why they rely on stereotypes to describe others. It's easier than having to think about every person they already know in a new way each time that they see them.

> This is why a **First Impression** sticks to you like glue and is all but impossible to shake off without an enormous 'public relations' effort!

Of course you realize this cuts both ways... a *bad* first impression will also be on you like atomic dogshit. You will never get a chance to go back and "undo" a lousy first impression – so it's imperative that you get off on the right footing when it really matters. Punching through your shame takes courage, and it will all be for naught if you don't follow through with a great first 4 minutes. This is where she will create her critical first impression of you and file you away mentally under the category of either INTERESTING GUY or BORING ZERO.

The idea behind rapport building is to develop an area of overlapping interests between the two of you that can serve as a common ground upon which to base any possible future relationship. Later on, when she's replaying your "encounter" over again in her mind, she'll be able to reflect on how much the two of you seem to have in common.

You begin the rapport building process simply *by drawing her out...* listen and get a feel for what interests her. Guide the conversation towards hobbies, lifestyles, common friends, hang-outs, etc., but let her give you the cues as to what she's willing to talk about (those lifelines!). Then show her that you either have a similar interest or that you are open-minded enough to learn more about whatever it is that interests her.

IMPORTANT: Make sure that your interest in a particular topic is genuine, or you'd be better off to just say nothing and press the conversation forward in hopes of finding some other common ground with her that's more to your liking. Some topics (like for instance shopping....) are just too feminine and you wouldn't be expected as a normal dominant male to be too excited about them. She understands this, and in fact she could be slipping you a sophisticated test to see if you're full of shit. Be careful because, if she detects that you're being dishonest with her, the seduction is over... as it should be. Evidence of dishonesty when you're only just meeting someone for the very first time is a super red flag to any woman, because she knows that this bad habit will only get worse.

The ultimate goal of all this seeking of commonality is to give her something positive and intriguing to think about... *later on*. **This is very important since we tend to convince ourselves about our insights into someone when we're off alone with our own quiet thoughts.** Yes that's right... we fall "in like" and then later on "in love" on our own. Why?... because falling in love is actually a self-hypnotic process that liberates fun-loving neurochemicals in our brains that make us high – and we keep going back after these drugs like any addict would. Women are especially fond of this "love drug" and will latch onto any guy big time who promises to keep it flowing!

Focusing most of your attention on this search for common interests also acts to help deflect your shame, because it keeps you immersed with a task that occupies your mind. It prevents you from back-sliding destructively into the zone of pain-loving self-centeredness *("I'm blowing this; I'm too nervous; does she like me?; what should I say next?; should I ask her out now?; is that a snot I feel hanging out my nose?; I hate myself; I should have never said anything; how do I get out of this?... etc.).* The fact that you are **tasking** instead of shame spiraling will calm you and make you seem more like a confident, High Status Male. Baby steps.

Visuals, Auditories and Kinesthetics

There's a really cool psychological technology that you can use to create an intuitive feeling of connection with someone you just met. It involves **reading their eyes** to see what kind of sensory input they prefer to use when constructing their thoughts

– and then *matching their favored thought preference!* People tend to fall into three distinct categories when it comes to using one of their primary senses to form thoughts – those that use their eyes, their ears *or* their feelings.

By far most people are **visuals** (60%) who tend to rely most heavily on their eyes to create pictures in their minds when they imagine things. Some people though (30%) are **auditories** who depend heavily on the use of remembered sounds and re-constructed dialogs in their brain to do most of their thinking. These people are often heavily into music or are often musicians themselves. The rarest group of all (10%) are tough to find... they are known as **kinesthetics**. They prefer to rely on emotional feelings and sensations to guide their thought processes. You can really have fun with a kinesthetic girl if you can find one, they are very easy to get a rise out of.

Your ability to use sensory-matching to gain rapport with someone will tend to vary inversely with how common that particular form of thinking is to be found among the general population.

Huh?... I know, I get carried away with the professor-talk sometimes. What I'm trying to say is that, since most people are visuals for instance, they tend to find a lot of natural rapport with other people on a day-to-day basis merely by chance. Since 60% of everyone is a visual (like me), we're bumping into other visuals all the time. Finding rapport then with another visual isn't such a big deal. Therefore, matching your figures of speech with a visual by using all visual terms like "I **see** what you mean... that **looks** like a really great magazine you're reading..." may not even get noticed, especially in an emotionally-charged situation like a pick up. So this trick will not be very effective, *for visuals.*

However, the other two types of thinkers – auditories and kinesthetics – are found more rarely, and are therefore more intrigued and favorably influenced by an encounter with someone who seems to share their thinking style. This is especially true of the *kinesthetics*, who are notably more emotional than most people to begin with and can often be manipulated with a come-on that seems passionately charged. Now, now... just because you'll soon know how to psychologically manipulate someone doesn't mean you are ethically free to do anything that isn't in her (as well as your own) best interests. Play nice!

But more on all that in a minute. First let me show you how to read someone's eyes to find out what their preferred thought process is. It's really pretty simple. You've seen how people will **cut their eyes** in one direction when they're thinking about something or working over an image in their mind? We all do it, it's very common. *Well, it turns out that the specific direction that we turn our eyes tells us what part of the brain is being accessed.* The eyes act like a pointer... revealing that an individual is stimulating a particular portion of his brain where visual memories are being stored, or that segment used to create audible dialogs, or remembered feelings etc. **Eye cues are very reliable because people perform them unconsciously and therefore they are beyond being faked.**

For instance, when you ask someone a question that causes them to imagine something in their minds, their eyes will move in a direction that reveals just exactly how they prefer to frame their memories. There are only three ways that it can happen... either they form a *picture* in their minds to look at, or they hear *sounds* or a verbal *dialog* of people speaking, or they try to recall how something made them *feel* when they experienced it.

For example, let's pretend to ask some hippie-looking girl that we're trying to establish a rapport with, "Have you ever been to a Grateful Dead concert on a hot August night?" Now watch her eyes. A visual thinker will always *look upwards* when they ponder something, forming pictures in their mind and viewing them on a mental 'screen' that only they can see. Whether they look to the left or right doesn't really matter that much. Our little hippie chick is seeing a picture of Garcia and the boys jamming on stage.

Either she pulled an image up from memory (if she's actually been to a Dead concert), or she's trying to imagine what it must look like if she hasn't. What's really important is that you've identified her as someone whose thinking mode is primarily visual in nature.

This is the way that most (60%) of us commonly think however, and therefore isn't really all that useful because it's too conventional to exploit.

Eye Cues: *All visuals look **up** (to the left or right) when they think.*

Okay. A more rare find is an audible, a person who prefers to think in sound patterns. Thinking audibly forces a person to cut their eyes either to the left or right, **but they keep their eyes level when doing so,** they don't look upwards. This can be tricky to spot but if you watch carefully you can make the distinction. Our cute little friend is *listening* to a Garcia guitar rift in her mind... hearing the Dead play. Perhaps if you had asked her a question that involved recalling voices instead, she would have heard the dialog in her mind as opposed to seeing people speaking. The auditory's world is dominated by remembered sounds, voices and music... *she's undoubtedly into music quite heavily and could likely be a musician herself.* This would be a good guess to make about her, and it makes you seem **intuitive** and maybe even a bit **mysterious**... all good stuff to have dripping off of us!

Eye Cues: *Auditories look to either side with **eyes level** when thinking.*

This kind of intimate clue about a girl can be very useful in the early stages of a seduction. It allows you to capture that all important intuition about her that should have a good chance of being accurate... *"I have a sense about you... you are into music pretty heavily, do you play some kind of instrument?"* you ask knowingly. Her return look is one of amazed curiosity. *Bingo!*... how the hell did you know that? Women love to discover this kind of mystery in a guy... especially one they're just meeting. It's straight out of a gooey romance novel. It's what they live for!

Once you know someone's thinking preference you can make a pointed effort to match their pattern by inserting **conversational cues** that suggest that you too share the same cognitive bias. This creates an instant feeling of closeness and comradery because the basis of all romantic attraction is simply this: people like people who seem similar to themselves. Finding someone who seems to be on your wavelength – who holds the promise of one day being able to communicate with you in shorthand and discerning glances – can be quite thrilling, for either sex. Finding someone so in tune with your own way of seeing the world validates your viewpoints and opinions... doing so in a way suggests you're a pretty smart person without actually coming out and saying so. *A person who seems to mirror your thinking style is appealing on a subconscious level.*

This notion of being subconscious is very important because you'll want to impress a girl with your similar outlook and style below the level of her awareness, since this is where she will mull over her feelings and conjure up that "delicious sense" about you later on. She'll realize that you were saying things like *"I **hear** what you mean"* instead of I *see* what you mean, and so on. I know this takes some swift thinking on your feet, but it's well worth the effort. And remember that you can practice with anyone, not just a cute girl, so the pressure is off.

Once you've identified an auditory girl – try to sprinkle your conversation with a lot of "sound" words like... hear, rings true, talk, tell, harmony, tunes, clear as a bell, music to my ears, etc. On a subconscious level, she will begin to get a sense that you prefer to think in sounds just like she does, and this will begin to forge a sense of connectedness between the two of you. **All seductions are a masterful cat-and-mouse game of Psychological Persuasion... and much of it is subliminal like this.**

When an auditory-type girl bumps into a guy who says things like "That **sounds** so cool when the guitar **echos** off the back wall of the stadium and comes **humming** back down over the crowd like that... it makes your whole body **pulsate** in the same **rhythm** with everyone else. The music just seems to **muffle** everybody else out..." it makes her stop and take notice. Hey, you're different... you're a lot like... *me!* Are you following how powerful a persuasive technique this is? The actual statement I just used might be corny or it could be appropriate. The exact content of this sentence doesn't matter – but look at how I've deliberately salted it with words that evoke the sense of sound vs. pictures.

Before we move on, let me tell you briefly about the kinesthetic.

Kinesthetics are even more rare than auditories, but you'll want to always be on the lookout for one when you're doing the "eye check" part of your pick-up routine, *because it can be really easy to establish a deep emotional connection with this kind of girl almost immediately on a first encounter.* Kinesthetics think with their feelings first before ever getting into sights or sounds. When you ask them to recall something, they will first go back and get a sense of how whatever it is they're trying to remember *made them feel* at the time it was happening. It's their feeling and emotions that have the greatest influence on them. When she forms thoughts and concepts in her mind, recollections of emotions will always be prominent.

The kinesthetic has only a single eye-movement signature that's easy to spot if you watch for it carefully. She will always move her eyes **down and to her right (*your* left as you look at her)** when she ponders something in response to one of your clever questions (you know, the ones that get her to think deeply about something, like "would you describe most of your friends as being loyal?" or something similar that stops and makes her go far into her mind to dig out an answer...). This particular eye movement links her directly to the emotional centers in her brain. Watch for it!

Eye Cues: *Kinesthetics look **down and to their right** when thinking.*

Later, I'll demonstrate how you can exploit this quirk of neurobiology to give any girl (no matter if she's a visual, audio, stereo or DVD) **a super-charged orgasm** that will have her calling you Master in no time at all! For now, let's get back to work on our seduction...

Romance is a Trance

Once you believe that you've picked up on her thinking style, your follow-up move is to make a conscious effort to use language that supports it – giving her the perception that you too take in the world through your physical senses similar to the way she does. This confers a powerful sense of connection between the two of you on a subliminal or unconscious level, making such feelings **profoundly hypnotic** because it slips beneath the judgmental radar of the conscious Mind. For example, consider the rare (10%) kinesthetically-centered girl that we just spoke of. She is likely very sentimental and relies heavily on her emotional interpretation of events to create and process memories. The tendency to think in this way has always placed her a little bit out of the mainstream though. She's always felt something of an outsider... a little uncertain of how she's supposed to fit in with the rest of the world. Depending on how old she is, she may or may not have come to grips with the constellation of feelings surrounding her relationships with others as seen through the prism of this type of unique mental identity.

All that aside, this tidbit of 'inside' knowledge about her thinking preference provides you with an opportunity to make a strong, almost *magical* connection. Simply by modifying your choice of words as you talk, you can give a kinesthetic girl the sense that she's finally met someone who understands her... a kindred spirit. Even when a woman has a one-night stand with a guy, she feels that she's made some type of instantaneous connection with the lucky dude. Otherwise she would've never let it happen. This deep, unexplainable, invisible 'something' that seems to reach out through space and favorably connect two people together as if they were magnets, is what is commonly called *chemistry*. Simply by being observant to the clues she sends with her eyes, you can establish this 'chemistry' artificially merely by changing the way in which you speak. It's done like this:

Back to our Deadhead concert example – "I remember **feeling** the warm buzz going through the crowd that night just before they took the stage... it was like everything was in perfect **harmony** and there was just such a **cozy peacefulness** about the entire evening that made me wish it would never end..." This might sound like a bunch of hippie hooey to you, but the important thing is that by making use of the words that I've highlighted, you've just demonstrated a tendency to *think with your feelings and emotions*. If you've correctly read her eye movements and identified her as a kinesthetic-type thinker, then you can be sure she's thinking that she might have stumbled upon a soulmate. She won't be thinking this *precisely* of course – but she'll have a 'sixth sense' about it.

Listen, I know some of you might be thinking this is unethical, but even if you're not really a kinesthetic or an auditory thinker, there's no harm in modifying your words in order to establish a groundwork of connectedness with a woman that you can build on later. Remember, when meeting women that first impression has to be strong because it's really all that you've got. Later on as she gets to know you, your shared experiences will endear you further and you can both build your relationship on more genuine ground.

But for now your job is to ring her bell somehow or you're going to get the boring guy brush-off. Don't ever think that you're being harmfully manipulative merely because you're putting on a bit of a charade for her benefit. That's just your toxic shame manifesting itself as self-righteousness i.e., *'Since I'm better than everyone else, I'm above "cheating" in order to get what I want from women.'* That's raw bullshit. It's exactly that kind of thinking that's kept you off the playing field your whole life.

* * *

In that spirit, here's a few more ideas to keep in mind. After you've connected non-verbally, tamed your shame, and gotten a bit of a snappy conversation going, don't think you've got it made just because you actually got her talking. There's a big difference between pointless chatter and a guided seduction...

Use Your Voice Like a Drug

Influence a woman's imagination not just with your words, but by **deepening the tone of your voice** every so often. Drop your voice once every couple sentences (slightly) as you make your point. (But be careful not to come off sounding like some kind of old vampire!) **Pause** once in a while (again, not too much) to get her hanging on your words just a bit. If you need an example of what I'm talking about, check out the lead character Ned Racine played by William Hurt in the movie Body Heat (1981, rent it, it's a really good story) and observe how he chats up Kathleen Turner. Study the way he plays this sleazy, Miami lawyer – now there's a guy with a seductive come on!

Women long to feel a deep sense of connection with a man... you have to feed this desire through the vehicle of her unconscious mind.

Falling in love is something that we do to ourselves in the privacy of our own thoughts when we're alone. During the interlude between your next encounter with her, she should be daydreaming about you and gradually convincing herself that you're a great guy with lots of relationship potential. Maybe she'll even go off the deep end and completely fall for you. Make sure that you re-enforce these fantasy images when you're together on subsequent dates by continuing to be charismatic and charming.

Don't Let Her Imagined Social Situation Stop You

Almost all really great looking women are involved with some guy most of the time, but not all of them seriously. And that's the important key to seducing great looking women – you must not be put off by the fact that she could be involved with someone else. They're usually ALL involved with someone else! Attractive women don't spend a great deal of their time floundering around between relationships. Instead they are often in some kind of relationship, even if it's just a casual dating deal, always testing to see if this guy's the 'one'. A beautiful woman's dating and mating dilemma does not consist of finding someone – anyone – to go out with her (like us social cowards), her problem is locating a suitable male. They're searching for that knockout dominant male who can give them the kind of terrific emotional states that they crave!

So don't let the excuse that "she's probably already got a boyfriend" stop you from flirting with any foxy chick that catches your eye. They'll always be flattered by a classy approach and willing to entertain your 'sales pitch'. The only exception is if they're newly married – then they send out STAY AWAY signals all over the place to every guy on the planet.

Don't Judge, Be Profound

One of the worse things you can do around a woman is to start acting all opinionated and judgmental about everything she says. Your know-it-all act may not fly, *but she sure will!* Try not to come across as the type of guy who's so certain his view of things is correct that he's constantly telling people that they "should" do this and "should" do that. I know I said this already, but it's such a common faux pas I'm saying it again. It might be such a bad habit that you don't even realize you're doing it... turning people off every day with amazing efficiency. Take some time to assess how you interact with your friends and family. Try to step outside yourself and objectively observe your behavior for any chronically obnoxious habits such as this. If you find any, put a sock in it.

No girl likes having her opinions summarily rejected by a guy, it shows that he sees women as mindless little children who need to be moved around and shown how to do everything. No decent woman will put up with that kind of disrespectful horseshit any more.

If you must, offer up your wisdom in a non-intrusive way that gets people to think about things from a different perspective. Don't try to force others into accepting your viewpoint, lure them over by to your camp gently offering a way of seeing things through your own unique experience of life. No one has a lock on the best way to view and do everything (except me). The classiest way to endear yourself to someone is to validate their point of view by being open-minded enough to accept advice from them.

Have an air of wonderment about you, but strike a balance. You don't have to pretend to be a befuddled dumb ass to seem like the kind of easy-going guy she'd like to get to know better. Just don't go and suddenly find yourself to be acting like her "I-don't-want-to hear-it-cause-I-know-everything-there-is-to-know" **father** either!

Touch Her at least Once

People are absolutely starved for touch in this uptight, politically correct world that we live in – and a touch shared between a man and a woman sends a very powerful, primal signal. The very best kind of non-verbal signal. Of course I'm talking about a light, friendly touch in a socially proper spot like her arm, shoulder or upper back – not some lecherous grope! The absolute perfect situation occurs when she touches you *first*. This is a clear signal that she's willing to up the ante (that all-important *escalation*, which we'll discuss in greater detail in chapter 6) and take the potential seduction further.

She might be shy or unwilling to do so however, therefore you'll have to settle for the second best deal which is you initiating the touch. **Only touch her one time, lightly and for a few**

seconds duration. Try to slip in this casual touch as a natural part of the conversation you're having... as if you're swept up in whatever you're talking about and you just felt the need to feel the warmth of her body without really thinking about the consequences. You should perform the touch nonchalantly without fanfare as if you're old friends. But be sure to hold eye contact and give her just the slightest, knowing smile while you're doing it.

Don't let the casualness of this action fool you into thinking that it doesn't have any impact. She understands what you are saying: ***I am interested in you as a Man!*** This fact is extremely important to establish as early as possible. I'm sure you know the consequences of not doing so since you probably have a long list of friend girls and a short one of ex-girl friends. One major reason for that is that you failed to establish a man-woman sexual based interest with her right at the outset, and so she pigeonholed you in the sexually-neutral "buddy" category in short order. And once you get yourself trapped in that prison there is no 'get out of jail' card to be had. That's why I keep hammering away at the importance of the first impression... it's absolutely decisive to your chances of having any future relationship-style success with her.

Touch is a compelling tool when you need to establish your "manly" interest in her right away -- it sends a clear and unmistakable signal that you're not willing (as a High Status Male) to tolerate becoming her buddy boy. This is a critical aspect of the proper dominant male attitude that you should always be striving to exhibit. Use the power of touch, but use it properly.

Be a Space Invader

At some point where you sense it might be appropriate, casually invade her personal space for just a moment to get a read of what she thinks of you. Lean into her while talking, or step in closer for a few seconds. This creates a sense of intimacy that she'll either react to favorably, by holding her ground or leaning into you even closer (yeah!), or by stepping back and recovering her space. The later means you're either coming on too strong, or you stink, or whatever. Not good. In any case, it allows you to either adjust your approach or to cut bait and move on without further waste of your time. It's a nice way to get some feedback on what's happening between the two of you chemistry-wise, only make sure you don't do it too soon before she gets a chance to get a sense of who you are – otherwise she'll certainly flee and you'll be standing there talking to yourself. This stuff is all common sense, so just use your head.

Do a Quick-Flash Check of her Bod

Checking out her bod is a great way to demonstrate that you're a real man who appreciates her female charms – but you've got to do it just right. You know that ogling and leering at a woman is impolite, and in a situation where you're trying to impress her it's downright suicidal to your chances of making out. Keep trying to stare down her shirt like that and you'll soon be watching her ass as it sashays away into the sunset. Here's the secret: *you have to move fast.* Look fast, actually. And, more importantly, you have to **get caught looking**. That's right, you're doing this to communicate your growing interest and desire in her sexually, so she has to see what you're doing in order to get the signal.

The correct way to sneak this highly-charged 'peek' is to pick a moment when you're standing facing each other engrossed in conversation. When the chit-chat lulls for a second, break eye contact and sweep your eyes down her body, and then back up to her eyes. Let your eyes wander for only about 3 or 4 seconds, then go back and lock into a steady eye contact with her. *Don't leer or stare!* The idea is to let her see you appreciating her body. Make it seem as if you just couldn't resist snooping at her goods because she's so foxy and you just slipped up for a moment. This communicates your sexual interest better than anything you could possibly say, and beats the hell out of any kind of "you've-got-a-great-body" compliment that you could possibly lay on her.

Now she knows that you're a man with potential desires for her, but you're also a classy gentleman because you "caught" yourself and didn't leer at her like some horny lamebrain. She'll allow you this one slip-up. Trust me she'll be more than a bit flattered, and most importantly, you've taken a giant step **away** from the Buddy Zone. Either this thing between the two of you will now grow into a romance or it won't... but she's been put on notice – non-verbally – that you will not accept becoming her ball-busted "friend".

Read Her Body Language Feedback Signals

So much of the communication between men and women remains unspoken, even after you've actually begun talking. You have to be aware of the signals she's sending you and adjust your performance accordingly. Don't just stand there blabbing away lost in your own brilliance... watch her and *observe* how she's reacting to your approach. Here's some things to look for:

Positive Signs – She holds your eye contact & smiles; primps her hair or plays with a lock of it; straightens up her posture (to make her breasts look bigger); breaks eye contact by looking down, then away; tilts her head 'cutesy' style; mirrors your movements or stance; narrow, bright eyes; holds her body facing you straight on.

Negative Signs – Fleeting eye contact; body turned sideways away from you, dull, uninterested eyes; crossed arms or legs; sagged posture; nervous tapping; head held high.

Most of this stuff is common sensical and you probably recognize a lot of it unconsciously already. The thing to remember about body language is that you should always look for **two or more** of these signals grouped together in order to get a truly accurate read. Isolated signs aren't always that reliable. I don't like to harp on body language too much because most of it is obvious and I'm not sure how useful it really is when it comes to seduction. Unless you're a complete simpleton, I'm sure you can tell if a girl is warming up to your approach or if she's blowing you off with the cold shoulder. Just stay alert.

Don't EVER Break the Trance!

The *Trance of Romance*, that is. I know a guy who starts to come on to a woman as if he's trying to pick her up, then makes a joke about the whole thing by admitting what's he's doing, like... *"isn't this all so stupid how men and women behave? Why don't we just skip all this talking bullshit and just fuck? I'm only after one thing, I admit it... don't you like my honesty?"* Needless to say, this guy is a royal asshole who never gets laid – and the really sad thing is he probably could once in a while if he didn't feel the arrogant need to demonstrate that he's "above" all this courting ritual and romance bullshit. It's for all the rest of us little people to occupy ourselves with... he can't be bothered. This guy displays the classic Disabled Will – he imagines himself godlike and transcended beyond all these tiresome mating games that us puny little humans must endure and therefore won't participate in them.

Of course, what he's really scared to death of is being *rejected*... so he deliberately crashes and burns any seduction before it can reach the point where he's in danger of becoming vulnerable to the woman's judgement of him. No mortal may be allowed to judge him, after all! But the 'Romance Trance' is important to women and it's not to be trifled with. This is what they fantasize about -- in the same way that all us horny bastards dream about having sex with every hot chick we see strolling down the street. To diminish and mock it in this way will gain you nothing but the eternal scorn of every woman you meet. Imagine if some chick came right out and told you that she hates sex and would never dream of ever having sex with any guy, even if he married her. Still want to take her out? Talk about a complete turn off. You'd split away from her without so much as a wave goodbye. Once stripped of her sexual allure in this way, a woman becomes completely uninteresting. Well that's how *you* become to her when you blow off the Trance of Romance like it's all a lot of stupid horseshit!

Anyway, if you're this deep into self-sabotage and flopping around in your toxic shame like a muddy hog, why don't you just stay in your room and watch pornos all day and just forget about ever getting a real woman? Spare us all the pain of watching you play out your ridiculous charades.

Always Leave Her Wanting More

Just like a great comedian makes his exit while the audience is still in stitches, you should make a exit on your terms while your stock is still high. Don't drag things out because you're so happy to be getting a positive reaction from her that you end up throwing a wet blanket over the whole seduction. **Timing is everything!** In this case, the timing involves knowing when to quit while you're ahead. If you hang around gabbing too long, you'll invariably run out of things to say and end up talking about your hemorrhoid surgery or something similarly grotesque. At that point the mystery is gone and the Trance of Romance has been popped like the delicate soap bubble that it is.

You have a life, things to do. At the point where you sense that she's really come around and is beginning to take a liking to you, that's when you excuse yourself. At this moment it's very natural to ask for a date or her phone number since it will only seem like a continuation of the fun that the two of you are already having. If you've read her signals right and mirrored her thinking style and found common interests, then she should be beginning to feel the stirring of that mysterious 'chemistry' forming between the two of you, and will want to see you again.

See how if you perform all the steps in their proper order and respond to her cues appropriately you can almost insure that you won't get rejected? It's only when guys refuse to go through the steps of seduction properly – because of ignorance, laziness or stubbornness – that they set themselves up for being rejected. When you try to bull your way through all the "chatting-up bullshit" and just cut right to the chase and start coming on too strong... that's when you just about insure failure with all but the most heinous pigs. And we're not interested in mopping up the 3:00 AM drunken leftovers here – leave all that for the low status males. Our goal is to elevate your game to the level of the dominant male who has a clean shot at the best women available.

*   *   *

So now you know the "secret" to not getting rejected – **play the game correctly by her rules and she will be compelled to respond to your advances.** Why? Because women, when it's all said and done, are genetically programmed to react favorably to a mans' mating advances. The signals that you send provoke reactions within the deepest recesses of her mind... responses that stem from her most primal need to reproduce. Rejection is reserved only for those males who fail to follow the proper steps. For those who do know how to play however, acceptance becomes almost a reflex on her part.

Five Minute First Contact Scenario

Okay, I've dumped a ton of stuff on you in this chapter and I wouldn't blame you if you're feeling somewhat overwhelmed by now. Allow me to tie this whole thing together by making up a quick outline of all these steps for you in a way that you should be able to study and memorize more easily. The best way to learn anything is to actually **write stuff out** for yourself with pen and paper. Writing in longhand seems to fix information in your brain much better than just reading it. So why not make yourself a 'cheat sheet' and refer to it every day until the entire procedure and all the important highlights are burned into your mind like a bunch of song lyrics that you can't forget.

When you get an opportunity to make a lasting first impression with a good looking woman, here are the critical things to remember in order to move from a perfect stranger –> to an interesting guy –> to a potential lover...

Your Pre-Game Attitude Adjustment

1) When Flirting, think Fun, not Outcome... Develop the mindset right now that you are going to flirt for fun's sake and that's all. Do not concern yourself with any preconceived notion of what the definition of success ought to be, let Nature take care of that. You're just playing. It's never Game 7 when it comes to flirting... it's always just the preseason. Reject the pressure to "score" from your mind permanently.

2) Stay Alert for all possible opportunities to meet and flirt with women. This requires that you pull your head up out of your ass and see the world in a whole new way. A way full of promising women who could be yours if you only choose it to be so.

3) Don't Let Her Imagined Situation Stop You... Fuck whatever possible goofy-ass boyfriend might be hanging around in her life. Unless they're recently married, girls are always shopping for the "Right One"... especially if she's grown bored with ol' Johnny boy. There's no way that you can know what her current relationship status is ahead of time (hell, even her clueless fuckin' boyfriend might not know that!...) so you must act like it doesn't exist. This is how the "pros" do it. It's a mindset baby, an *attitude*.

First Non-verbal Contact

4) Get Caught Looking... You should always try to make non-verbal contact first by maneuvering yourself into her field of view somehow. When she catches you peeking at her, (a cool, casual checking-out...) *hold on for a few seconds* and resist the urge to look away. Train for this pressure eye-contact moment like a prizefighter using dogs, cats, and old ladies as your foil wherever you get the chance to. Learn to defeat the shy 'look away' reflex that we all have without having to *think* about it when you need it most.

5) Get a "GO" Signal... Women control the meeting & mating enterprise because they are the ones who do all of the actual selecting. What?... you thought guys carried the burden of making the first move? Guess again. Men simply offer themselves up for inspection, but it's the female of the species who always makes the choice. *That's what makes this whole event so goddamn terrifying – it's a test of your value as a man.* Your attempt to make contact is really an offer to have yourself so considered. Socially, the unspoken relationship between men and women is very important to understand. Because in the absence of a clear "Come Hither" signal men are almost universally rejected by women. The exception being if the man happens to have extremely good looks, or some other overwhelmingly attractive characteristic (i.e., $$money$$, $$money$$, and $$more money$$) that will cause a woman to overlook her normal rule of rejecting the unsolicited advances of a male.

If you don't have these qualities, your ego is nothing more than a hanging softball waiting to be knocked out of the park! What to do? Get a smile or a long eye contact that signal's she's interested and willing to listen to your 'sales pitch' before moving on her verbally. Protect yourself from a nasty bout of toxic shame and back off with your dignity still intact if you can't get the proper signal. Unless, of course, you feel like taking a risk that day (the ultimate in high status male behavior). Then don't let me stop you... *go for it!*

Control You Inner Game

*6) **Snap your Rubber Band...*** Fire that anchor. This instantly provokes the Pavlovian trigger that you've been creating for yourself -- switching on those magnificent emotional sensations that you have pre-programmed into your subconscious mind. It will elevate you into the proper attitude necessary to help alleviate your shame, so you can start making the connections you desire. What?... you think it's all bullshit? JUST HAVE A GODDAMN OPEN MIND FOR ONCE IN YOUR LIFE AND TRY IT!

*7) **Use the Post Sex Visual*** to boost your confidence and knock her down off her pedestal. This keeps you from being in awe of her so that you can function with the attitude of the dominant male instead of some sniveling little boy. Here's how it's done: visualize her all sweaty and exhausted just after you've given her about 5 smashing orgasms. *Imagine the look of total devotion and supplication in her eyes as she gazes at you lovingly through your buttermilk bath.* You know that you could do this to her if you can only make the proper psychological connection first. Let her read the confidence in your eyes as she sees you contemplating this very mysterious inner fantasy!

WARNING: *Don't leer at her like some kind of pervert!* (And wear baggy pants to conceal your woody!) Practice this mental-fantasy maneuver with a porno mag photo while watching yourself in a mirror so that you can control your expression to the point of showing off just a hint of lust. Remember, women often don't understand how hot they really are. Your sexual interest in her is flattering as long as it's done very obliquely. This is a very fine line we're talking about here... cross it too far and you're dead. This is a dangerous point for all you self-sabotaging bastards who would like to deliberately crash and burn the seduction and run home to mommy. Men have to be **tough**... wimps lose!

First Verbal Contact

8) Open Up... Showtime! A bright, friendly, enticing expression will be the first communication of both your interest in her (as a man) and your availability. Try to keep your eyes locked onto hers, even if you have to use the old "shy salesmen's" trick of staring at the bridge of her nose, but try to seek out her pupils and make a solid psychological connection if you can.

9) Show you are Harmless and Interested... It's as easy as saying "hi!", commenting about a common environmental experience going on around you, or making a light, self-depreciating joke. Just say something non-offensive to get the ball rolling, and remember... *Use No Stupid Fuckin Pick-up Lines!*

10) Get her to Toss you a Life-Line... Listen closely. Let her provide you with a safe subject to talk about that is interesting to her.

Remember, it's your dominant male attitude more than your words that makes the greatest impression – because her head will be reeling and she probably won't even hear what you're saying anyway! Be naturally curious about her, *but not blatantly interrogatory.* Pretend that you're the host of a party and are making the rounds – be informal and at ease like you imagine Hugh Hefner must act at the Playboy Mansion. Ask questions that demand a thoughtful answer instead of a simple yes or no. Give her a chance to *converse.*

11) Exchange names; use the Handshake Trick... Rotate to the right. And use her name *exactly* as she speaks it to you.

12) Establish rapport... seek out common interests to which you pretend to be always agreeable. You like _____ (whatever it is she likes) _____ too! Let it be known that you make no excuses for your desires to get to know her... and you don't feel the least bit ashamed to be doing this (even if you do).

Don't trigger all those tired old dating associations by asking for her phone number, or if she's available, etc., too soon This only sets you up for a reflexive rejection. Instead, ask what she finds most compelling about some aspect of her life, something that makes her think and thus begins to evoke the romantic trance. Find out what's missing in her life right now – what her dreams are. Talk in a comforting voice and **pause** at random moments (but don't overdo the pausing) to get her hanging on your words a little bit. Be fascinated and interested in her... but keep some mystery about yourself in reserve. Focus the conversation on her and only dole out bits and pieces about yourself. *Mystery, mystery... mystery!*

Advanced Maneuvers

13) Use Eye Reading Tricks to uncover her thinking process – visual, auditory or kinesthetic – then adjust the use of your language (the action verbs when you're describing things to her... "I **see** what you mean"; "I could **feel** her delight") to establish yourself as "one of those ___X___ types too". You can make an incredible connection with her on an unconscious level by using this simple trick. It is very powerful because it's subliminal.

14) Always make 'em laugh... Utilize humor, but always cleverly, gently and with some *scarcity* (don't be a non-stop jokin asshole!). Mildly self-effacing (a small joke made at your own expense), or conspiratorial humor (share a laugh about someone or something else in your immediate environment) is always the best application. Humor should be used like a spice... just a little bit makes the food taste great, but if you pour on the whole bottle you'll gag on it. Two or three light moments is enough – and be sure to never make a joke **at her expense** like some kind of super-cool lunk. Not everyone understands that you're joking... especially if your delivery is deadpan (seems serious) or you come off as being aloof or even somewhat cruel. This kind of "humor" is known by psychiatrists as having a *hostile wit.* It's nothing more than a left-handed way of sticking a dig into someone while trying to seem like your just a joking, lighthearted sort of guy. Very deceptive. Women see through this nasty shit like it's made out of glass.

15) Give Her a Sincere, Personal Compliment using her Name (but only *one* time). You perform a little bit of social magic merely by honoring her experience of life. Talk with her and get a feel for what her passion is. Then craft a sincere compliment that is unique to her, and deliver it in a way that is intriguing. The trick is to make it seem as though you were just struck by the notion to tell her this "something" about her that you find so utterly fascinating. *Remember, you radiate charisma by making people feel better about themselves after having encountered you, as opposed to feeling worse.*

Begin by observing the "3 A's"... **Appearance, Appliances** (jewelry, tattoos, piercings, hairstyle), and that "air about you" **Ambiance.** You re looking for something unusual about her that really ties into some aspect of her persona which she seems to either be promoting (perhaps unconsciously), or is some central characteristic of her general presentation. I can't really describe for you what that might be since it will be unique to every woman. This is where you have to practice thinking on your feet. I can tell you that one of the greatest compliments you can pay someone of the opposite sex is to *exhibit an interest in them that seems so overwhelming,* all thoughts of conventional restraint go out the window and your normal inhibitions disappear...

...and then act a bit embarrassed about it. This will seem cute and disarming! Most people are a bit ashamed to admit to being suddenly smitten by someone. But women find this kind of endearing!

Deep Complimenting 101...

1) Discover a key passion of hers by listening carefully, or...
2) Pick out something about her that she's trying to show off.
3) Make an off-hand sincere compliment about this characteristic.
4) Never mention it again (trust me, she heard it!).
5) Make no further compliments during this encounter.

16) Be a Space Invader... Invade her personal space briefly to see if she's feeling any kind of connection with you. If she holds her ground or even leans in, this is a terrific sign! By getting a little physically closer to her, you're creating a bit of nascent intimacy and demonstrating your ability to focus and give her your undivided attention. Women love this. You're also allowing her to get a little *whiff* of you... and you know that the correct scent has a powerful subliminal effect on her, either good or bad. You may as well find out right away where you stand with her biochemically before you waste any more time chasing her, right?

17) Touch her... Light touching on the arms, shoulders or upper back forces her to think sexually about you and gives her permission to touch you back if she wishes to 'up the ante', so to speak. If she responds favorably, then she is at least somewhat interested and possibly attracted to you. Failure to initiate at least a little bit of casual touching will get you categorized as a non-sexual 'nice guy' -- and we all know how much we hate him!

Effective Closing

18) Exit like Bond, James Bond... Always quit while you're ahead and leave some mystery about yourself hanging in the air.

Use any reasonable excuse to cut short a first meeting because you simply must be somewhere else, making this the perfect time to ask for her phone number. Now you will experience **no shame** since the revealing of your affection needs occurs within the framework of being the logical next step to the thrilling sense of connection that you've begun to build with her! *Discreetly snap your anchor band if you need another boost of courage at this critical moment.* Using 'reverse psychology' to make yourself scarce will invoke the "people-only-want what-they-can't-have" sentiment in her. *Strike while the iron is hot!*

19) Get her Thinking about You when she's Alone... That's right, you're not even around for this last step! People fall in love when they're off by themselves. Love's an internal process that goes on in the absence of the person who is the focus of your affection. Why do you think women fall in love with rock stars and movie actors from afar? Because they feel they know them somehow through their music or performances. *Your only real task on any first encounter is to plant the seed of romantic possibility in her mind!*

Okay, here are all the cheat-sheet highlights:

Get Caught Looking
Snap Your Anchor – Post-fuck Visual
Get a "GO" Signal
Smile and Make Verbal Contact
Exchange Names -- The Handshake Trick
Seek out Common Interests
Use Clever Humor
Mirror her Thinking-Style to Establish Rapport
Offer One Sincere Compliment using her Name
Touch her at least once Non-offensively
Be a "Personal Space" Invader
Quit while you're ahead!

And so there you have it. These are the major things to keep in mind when you're trying to *meet* a woman. Again, the best way to fix these steps into your subconscious mind is to write them out for yourself in longhand. Print them on a small card that you can keep in your wallet, and get in the habit of reading through them whenever you get a chance. Burn them into your brain at least once a day for a month or so. Twenty-one days of repeated exposure to any sort of new idea permanently fixes it into your deep, reflexive memory.

Central to all the difficulty that you've been having is the fact that fear and shame have turned the entire process of meeting women into a deadly serious burden for you. Once you learn to step away from all that toxic shame bullshit and discover how to achieve a more light-hearted approach towards everything, the game of romance returns to what it was always meant to be... fun!

Chapter 6 : Closing the Sale

If you're the kind of guy like I used to be who was so totally stymied by his inability to get beyond his fear of rejection that it was impossible to even think about getting a date with a woman, there's a tendency to believe that if you could only *somehow, someway* get through this wall of impenetrable terror that all the rest of it will be simple by comparison and would pretty much take care of itself. Nothing could be farther from the truth. It turns out that your challenges are only just beginning once you've gotten past the stage of making initial contact with a woman.

No matter how favorable a first impression you make, it only really just gets your foot in the door -- gets you an 'audition'. Now the real work begins. One of my major problems once I started successfully moving past my paralyzing fear of rejection, was that I couldn't figure out how to get any *passion* stirred up between us that would eventually lead to the bedroom, which – let's not forget – is supposed to be the whole point of going through all this agony in the first place!

My maddening failure was that I always ended up being friends instead of lovers!

The hated 'buddyville' dilemma. This problem was a real curse for me. I've already had a lot to say about it in previous chapters... drawing upon my frustration and anger as my muse, which often finds vent in this writing project! I finally came to the conclusion that there exists a **series of critical steps and behaviors** that you must always be aware of – along with the proper timing and sequence to perform these steps in – if you're going to have any hope of turning a girl onto you sexually.

Look, we all know there are jokers roaming around out there who have absolute balls of brass when it comes to approaching women, but *still* only manage to get laid maybe one out of every 20 tries or so. That's because a lot of them don't know exactly what steps have to come next in the game, and how important those steps are to the overall scheme of a well thought out seduction. Again, because the fear of rejection seems so insurmountable to guys like you and me, we think that if we can just get around this life-murdering fear the rest of it will be a cakewalk. Not a chance. Once you've fought mightily to get over your rejection fear, you're really in no better shape than the guy I just described who never had this kind of massive rejection fear stopping him in the first place, but still gets nowhere with most of the women he moves on!

Sheesh! What a pain in the ass this seduction stuff is! Once we get over our fear of attempting it, now we've got to actually demonstrate some skill and knowledge to "close the sale" and maneuver her into a sexual relationship. I guess it's really no different than learning to fly an airplane or something – once we get over our fear of flying so that we can climb into the cockpit, now we've got to actually *learn* what the hell all those switches and controls do. Becoming a pilot requires a certain degree courage to even attempt at first, and then the proper training and acquisition of actual skills to complete the job afterwards. Welcome to flight school 101.

*   *   *

If I could sum up the gist of what is most important to understand from the last chapter, it would simply be this: **women are far more interested in how you make them feel than what you look like.** Of course, this assumes that you aren't completely off the scale in terms of physical or hygienic grotesqueness. But if you're a fairly decent looking guy who's clued in on how to take care of himself then you should begin to see your shyness and reluctance to approach women as having a **diminishing basis in reality.** In a seduction, all your efforts will be focused on creating the intense feelings and emotional states within her that she craves from a man. It isn't all that mysterious once you obtain a clear understanding of just what those needs are, and how to go about fulfilling them with your behaviors and attitudes.

> *If you can get her to see you as the pathway to achieving all those desires, then you are home free as far as drawing her into your web of seduction. In fact she will gladly leap into your web!*

The time has come to step back and expand our view of things. We've dealt with the most troublesome aspect of seducing women for many of you, the actual act of approaching and speaking to them. Since it is highly unlikely that she's going to jump your bones in the street a few minutes after you've first met her, we must continue to escalate the process of *psychologically bonding* her to us until we reach that point where she decides to transform the relationship into a full blown sexual romance. Layer by layer we build a foundation for the two of you to stand upon – bit by bit we draw her into our lives and vice-versa.

Escalate When the Time is Right

Recall earlier when I first spoke about the idea of being 'passive-aggressive'? It's a psychotherapy term that describes a technique by which a person can exhibit aggressive or hurtful behavior towards someone not necessarily by doing something to them, but by *withholding* something from them. You withhold the full expression of your personality in some way... give half an effort, drag your feet on the job, give someone 'the silent treatment' – whatever it takes to inhibit their efforts to accomplish something that requires your *cooperation* as a way of punishing them. Teenagers are great at doing battle passive-aggressively with their parents, and some women I know have this technology down to an absolute science!

I mention this only to demonstrate that you probably already know how important the concept of *escalation* is to a seduction, because you've likely used some fashion of its 'anti-matter' form – the ol' passive-aggressive routine – to strangle off a troublesome relationship in the past that you simply didn't want to deal with. You know... like some goofy chick in high school that you didn't find attractive took a liking to you and kept hanging around and flirting with you after class. Embarrassing you in front of your friends and so forth.

You got rid of her by steadfastly **refusing** to take things to the next level – by stonewalling all her signals and frustrating all her efforts to get you to respond to her in an appropriate way that would lead to a relationship. When it was time to hold her hand, you refused... when it was time to ask her out to the prom, you declined. See? That's passive aggressive behavior, and you manifested it in this particular situation simply by refusing to escalate the romance to its next required level. You did this without ever directly confronting the issue or getting into a nasty scream-fest with her, etc. *Passively.* Eventually, she gave up and went away (I hope). This worked because any potential relationship between a man and a woman **must escalate forward within a certain time frame,** or it will run out of momentum and die.

A failure to take things to the next level chokes off the oxygen of romance and ultimately kills all hope of seduction.

When you think about it, every stage along the way from first eye contact to marriage vows requires one partner to initiate an attempt to move the relationship forward to a new level, and the other partner to eventually join in. From first glance to smile, to an opening conversation, a date, a first meaningful kiss, sexual relations, an engagement ring, a trip down the aisle and finally a decision to have kids. At each step along this path, if one or both partners refuses to advance onward to the next phase of the seduction, the two people will invariably separate and move on with their lives in different directions.

I mentioned earlier that seduction is a delicate bubble which can be shattered quite easily, especially in its early stages. Now you can see how this fragility is related to the length of time each person has invested in the potential relationship... the more *tentative* the relationship, the more easily it can be destroyed by a failure to escalate properly at the correct moment. **With little invested, our patience is thin.**

For instance, at the instant of first eye contact with an attractive person, the bonds holding two strangers together are virtually non-existent, so the signals exchanged between them must be clear and unambiguous, and happen fast. Eye contact must immediately *escalate to a smile and then to a friendly exchange of words,* or the opportunity to interact is over in a flash. Since there was nothing of any value invested except perhaps a fleeting hopefulness – there was no "cost" to a cursory dismissal of the opportunity. Later on in a dating relationship, you might be allowed to miss your first chance to deliver a great first kiss and still have a green light to go for it next time, but if you wait *too long* the momentum will drain out and the seduction will crash.

Now if we consider a more matured relationship (in terms of the length of time that two people have been dating, not how mature the individuals may or may not actually be), the woman will start angling around and nagging the man for a wedding proposal. A clever guy can forestall this "final escalation" of the romance for months or maybe even years, but not forever. His elaborate tap-dancing will be tolerated by the woman only because a lot of time has already been invested in the relationship, and she clings to the hope that it's not all been for naught. Tolerance is available, but it's not unlimited. Eventually this relationship will break apart if the escalation to marriage fails after a reasonable amount of time has dragged out.

See how it works?... in the first moments of meeting you have no more than a few seconds to make the proper move, then – f successful – perhaps days to make a good romantic first impression, and then weeks to elevate things to the level of sexual intimacy, then possibly years (but not forever!) to advance the affair along to an engagement and an eventual wedding. The bonds between the two of you may grow stronger as the relationship matures, but they can always be broken by a failure of one party or the other to take it to the next level once a certain amount of time has passed. Relationships between men and women are always fully dynamic in this way:... if things hit a plateau or a rut, they will fall apart. Remember what I said about comfortable wimps? The wimp attempts to get all aspects of the relationship settled into a cozy routine as quickly as he can because he doesn't like the discomfort of having any uncertainty in his life.

Trouble is that if you try to get all the important aspects of your life locked down before you're married and have kids, the one inevitable change that you'll end up with is a failed relationship. Why? **Because experiencing the full range of all the various and diverse stages of seduction and romance cannot be denied.** They must all be played out, and in their proper order. To play this game you have to become a tough man and be willing to welcome the emotional discomfort that occurs when two lovers fight their way through the various trials and heartbreaks of a romantic affair. True comfort does not occur until after you've grown old together and have built up a vast inventory of shared experiences that will bind you together magically for the rest of your days on Earth.

This is not something that you can ever realistically aspire to obtain during the early stages of any relationship, certainly not during the often tumultuous seduction phase. So flush that childish dream out of your head right now and get real! And don't even think about figuring out some clever new way to navigate around all the rocks and potholes. Instead, learn how to revel in them and drink 'em up! Think of it all as a great competition... the greatest – and most rewarding – battle of your life. Bring it on!

You Must Disclose Sexual Interest

No, this doesn't mean that you're free to fly off on some lame, clumsy gropefest in an effort to show her what a real "man" you are, but... going off the deep end in the *opposite* direction and **not** displaying any sort of sexual interest in her is just as deadly. One gets you a slap in the face (or a knee to the nuts) and the other gets you a free lifetime ticket straight to Buddyville. The solution?

You must strive to create situations that will make her experience romantic feelings and think romantic thoughts about you right away, or you will disappear into the tar pit along with all the other boring guys who she never felt any chemistry with. Women are into the whole 'chemistry' and being 'swept away' thing... they love it!

Remember how I said they get off on how a man makes them feel as opposed to how he actually looks? This is the truest thing that you will read in this entire book. The point is that if you **don't** demonstrate very soon that you are the kind of guy who can create romantic feelings in her, you have no chance of becoming her lover. The typical woman in this modern age of ours is just awash in a longing for emotions and feelings... the same kind of stuff she sees on TV (Lifetime), movies (*When Harry Met Sally, Titanic, Ghost*, etc.) and reads in all those romance novels they churn out every year (annually the highest dollar grossing niche market in all of fiction publishing). This kind of thinking is entirely alien to most guys because we usually try to design our lives to avoid strong, disruptive emotion whenever we can.

But girls *love a good cry* – they think it's therapeutic (hell, maybe it is!... What do I know?) With the exception of their parents' or a close friends' funeral, guys will attempt to spend their entire lives figuring out ways to avoid ever having to cry about anything. Face it, we're "emotion-duckers", and we like it that way!

Women crave emotional experiences the same way guys crave sexual ones.

Look, mating drives are controlled by the primitive hindbrain and by glandular secretions, not by the "seat of consciousness and reason" located in our cerebral cortexes. In this aspect of our being we are little more than very fancy animals. This means that one of the most important skills you can have as a seducer of women is to be able to create the kinds of warm, loving emotional states *that their animal natures hunger for.* If you can get her to begin feeling these powerful emotions by whatever means and behaviors possible, she will become enamored of their source... *you!* In a very crass sense, she will be like a junkie that's become addicted to a drug that only you can provide – you will have become her one and only "dealer". Like any dealer-addict relationship, you can imagine **who** has all the power here.

This is why 'nice guys' and wimps and polite little mousy-men don't show up on her radar – none of them 'trip her trigger' in the sense that they don't hold any promise of ever becoming the source of the main thing that she craves from any relationship... *emotions!* It's the same with men too. The most important thing to men when it comes to relationships is sexual fulfillment. Therefore, we size women up in terms of attractiveness by imagining just how potentially awesome it would be to have sex with them. That's why fat ugly chicks don't get a second look from us... we instantly recognize it would be unlikely that they could keep us sexually interested and erotically stimulated on a continual basis with bodies that don't turn us on visually. Same basic principle, different drug.

Which brings us to another pivotal male-female understanding. When it comes to rating each other for romantic attractiveness, men can make the most important assessments they need for the most part just by looking at women. Anything in the way of added erotic enticement that emerges from the nature of her personality once we get to know her is just a lot of whipped cream on the cake! Women however, since what they are after is a more complex source of exhilarating emotional states, can't make such an assessment of a man's potential for delivering "the goods" (feelings and emotions of romantic excitement) without first getting *a feel for who he is, personality-wise.*

Our visual appearance to them is only part of the equation, and not necessarily a very meaningful one at that. This is why the game of seduction is rigged in such a way as to **force us to speak up** and make that romantically charged great first impression! It's our first test, and one that hinges on a frivolous snap judgement. Ah-ha! See how clever they are? Do you understand now why your fear and shame and all the other various trouble that you have with this subject have come to focus themselves directly on this issue of having to be the first one to open your mouth and start a conversation? You certainly realized how *this moment* – unlike any other in the world – is the most **important appraisal of your manhood** that you will ever encounter. In that split second with no hope of rebuttal, you would be judged on your acceptability as a potential lover. It is your audition for a woman's heart! The dilemma is that you may not have had a sincere appreciation of just what it was you were being graded on when you attempted to speak to her (**answer**: you do *now*... your dominant male attitude!). The combination of these factors created too much pressure for you to operate, and so you froze up!

Thought experiment time... Let's turn this thing around for a moment and see what happens, then maybe you'll understand that your fear reaction is not so cowardly and unusual after all. Imagine if our cultural situation were such that women were normally *hidden* from the view of men until, during some grand social presentation, they were forced to step out from behind a curtain wearing only a thong bikini to display themselves for an audience of men to be evaluated and judged as acceptable sexual partners. How many women do you supposed would be terrified to step out from behind that curtain and expose themselves in such a ruthlessly candid way?... To have their value as women judged within mere seconds by the snap impressions of perfect strangers who have no investment in protecting their egos from any harm?

Probably every woman alive!

Well, isn't this exactly what happens when we are asked as men to expose our egos for 'naked' evaluation when we attempt to 'pick-up' a girl and risk being rejected by a woman who's nothing more than a perfect stranger? *Can any evaluation be more painfully genuine?* There is no doubt as to why this situation is so unbelievably problematic for low status males who instinctively understand that they don't have what it takes to impress most women. They are like 300 pound fatties fidgeting nervously behind the curtain in their tight little thongs, waiting to step out in front of an all-male audience to an almost certain chorus of laughter and ridicule. Would they be scared shitless? You bet they would! Are you? Well guess what... it's really all the same thing! Your fear is normal.

So what's the solution? Well just as our hypothetical fattie has to lose some weight, you need to get a clue as to what women really want from men – **great emotional experiences** – and how to quickly and certainly demonstrate that you have what it takes to deliver those great vibes. I'll now show you how to build this compelling impression of yourself brick-by-brick in order to draw her into your snare of seduction.

Be the First One to Touch Her

There is nothing that conveys a deeper sense of intimacy and warmth between two people as does physical touch – and between and man and woman, touch can become electric if handled correctly. We already discussed how important it is to get some kind of touch on her as soon as possible to keep yourself out of the dreaded "buddy" category. **In most every culture, it is always the more dominant person who initiates a casual touch.** It's okay for the big boss to put his hand around the shoulder of the (male) employee, but never the other way around. A parent embraces a teenager or a child first, etc. So initiating the first touch flags you as a dominant male who's comfortable being the 'toucher', rather than the lowly 'touchee'. Get it? She does.

There are a few important points to remember about this *touchy* subject (ha, ha!... my comic talents are boundless, are they not?...) that I'd like to *touch on* (...stop it... I'm killing myself...). Ahem, here they are:

You must always be the one to initiate the touch
Touching can only occur on the appropriate places
The timing and frequency of your touches are critical
The ultimate goal is to get her to start touching you back

Remember, dominant males are comfortable being 'first touchers'. When you're getting to know a woman, it's appropriate only to touch her hands, arms, shoulders and upper back areas. Never touch her anywhere below the waist. At first, your touches should be fleeting. Don't allow any initial touch to linger because it becomes uncomfortable and eventually offensive. It is inappropriate for newly acquainted strangers to engage in lingering touches. **All the magic lies in a brief touch.** Touching her imparts an electric jolt straight into her mating and lust centers – subconsciously telling her that a seduction has begun. A classy move you can make on a first date is to brush a stray lock of hair out of her eyes when talking to her. This is straight out of a romance novel!

Realize that what you're really after is to get her inspired to begin *touching you back*. Even a brief touch of your wrist during dinner, a squeeze of your arm while walking together, or something as innocuous as picking a piece of lint off your jacket can send a thrilling return signal of acceptance and elevated interest back to your heart. *This is what we live for!* **Touch from a woman is a clear signal of growing desire.** Not the "I have to jump your bones right now" kind of desire, but a genuine interest that you can properly interpret as meaning that you've passed her first real test... i.e., she now views you as having some kind of serious mating / relationship potential. You've moved along in her mind from stranger to intriguing guy. Now she's thinkin' about it!

* * *

Alright, so you've passed the point where a frivolous rejection is no longer likely. Now you'll have to really work to screw it up by doing something completely offensive, or by deliberately failing to escalate to the next level when the moment is right. This is where you have to keep your head and suppress any urges to start sabotaging yourself. **Self-sabotage is a "power tool" used by your shame... remember that.** Don't let your shame do your thinking for you at these most critical times in your life! If it "succeeds" in ruining your chances, your shame will feed off the failed event and grow even stronger in the future. But look at it this way... if you perform the steps of seduction with light-hearted flair, your efforts will always be respected by a woman – even if she's ultimately not attracted to you.

Any woman is flattered by the attentions of a classy man who takes the game of romance seriously, and does not try to diminish it by turning it into a joke.

Always remember that if you keep the level of your game high you have nothing to be ashamed about and no reason to get down on yourself. By keeping your cool and giving her no easy reason to reject you, any rebuff that does occur cannot be blamed on you. It's her issue, not yours. Your goal should be to keep everything you do classy and appropriate, thus draining all the legitimacy from any shame that your goofy unconscious might try to burden you with later on. You can 'starve' your shame in this way by giving it fewer and fewer opportunities to make its' embarrassing appearance.

Think of it this way... from now on you'll have to *'earn' your right* to feel any shame by performing like a totally inappropriate jerk. If you strive to keep your actions cool and classy, it is illegal to feel any shame about what you did, get it? You can't just wallow in your cozy familiar old shame just because you exposed your secret need for affection. Not good enough any more. You must set higher standards for your shame. By raising the bar, you'll have room to work freely underneath it without worrying about the "horrifying" consequences of what you're doing. You'll have plenty of slack to have fun and let the chips fall where they may, which is the most effective way to approach a seduction.

The Tools of Toxic Shame

Let's digress for a moment, because I know that when you read this stuff you're thinking of dozens of reasons why your own rotten situation is uniquely "special" and therefore why none of this shit will work for you. *Resistance to change occurs because your shame is threatened with annihilation if your fundamental style of cognitive behavior is ever permanently altered.* Your shame is literally fighting for its own survival! To defeat an enemy you must understand it. To that end, here's some flawed thinking styles that you might be using to torture yourself with in the service of your own shame:

All or Nothing Thinking – There's no middle ground with you, no partial successes. Either you win the gold or you're a massive, humiliated failure who deserves to be put to death.

This kind of on-off, zero-one, black-white thinking puts colossal pressure on you to succeed, since the punishment for even the slightest amount of failure is to shame yourself mercilessly. With the stakes so high you are, of course, **paralyzed by fear** and therefore cannot take any action, especially in a situation where your very self-identity as a man could be put to the test. What this does is make it impossible to learn a new skill (especially one as emotionally charged as seduction) because you have to be willing to accept the inevitable flub-ups that will occur during training as you work your way through your novice period.

Too old to let anyone see that you're only just a trainee? Too bad... you should have thought about that while the years slipped away and you allowed your skills to atrophy because you were too prideful to make your first rookie mistakes. Pride is, in fact, the root cause of your condition. It's the old disabled Will again... to keep from thinking of yourself as a lowly subhuman worm, you must instead believe that you are godlike and floating above it all. And gods don't fail at anything, right? Otherwise they're really just worms. See how this rat trap works?

Inadequate Self Image – Either you act like a jerk half the time and don't realize it – or your behavior is acceptable but you *think* you come off as a complete asshole because you're too hard on yourself. Got a camcorder? Set it up on a tripod in the corner of the room when you're alone sometime and start recording. Shoot about an hour of yourself just doing ordinary stuff... cleaning up, working out, talking with a friend on the phone, singing with the stereo, working on your car, etc. Try to forget that the camera is going. Then watch the tape by yourself. This can be an eye-opening exercise in seeing yourself as others see you. Not so horrible, is it? This is what women see.

Perfectionism – an overwhelming need to feel like you must have every aspect of a situation completely analyzed and in control **before** you can take action. This mental disability stems from a deep-seated **lack of confidence in your ability to think on the fly** and then respond to whatever unexpected things occur once the bullets start flying. Almost nothing in life goes down the way we hope or anticipate that it will. Did you predict the construction project on the freeway this morning that made you late for work? Why not? I thought you were on top of everything? The truth is that we have to react and adapt to the unexpected on a daily basis... there's just too much going on and too much random chaos for it ever to be otherwise.

Dealing with women is the same way. You can't predict how they will react to your actions before they take place. We are dealing with interactions between two human brains... the most complex systems in the known Universe! How in the hell can you assure in advance that anything specific will occur *for certain?* You can't, that's how. And you will be rewarded with complete and total **paralysis** if you try to get the table set perfectly each time before you feel comfortable taking any action. Seduction is a skill – it's like shooting free throws or putting. You don't start out at the top and stay there forever. You start at the bottom and crawl you way upwards *on the stepping stones of failure* until you reach an acceptable level of achievement. You never get to the top in this game. No one does. There are just way too many variables. Relax, fuck-up, and learn!

*   *   *

Okay, time-in. Back to our discussion about the importance of touching. Since it's easy to cross the thin line into offensiveness if you don't know what you're doing, you have to be a bit careful. Still, you must risk some touching in order to demonstrate your male status and keen interest in her *as a man*.

Pay attention to her non-verbal signals. Is she holding your eye contact easily without a lot of 'get-away-from-me' cutaways? Smiling? Laughing at your funny junk? It doesn't take a rocket scientist to figure this stuff out. Here's a really terrific escalation... **she touches you!** Don't go nuts and blow it by thinking you have carte blanche to put your arm around her ass now. It's only a medium 'I-like-you' signal, a sign that you've made a good first impression on her, so far. Stick to the "one touch rule" for *first* meetings and keep it appropriate.

If you think you've been issued free groping rights, it only makes you seem desperate and lonely for contact. **No High Status Male is starved for the casual touch of a woman.** *She's testing you!* If you respond like the kind of clueless nerd that you used to be before reading this book, then you are on your way down rejection road. If instead you react with the proper attitude of the dominant male and accept that her nascent interest in you is the *usual sort of reaction* that you're **used to getting** from women, then you've communicated tons of crucial unspoken data to her that you are the kind of guy who *expects* to have women take an interest in him. This is HSM attitude!

Alright, a quick review:

Touch only the **appropriate places** of her body like arms, upper back, hands, and perhaps her hair (but not her head, like she's a puppy...).

Keep your attitude **casual and expectant**... you expect her to enjoy being touched warmly and appropriately by an attractive man like you.

Get a clear signal of "like" before touching her, but if you can't, just **assume** she wouldn't mind being touched unobtrusively and warmly anyway (more on the amazing power of assuming in a moment).

Touching is a dependable way to get a sense of how she feels about you in a potentially romantic context. You can then decide whether or not it's worth continuing to pursue a particular woman immediately so you can save yourself a lot of wasted time and future heartache. If she's upset with a little non-offensive touching, then either she doesn't like you or is a **cold fish sexually**. Either way, I recommend you move on to greener pastures.

Sexual Tension Can Never Be Denied

The dynamics of sexual tension hold primacy over anything else that occurs between men and women, no matter how politically correct it might be to pretend to believe otherwise. There is simply no escaping the imperatives of Nature. A touch shared between two people can be thrilling in the proper context of growing sexual chemistry.

It's imperative that you establish some level of sexual tension between the two of you as early as possible. One of the quirks about women is that they rely on their instincts, passions and "love-at-first-sight" kind of emotional reactions in order to catagorize men within their own minds. And those categories generally break down into two groups: guys who make their heart flutter, and guys in which they feel no *sexual* interest whatsoever. Women change their minds about all sorts of stuff all the time, but one of the things which they hold onto with a bizarre certainty is their initial, snap impression as to which category every man they meet belongs in. Once you get pigeon-holed as either being a hot dude or an uninteresting nerd, that's where you are going to stay.

And if you think it's important to establish sexual tension with some touching on an initial meeting, it's extra doubly important to do so on a first date. If you don't break the touch barrier on a first date you are DEAD MEAT! If you've been the kind of guy who never gets anywhere with women on a date, this could be one of the big reasons why. If you're too respectful or afraid to touch her casually, this paints you as a sexless, bore in her mind. When women complain about dating boring guys, this is what they're generally talking about... guys who are too timid to crack off even a few little sparks of sexual tension.

The Assumptive Attitude

Remember what teacher used to say?... "whenever you *assume* (spelled out like this: **ass / u / me**, on the blackboard) you make an 'ass' out of 'u' and me..." Right. When you stop and think about it though, all of what we call 'attitude' stems from just a bunch of assuming. The stance we take and the non-verbal communication that we broadcast with our actions and facial expressions all rest on a series of assumptions that we make about the sophistication of the person that we are trying to signal. If it's a woman, we *assume* she will understand what we are telling her with our attitude because we assume she has gained enough life experience with people to interpret those actions appropriately. If she doesn't get it, then we have learned something about how socially clueless she might be. But if she does, then we have realized some valuable information about how wide ranging her knowledge of the world is likely be.

An good example of this can be found in the subject of touching that we just discussed. When you touch a girl just right, an abundance of unspoken communication is going on, critical romance communication. When you touch a woman, you are assuming a lot. You're assuming that **she will enjoy it**. Now, where could you have possibly gotten such an idea like that from? That's right... *your "vast" experience with other women!*

With a simple touch you can communicate a nonchalant ease and a casual understanding about women that no words can ever match!

Think about this... if you commonly have intimate experiences with women, wouldn't you be comfortable touching them because you know they enjoy it? You certainly would. To you, women are not the strange, alien creatures that they must seem like to all the other hopeless low status guys out there who never get any real action. Romantically inexperienced guys tend to compensate for their lack of real world experience by harboring worshipful fantasies. This places you at a huge disadvantage however, because when you suddenly come into the proximity of a woman that you consider a "pedestal-worthy goddess", you will freeze up as if you were in the presence of God himself. This is a sure way to creep women out. You'd be creeped out as well by some crazy chick who appeared out of the clear blue and claimed to "love you" or "adore you" (and you were hardly aware that person even existed up until then). Think about it.

One major essence of the so-called "dominant male attitude" can be stated thus: **the High Status Male always assumes that girls will like him.** This may not sound like much, but really it marks the demarcation line between those guys who do well with women and those who are inept. On one side are guys who act as if are *naturally accepted* by women – while on the other are those guys who believe they must 'do something', perform some kind of trick, to capture the favorable attention of the fair sex. This mis-belief places an enormous amount of pressure on you and leads to an inevitable resentment of women. Hell, who wouldn't be resentful of some special category of people who always demanded to be **pleased** in some *mysterious and unfathomable* way in order to gain their graces? *I'd be (and have been) pissed at them too!*

Here's how to re-frame this poor thinking habit... just remember that feeling this way is always a ***choice*** – that you've chosen to believe women don't like you and that you are eternally burdened to prove otherwise. And – whether you wish to believe that women desire you or not – that this choice is an *arbitrary one.* Meaning that no external factor of any consequence exists which compels either choice above the other. There is no basis in truth to support either belief about yourself if you think about it – although I'm sure during the course of your life you've gone through all sorts of mental gymnastics to convince yourself there is.

But if we're going to become masters of seduction, we can't continue to cling to crusty old ideas that make it impossible for us to operate. We must embrace an entirely new idea. Here's one that I call the **Arrogance of an Assumptive Attitude.** Huh? Look, we've watched the gorillas, mutants and various other pukes lumbering around with cute women at their side and wondered how the fuck they're doing it. Well, here's how: they simply **assume** (*arrogantly* I maintain, especially if they're ugly and they stink) that women will like them no matter how they look or reek. They merely blunder along like "bulls in a china store" unaffected by frightening waves of female rejection and disgust until their *arrogant, assumptive attitude of likability* finally clicks-in for one poor misguided woman... and *presto...* **gorilla boy got his ass a girlfriend!** Meanwhile you're back home rubbing one out to your latest porno rental. How come?...

Because gorilla boy doesn't *think* too much about how he comes off in the minds of women, he just does his lurch-like thing and some small percentage of women actually dig it! They think he's "cute" (like a hedgehog is cute I guess)...

Well it's time to tear a page from the mutant handbook!

Beginning today you must *stop* over-analyzing every little thing you do – paralyzing yourself with blinding self-criticism (shame food). Instead, *arrogantly assume that she will like you no matter how you look!* Act with this brash assumption guiding your behaviors whenever you can. If you do this you soon won't be afraid to display your sexual interest in her... touch her, and do all the other little things that will set you on the path to becoming her *lover* instead of her buddy boy.

One Quick Warning... you can display an arrogant attitude in your assumption that she will respond favorably to your romantic actions, but don't go too over the top and become a 'macho' asshole-cartoon character either. The basis of your attitude should always reside deep within your soul as a **hidden male power.** This is actually the kind of thing women can sense in our friend ol' gorilla boy, which eludes the superior intellectual understanding of us withdrawn, shame-ridden nerds. Now you understand how to tap some of that power for yourself and join in on all the fun!

Alright then, here are the four most important assumptions that you need to make when you are attempting to meet any woman. Write these down on a business card and memorize them by pulling the card out and peeking at it frequently:

Assume that...

She has **no** boyfriend...

She will **enjoy being approached** by you...

She will **respond favorably** to your classy advances...

That it **doesn't really matter** *what exactly* you say to her, as long as your words are **non-offensive** and indicate that you are a) harmless, and b) interested as a man. (*Fuck fretting over the perfect thing to say!* There is no such thing as a perfect, knockout opening line for every possible situation. It's a harmful and stupid myth. You always just have to use your head and **be playful**).

How's that for a little arrogance of assumption? These are the kinds of "shocking" thoughts that lie behind the romantic success of the gorilla boys of the world. I know it's enough to make your head spin because they stand in stark contrast to the kinds of shitty things that you and I normally assume about ourselves... how bad we suck, how ugly we are, and all that other worthless horseshit. *Transform this mental horseshit and you will begin to win for a change!*

Then maybe you can steal the gorilla boys' girlfriend and rescue her from a hellish lifetime of picking up beer cans and trying to get the encrusted skid marks out of his 4x briefs.

The Deep Look

An unmistakable signal that you find a woman attractive occurs whenever you can thrill her with increasingly long, soulful looks right straight into her eyes. There's a connecting of spirits going on that many women find intoxicating when a man stares deeply into her eyes. You've seen it in all the old movies, and it still holds true today. By contrast, one of the most effective ways to kill any passion is to display nervous, darting, uncomfortable eyes. *An inability to maintain extended eye contact speaks volumes about your insecurity and low male status.* You've got to learn how to defeat the bad habit of shifty eyes or you will never be able to light her fire. Shifty eyes convey distrustfulness to many women. It looks like you're being dishonest and trying to hide something. If you can't look into her eyes, simply stare at the bridge of her nose. It's difficult to tell the difference.

Deep looks should be reserved for moments when the two of you are either alone or at least isolated (like at a corner table in a restaurant) and aren't likely to be disturbed by others. Use the deep look as you ask thought-provoking questions about her life, dreams and fantasies – or whenever you reveal things of a similar nature about yourself. Watch the way her eyes move... is she a visual, audible or kinesthetic? *Mirror* her viewpoint with your word choices. This is the kind of exposing of the soul that really turns her on! Remember, you must establish an ever deepening psychological bond with any woman before she will feel right about getting intimate with you. There is no shortcutting this process – despite whatever bullshit you might've read about 'hypnotizing' women and seducing them in one afternoon. The average joe doesn't stand a chance playing such parlor tricks.

Make sure you don't confuse the Deep Look with some kind of wild-eyed, psycho "Charlie Manson" stare that's likely to scare the shit out of her! Keep a light-hearted playful manner about you at all times. Don't get all goal-oriented and start feeling pressure to 'win' or 'score'. That's exactly the kind of anal-retentive bullshit that's been getting you nowhere with women. It stinks of desperation. And who are all the desperate guys out there? That's right... the lousy, low status, subjugated males. Do I have to keep repeating over and over again how women universally despise them? Good. So just relax and remember that the idea is to have fun and make her start feeling fuzzy thoughts about you.

Look, I know you may not want to hear this because you're so desperately horny, but you don't want to just bag some chick who doesn't care about you. It sucks. The sex is bad, and the aftermath is even worse. The best sex in any relationship doesn't begin to happen until after the third or fourth hayride, when the two of you begin to get comfortable with each other and she really starts to let loose. If you try to zoom right into the bedroom as fast as you can, you'll only end up cheating yourself out of some truly erotic experiences. You won't see her best work on the first lay – not gonna happen. So slow down, do it right, take your time. *And seduce!*

Deliver a Knockout First Kiss

There are a couple of gestures in the seductive dance that cultural convention insists men must always be the first ones to initiate. The most difficult "gesture" of course is the one that lies central to most of our problems with women... i.e., being the first one to have to *speak up* and say something! However, there is a second action which is equally as crucial... one that you may not fully grasp the importance of possibly because you've never gotten this far... the critical action of which I speak being the delivery of *a superb first kiss.*

The romance novel / chick-flick movie industry is built up around the secret longings all women harbor to be kissed in a way that makes them weak in the knees. *Kissed by a man who is taking the daring chance to **escalate** their relationship at just the right moment!* Men don't ordinarily attach any special significance to a first kiss. For us it's little more than pre-game maneuvering that we must get through. This is another great example of just how vastly dissimilar the brains of men and women are when it comes to seduction, and how having a keen understanding of these differences is what can give you the tools to separate yourself from all the other simple-minded chumps out there taking up space on the field!

For a woman, the first kiss with any guy is always memorable... whether it was her first kiss *ever* (when she was a teenager) or the first kiss she had with a guy who eventually became her boyfriend or husband, or whatever. To note... though she may perform some rather shocking sex acts upon a perfect stranger who shows up with enough cash in his hand, few prostitutes will ever allow a "john" to actually *kiss* her. *That's because even a whore views kissing as something* **far more intimate** *than actually blowing the horny slob!* I believe it all has to do with The Kiss being the pathway leading to the act of genuine, emotionally meaningful sex. For any woman, sex can be just sex. Emotionally connected, *meaningful* sex is a whole different ballgame. Passage into this wonderful world for women comes only by way of the *Passionate First Kiss.*

As a master seducer then, you must learn to exploit this aspect of the female psyche by doing all the little things that will make *your* First Kiss one that knocks her socks off! A great first kiss will place you on the glideslope to a hot sexual experience. **In fact, she may actually take over the seduction from you once you've passed the final test of the First Kiss.** (More about this in the final segment of this chapter.) For now, let's examine what goes into the making of the knockout first kiss and *exactly* how a schlep like you can pull it off cleanly and seem like the master Don Juan of the Ages! First allow me to list the salient points that you need to understand and then I'll discuss them each in finer detail:

> You must **lay the proper groundwork** before attempting the First Kiss by developing a deep sense of *emotional connectedness* with a woman. No 'stolen' kisses, or the entire seduction can be ruined!
>
> You must **read her cues** properly, and then boldly seize the moment to deliver the First Kiss. No fumbling uncertainty allowed!
>
> That moment must seem to be **spontaneous** and thus romantic.
>
> No **wimpy pecks** allowed! Save those for grandma!
>
> Never ask for **permission** to kiss her. Just do it!
>
> **Buttery lips,** but no forced tongue!
>
> Follow up quickly to keep the **momentum** headed towards the bedroom.
>
> **Details, details...**

You must lay the proper groundwork before attempting the First Kiss by developing a deep sense of emotional connectedness with a woman. If you spring a first kiss suddenly on her without having first created a sense of connection that makes the kiss seem like the *next logical move* in the relationship, the kiss will be a total flop and the seduction could be dead in the water. The first kiss is a pivotal moment in a seduction that's very much like a pre-sexual climax, and it must occur as a sort of climax to a growing sense of excitement and passion flowing between the two of you. Whatever you do, don't waste the first kiss on her before this incredible sense of connection has been established!

She knows about the importance of the first kiss – so you must never treat it as if it's no big deal... or soon *you* will be no big deal! Play the game of seduction properly and she will be mesmerized by your actions, especially if you keep things flowing right along at a reasonable pace. **The first kiss acts as a major point of escalation** and cannot occur until you've already gone as far as you can go building closeness with her through conversation and shared experiences. At that point you must escalate to the next level and the passionate kiss is the only way to do it. She understands that the kiss must happen when the time is right, and will accept your challenge to move forward to the next level. If you've done the foundation laying first, there is *almost no chance of rejection* at this point. Things have moved along too far, too perfectly.

You must read her cues properly, and then *boldly seize the moment* to deliver the First Kiss. During no other phase of the seduction is the **timing** so critical. There are two facets to this problem, 1) you must read her cues properly so as to know when she's ready for the kiss, and 2) once you get the signal you have to do it immediately... if you choke and get cold feet and fail to kiss her when the moment is ripe **YOU'VE BLOWN IT AND YOU'RE DEAD!**

I want to drum this point home into your thick skull one more time because this is a serious issue... *if you don't boldly take action when the signals are clear that she is ready to be kissed, the seduction is over and you've lost.* Just like *that* you will left with a cold fish or another 'friend'. There is no going back and recovering if you miss the moment to lay the First Kiss on her. Pound this into your brain because it's super important... **NO - GOING - BACK!!!**

One of the worst signs of low male status is *timidity displayed in the face of a female who is beginning to signal sexual submission.* Failing this test tells her that you are not a man, and that whatever thoughts she may've entertained about you as a potential lover were all wrong.

Want the male equivalent?... imagine a hot sexy chick suddenly swelling into a 300 pound fatso right before your eyes! You would instantly be aghast and immediately lose all sexual interest in her, right? **Well, that's what you look like to her when you wimp out of the perfect moment for the First Kiss!**

Of course a real-life woman swelling up to 300 pounds like a Road Runner cartoon is physically impossible so she's safe from having this sudden grotesque turn of events happen to her, *but you're not!* That's because a woman's attraction to a man is primarily psychological and not physical like it is for us. And unlike the physical world, our psychological appearance to her can change on a dime if we fail to effect the correct behaviors in the mating dance.

So what are some of the signals that you should be watching for so you know the time to act is near? Well, you should both be comfortably **touching** each other frequently and exchanging long periods of **lingering eye contact** (the so called 'copulatory gazing' that social scientists have identified as one of the preludes to intimacy in the human mating ritual). There might also be some **synchronization of your body movements** and postures. **Mirroring** each other both in terms of physical movements and thinking styles, emotional states, etc. This seems like a tall order when you read it written down like this, but I'm sure you'll have a sense of things just "feel" right to you. *That is the moment at which you must strike!...*

And that moment must seem to be spontaneous and thus romantic... do not let the chance to demonstrate your growing feelings for her with a perfect First Kiss slip away, or you will be kicking yourself in the ass forever! This is the most golden opportunity you will ever have to deepen the *Trance of Romance* that I talked about earlier. Women spend fanciful *hours* dreaming about the First Kiss – and you can tap into this lifetime of preliminary hypnotic work that she's done to herself by substituting yourself for the anonymous dream guy in her fantasies! Don't do too much pre-planning or the whole thing will seem phoney and contrived, which will ruin it for her. *Be spontaneous and take a risk here, it will pay off big time for you.*

No wimpy pecks allowed! Needless to say, one of the stupidest things you can do is pick the perfect moment to deliver the Kiss and then blow the technique of the kiss itself. How? *By being too timid.* If you dispense the kind of quick, antiseptic "peck" that you would give your grandma, your prospective lover will be disappointed and you will have done irreversible damage to your chances of further seduction. This is no place to lose your nerve!

Here's a great way to handle the First Kiss... I learned this from watching all those excellent old time movies. (This stuff never gets outdated, so listen up!) When the time is right, reach up and touch her chin lightly with your fingertips. As an almost unconscious reaction, she with tilt her head back and part her lips in anticipation of your kiss... a total green light and open invitation! This really works, you'll be amazed. Now just lean in and kiss her, but do it like this... keep your mouth slightly open and your lips relaxed and buttery. Let your soft lips just sink into hers and feel her melt into your body. This "tried and true" technique will produce a thrilling, truly memorable First Kiss for her... trust me. It dovetails right into all those romantic fantasies she's had since she was a kid. It will cause all the best dreams that she's ever had about a romantic affair with a man to come *rushing up to take control of her.* And those dreams will have little ol' nerdy you at their focal point!

Butter lips, but no forced tongue! I just showed you how to kiss her properly with "buttery" lips for maximum effect, but I want to make sure you get it right. This aspect of the seduction is important to understand thoroughly – don't go forcing a sloppy french kiss into her mouth right away. Swapping spit is reserved for when you begin to move along into more passionate kissing. The First Kiss is the *Romance Kiss.* It's objective is to trigger all those unconscious mental associations she's been harboring ever since her a teenage years... a magical time spent watching love stories and reading romance novels by the dozens. *You want to tap into these memories and link the good feelings they produce to YOU,* then you become the source of them in her present reality.

The First Kiss is the powerful opening kiss of the relationship which communicates to her that you are turned on and feel that emotional connections have deepened to the point where your lust for her is now possible to reveal. You are stepping deep into her exotic dreams now, this is amazing stuff! She almost has no control over her reactions to this kind of maneuvering on your part, it's like you're pulling her into a role that she feels compelled to play along with.

Never ask for permission to kiss her. This is a major, earth-shattering mistake! When the time is right she will signal that your kiss is welcome, and you don't dare break the Trance of Romance by asking for *permission* to kiss her! No dream lover in her fantasies ever asked her if it was okay to kiss her... how fuckin' lame! He just *knew* when the time was right and took her – and you must now do the same... *play your role like an actor!*

Rust me, she has a script rolling around in her head of how all this is supposed to go down... and if you can be the **one guy** who pattern-matches this hidden fantasy of hers with your real life actions, you will be "In Like Flint" and on your way to capturing her imagination! I have personally seen this happen – the transformation from suspicious-hopeful woman to melted kitten is stunning to watch. Remember, all the really important communications that go on between a man and a woman are expressed non-verbally.

Therefore...

...actually speaking words and *admitting what you're doing* is totally ruinous to your efforts and will completely break the Trance of Romance. This is a Jeffery Dahlmer-sized seduction killer! **At this point, the time for words has passed... just shut the fuck up and do it!**

Follow up quickly to keep the momentum headed towards the bedroom. This doesn't necessarily mean *immediately*, but you should get back in touch with her **no more than two days later** (preferably the next day) and set up another get together. No acting coy and calmly disinterested now... you don't want her to cool off. You only want to allow her enough time to think about the incipient new relationship the two of you are growing, and for her to build you up in her mind for about a day or so. One unfocused afternoon of daydreaming at work should do the trick. She will literally hypnotize herself into your social-sexual influence. Remember what I said before... we fall in love while off on our own. The psychological state of "being in love" is molded in the crucible an internal, solitary process that happens when we're off by ourselves obsessing about the person who's been creating these feelings in us. That's how women have fallen in love all throughout history... by exchanging passionate love letters with men who were off at sea or fighting a war! (Today we text... blah!)

For both men and women, falling in love is a self-sustaining mental process that you merely have to **_trigger_**, and then step aside and allow to work on its own. Then you move in and pick up the seduction again in the real world -- predicating your next actions carefully on her starry-eyed, more captivated, point of view.

Cruise Control: Now She Takes Over

Once you've made it to the First Kiss the ball is solidly in her court – and whether or not the two of you will go any further is pretty much her to call. No matter what happens now the one thing you've saved yourself from is a trip to 'just friends' hell. There's no longer any basis for buddy-buddy stuff. She respects you as a Man now and knows she can't play that bullshit game with you. Believe it or not, this a great victory in and of itself. One that many, many men can't lay claim to.

And don't think this doesn't matter because it matters greatly in terms of your future confidence, which stacks up with each positive step forward. The next girl you set your sights on will pick up on it because that's what her sensitive antennae are trained to do! Always remember that how you look to a woman only translates into about 30% - 40% of the calculus that she uses when it comes to deciphering your attractiveness. The rest of your "appearance" is made up of your Dominant Male Attitude.

See how the momentum of the seduction can sweep a woman up? One by one she opens up the gates that lead to her heart – _"...he seems normal and fairly safe, not an addict or a drunk, fairly attractive, funny, cares about his appearance... I guess he could be my type, nice guy but not a pushover, good job, makes money and isn't lazy, my parents and friends would probably like him, good listener, seems interested in me as a person, is definitely turned on by me!... we have the same values, I think I can trust him..."_ That last one incidentally, **_trust_**, is the big Kahuna. When she thinks she can trust you, that's when you'll get laid. Women make a vastly greater emotional investment in relationships than do men, and she needs to feel that if she takes the big scary sex plunge with you, you're not setting her up for a broken heart.

The ideal man for her is just the collection of all those imagined characteristics that have been rattling around in the back of her mind all her life. She pulls them up and examines them anew whenever a prospective new lover starts sniffing around, and the more of these qualities that you can match for her, the more likely it is that your seduction will be a successful one. If you can respect her need to go at her own pace without seeming impatient or throwing a pout, it won't be long before the two of you are into some molten sex.

Putting it All Together

Okay, let's see if I can summarize everything into another one of my famous 'cheat sheets'.

Don't act weird. Sounds obvious but it's not. Many single people tend to have a disturbing strangeness about them that tags them as individuals to be avoided. I know you've met women that you can tell almost at a glance are "lifetime virgins". In a man, "single guy weirdness" signals that he is a neophyte when it comes to matters sexual and emotional. It also implies that you're a low status male who's been roundly rejected by women all your life!

Women are experts on picking up these signals, far better than you will ever be. So while you're standing around socially incapacitated because you're afraid of being rejected, what you don't realize is that you already *are* rejected! You "auto-rejected" yourself before she ever had a chance to. See how much about yourself is on open display... communicated only by your appearance and attitude without you often realizing it?

Try your damndest never to send the weird-o signal, ever.

Act a bit guileless when you first meet a woman. Say what? Okay, here's some of the synonyms that I'm getting for guileless from my spell checker... genuine, innocent, honest, sincere, aboveboard, natural, unfeigned, open, trusting, casual, unpretentious, etc. etc. Get it? Just the *opposite* of how uneasy and cautious most people often act around someone they don't know. Why guileless? Because being this way makes you seem **approachable and harmless,** two qualities that will encourage a woman to strike up a conversation with you. You're just having fun flirting, right?. Remember, when you act like you don't need something... *that's when you get it.* This is the "perverse-reverse" law of the universe that keeps heaping more riches and rewards on the wealthy while stomping on the poor. Don't ask me why it works that way, all I know is that it does. So work with it.

It will always and forever be **your job** to make the first move and start a conversation. There's no manner of trickery or treachery that you or I will ever be able to dream up to relieve ourselves of this dismal burden which taps straight into the core of our shame. Truthfully, I wouldn't worry about it though, because most women are even more self-conscious and self-loathing than are men. If a guy walks by and fails to pay attention to her, a woman isn't thinking that the reason has to do with the fact that he's probably scared to say something. She probably thinks you're ignoring her because she's so plain looking or dressed like shit or whatever that she can't stir your interest. Why is this important to understand? Because it gives you an upper hand in this game, so use it to your advantage.

Let your sexual energy control you for a change instead of vice versa. We talked about this already. Lacking this important natural power robs you of the motivation you need to overcome your fears. You know what you must do to change this situation, right? Give it a rest for a while and generate some positive horniness to help yourself out!

Ultimately, everything is her choice to make at every step along the way. Although it seems like the man is the one who does all the heavy lifting in a seduction, it's actually the *woman* who controls the pace of things – from the very first glint in her eye to her ultimate sexual surrender. She sends the initial 'approach me' signals that suggest her willingness to entertain a meet... she decides whether or not to give you her phone number, date you once, date you a second time, beckon for your first kiss, allow further escalation to passionate kissing and groping, and then finally acquiesces to sexual submission.

The idea that the man is in charge is mostly an illusion which probably exists because social convention seems to demand it. Guys who don't understand the responsive role they play in the seduction dance are viewed as socially awkward and get rejected more than they probably should. Just make sure you gather a feel for the balancing act needed between being responsive and supplying the energy for escalation. This is a skill that becomes refined only through experience and will grow as your romantic victories stack up.

Remember that above all else, the Dominant Male you are now swiftly becoming makes his own luck in life.

Chapter 7 : | The Big Picture

Well... we've come a long way together, haven't we? We tried our best to deal with the most vexing issues of enticing women into our seductive clutches. I repeatedly pounded into your head the notion that women grade men for attractiveness based on how they rank on the male dominance scale, and not on how they look, per se. I did this to show you exactly where to concentrate your greatest efforts in order to improve your stock in the eyes of the women that you will meet from now on. You should understand by now that it's more important to project the proper male 'power' attitude around women than it is to kill yourself in the gym or plunk down two grand for the latest bolt-on hair replacement.

It's all in the 'tude, dude.

So in this final chapter, I'd like to bounce a few more of my crazy ideas off of you concerning what might be called the **big picture**... i.e., the larger issues surrounding the man-woman dynamic. After all, what good is it to have the ability to seduce women if the relationships that you keep having are ultimately unsatisfactory? Sure you get them in the sack and have fun for a while, but sooner or later the same old conflicts arise and the whole thing ends up falling apart. Then you have to be miserable for a length of time (actually, you were already pretty miserable during the weeks leading up to the breakup...) until you finally dredge up the motivation to begin the whole process over again.

Now I know that some of you horndogs are into the thrill of the hunt and would love nothing more than to learn how to hop from one cute chick to the next. The breaking up part is only a minor inconvenience to you. But I also know that there are lots of guys out there who would just as strongly like to use this knowledge to find the perfect soulmate. There will come a day when all you horndogs will have to hang up your condoms and settle down, and when that time comes you'll want to understand what **secret elements** make for a relationship that keeps both of you happy and energized. Why be a miserable bastard? Why not have the best of both worlds?... sow your wild oats until you can't stand it any more, then settle down with a women whom you really care about and who can fulfill your needs and keep you happy until you croak off.

Anyway, enough of this blather. Let's break down the search for the perfect woman into three areas of knowledge...

1) what *women need from men* to feel fulfilled emotionally,

2) ditto, *what men need from women*, and finally...

3) how to put it all together in a complete sexy little package that you will immediately recognize as *"The Right One"*... that elusive little minx that you've been spanking your monkey dreaming about!

Well, you won't find her (and truthfully, hardly anyone actually does) if you don't know what the hell you're looking for in terms of qualities and characteristics inherent in her deep nature. Also, it's your job to train your potential perfect soulmate and *draw some of those qualities out of her* by using your own clever seduction skills. Finding the Right One is one part **searching** and one part **designing**. You need a piece of good clay to work with, and then you have to take specific actions in order to mold that raw material into your ideal life partner. Anything less and you're only playing the game of social roulette like everyone else.

While you may need to assume the characteristics of the dominant male in order to seduce her, it will take a deeper understanding of male and female psychologies in order to keep her happy so that she is motivated to keep *you* happy. Let's have a look at these factors now...

Delivering on Her Primary Emotional Needs

Did you ever notice how many couples always seem to be getting into little nasty arguments much of the time? You yourself, being socially withdrawn much of your life, might not have too much personal experience with this sort of thing – but unless you're oblivious it's hard not to see how much of it is going on all around you. I'm sure you've got lots of stories about how each one of your friends who's in a relationship or is married takes his turn at being pissed off at his wife or girlfriend about something. He said this, she did that, blah blah blah... and so it goes. It never seems to end... the bickering, the hurt feelings. What the hell is going on? Is this the price we have to pay for the simple desire to have sex with someone that we actually *like?*

Mars calling Venus... can us guys just get laid now and then without all the friggin' grief!

Is *this* the bitter payoff to all the time and effort spent seducing women? It doesn't have to be if you use your head and keep your emotions from running you into a ditch. Stop for a moment and truly consider a romantic courtship. This *transaction* is driven by the exact same kind of internal mental process that occurs when we consider buying any other kind of product or service. The first, last and really only thing that we desperately want to know is...

"What's in it for me?"

I'm serious. The 'what's in it for me' calculus is applied to almost everything that we decide to do, (or avoid doing). When someone tries to sell you a product the sales pitch is designed to dig out a so-called **'pain issue'** that the prospective buyer might be having with some aspect of his life, and then attempt to demonstrate how *this product* is the answer to making that pain disappear. That's why effective ad copy always concentrates on describing the benefits of owning the product in question, rather than simply describing interesting aspects of the product itself (the features). "Our Nuclear Stink-Rat Annihilators are baited with 5 pounds of irresistibly delicious warthog guts"... is a *feature* of the Annihilator, which is nice but doesn't necessarily make you want to run out and buy one. "Our **Nuclear Annihilators** will forever end the **reign of terror** that stink-rats have been holding over you and your family by vaporizing up to **700** of them per hour!"... are **benefits** of the Annihilator that demonstrates how it will solve a major problem in your life. Define the pain and then solve it.

All kinds of products are moved by selling the benefits you will get from using them. No one goes through the agony of trying to lose weight because it's the good and heathy thing to do... they do it to gain the approval of other people and the psychological boost that goes along with it. That's why weight loss commercials always portray not just the 'New You', but the exciting types of fun activities that the New You will be enjoying (frolicking on the beach, etc.) and all the beautiful new friends (babes or hunks) that the New You will have flocking around showing interest. *It's the stuff lonely fat boys can only dream about.* Well they know your dreams – and they paint the fantasy picture that you want to see, and then tie their product to it as being the gateway into that dreamworld. It's the psychology of selling, and it operates by ruthlessly identifying the weak areas of your life-body-mind-experience and crafting benefits that provoke the solutions to those weaknesses.

Anyway, what I'm suggesting is that this kind of *'**benefits first**'* thinking goes on all the time in everyone's head concerning just about *everything* that we do, not just buying stink-rat annihilators. Dating and mating is no different: when two people consider each other in terms of their romantic possibilities, they use the same kind of ruthless, process. *What's in it for me?...* is this the girl of my dreams?... does she turn me on?... what will my friends think of her?... will she support my goals and aspirations?... is she a needy vampire?... and so on.

In the beginning, we are forced to make this assessment with very little to work with beyond our instincts, since we don't know a person well enough to be able to answer these kind of deep questions. That's what dating is all about – an opportunity to capture a sense of an individual for the express purpose of determining if our emotional needs and requirements have any chance of being met by this particular person.

The reason that most of us desire to be in a relationship with that "special person" is because we all understand on a very instinctual level that there are certain emotional cravings – primal human needs – that can only be satisfied by having an intimate connection with someone of the opposite sex. Other kinds of non-sexual family and friend relationships can only go so far in satisfying our deepest yearnings for intimacy. **Not having our intimacy needs met leaves us in a constant state of low-grade dissatisfaction with all the other aspects of our lives.** We begin to assume a miserable, negative attitude about everything around us which serves to push people farther and farther away. It's a classic descending spiral whereby the lack of having the need taken care of agitates our character to an increasingly more negative degree so that it becomes more unlikely that we will ever see that need satisfied!

Breaking free of this contemptible state of mind requires two attitude adjustments on your part:

1) you must **shatter the downward emotional cycle** in your own head by adopting the traits and attitudes of a calm, confident dominant male so that you can capture the interest and heart of a woman, and...

2) demonstrate that you are the guy who can also break this cycle of romantic failure *for her.*

And just what does this sort of relationship sorcery require? **Knowledge**. You must understand what a woman is genuinely seeking in a man if you are going to have any chance of showing her that you can be the man she's been looking for, right? And just as important, you need to know what you're going to require from a woman if you wish to stand any chance of being happy with her in the long run. Yeah I know... maybe your drought has been so dry you'll take any woman who shows even the least bit of interest in you at this point – but trust me, once the initial joy of bagging a few of them fades away you'll find that merely having a steady sex partner isn't good enough.

Let's begin by taking a look at what her needs are first...

Primary Emotional Need #1 – The need to Know that her Thoughts and Opinions are Validated by a Man. A woman needs for a man to show an interest in what she says and thinks, and not just blow everything she says off like she's some kind of child that must be squelched or corrected all of the time. Hey, there was a time when it was indeed a man's world and women were treated like overgrown children... their place was merely to nurture the *real* children and take care of all the domestic chores, while all the truly weighty concerns and issues of society were handled by men. Men possessed the real political, social and economic power as well.

But of course this caste structure has long since been shot to pieces and turned upside down, at least in most modern western societies. Most any woman who has half a brain in her head won't stand for an ounce of sexist bullshit from a guy anymore. Sorry to say but that war has been fought and there ain't no going back anymore.

How to Show Her that You can Deliver on this Need While You're Still in the Dating Stages: Simple (well, conceptually anyway) *shut the fuck up and really* **listen** *to what she has to say!* Stop bragging about yourself or endlessly yapping about only shit that's of interest to you, just like we discussed earlier. When she talks about things that *she* finds interesting and important, you have to make a serious attempt to engage her and react appropriately to what she's saying. You should be helping to expand and create excitement about the things she likes by helping her to see new facets of it... not brushing her off, acting bored, or treating her ideas about life as stupid "girlie" bullshit.

This is not "kissing her ass" or being less of a man in any way. All great relationships contain a large measure of give and take. If you show interest in her life, dreams and ideas she will be more than willing to develop a **genuine** interest in yours. *Now you've got a **real friend** in addition to a lover that you can pal around with and engage in activities that you both find mutually enjoyable!* This is far superior to suffering a mopey old girlfriend that you have to reluctantly drag around everywhere that you want to go... and who only passive-aggressively *ruins* whatever good time there was to be had anyway! Ever been in one of those relationships? Next time I'll just drink Drain-O.

Primary Emotional Need #2 – The Need to have a Man Available as Her Emotional Foundation. You don't have to become a complete sop for her every little bitch and pout, but she needs you to be emotionally stable enough to help her through the big crises in her life. This means that your role is to be an anchor of calming influence in the relationship, rather than becoming another source of aggravation! **Your male power and stoic grasp of life has to act as her "port in the storm" when she's being buffeted by the emotional rages that sweep through her life now and again.** If you're the "Nervous Nellie" type that reacts to stress by going to pieces, then you're basically no better than hanging out with any of her other mixed-up girlfriends. So why does she need you?

You've got to do better than that! Women have complications in their lives more so than men do because they maintain dozens of different close relationships with all sorts of people ranging from aging parents to suicidal girlfriends – and they emphasize and take on aspects of all these people's problems from time to time. When you start letting your life become interwoven with others, sharing in their problems is one of the prices you have to pay.

Two things to remember here... one, don't get in the habit of making a joke about the sorts of things she gets upset about, even though they may seem trivial to you ("think that's bad, you shoulda seen what happened to me at work yesterday"...). Her *impassioned* experience of life is very real to her, even if it sometimes seems out of perspective. Make an effort not to be constantly telling her that she's getting all worked up over silly bullshit. You're only cruising down the road to major resentments if you go this way, and you'll soon have a nagging bitch on your hands who will be more and more difficult to have sex with. Then you'll be faced with either having to dump her or play "kiss-ass and make up" all the time, neither which is very appealing. Of course, if she's often hysterical and you find yourself exhausted trying to keep her grounded in reality, then you might want to cut your losses and get out before she drags you down into mental hell along with her. You'll have to use your own best judgement here.

Secondly, don't go overboard with the "Mr. Solution" routine. Men tend to respond to people's problems by immediately offering up a litany of potential solutions. That's all well and good, but you have to realize that when a woman dumps her problems on you she isn't always looking to hear your instantly available laundry list of wise and clever solutions.

Most of the time all she wants is a **sympathetic ear**. That's right, you don't have to suffer under the burden of having to think up all those amazing solutions anymore! All you have to do is listen quietly and offer a warm hug now and then, maybe pour her a glass of wine and do something to take her mind off whatever's bugging her. Women want strokes and sympathy and lots of lovin' when things don't go their way. Your emotional support during the rough times is one of the big things that she requires from you. Provide this, and you will have one comfortable little purring kitten on your hands.

How to Demonstrate that You can Deliver on this Need Big Time While you're Still in the Dating Stages: Be decisive. Don't waffle around when picking out what movie to go see or what dish to order at the restaurant, "... oh I don't know honey, what do you want to do...". Be a man! Even if you don't know for sure what the hell you want most of the time take a guess and *stick with it.* As part of the exquisite dominant male attitude that you are always cultivating of course you'll always be looking to strike the perfect balance between **taking command of things and knowing when to yield** (as a gentleman) to her wishes. It always comes back to balance. Try to be the one part of her life that isn't always a constant source of problems and crises. Be the steadying influence instead.

Primary Emotional Need #3 – The Need to Feel that the Romantic Affection of a Man is Always Available to Her. Women are just plain out and out saps for romance, and it's one of the things that men just don't seem to fully grasp about them. *Romance is like oxygen to women.* They must have a breath of it every so often or they will wither away. It just isn't the same with men. A romantic touch or an evening out makes a nice change of pace now and again, but we don't need it like we need, oh, say... *football*! Now there's a much-needed gasp of oxygen, right?

The sad part is that being romantic really isn't all that hard – you don't need to arrange lavish dinner dates or smother her with expensive gifts. It's just the little things... a back rub(without no strings attached, such as sex), a surprise silly card, etc. A little shot of oxygen here and there and they are walking around high on life (and us!)

How to Show Her that You can Deliver on this Need Big Time While you're Still in the Dating Stages: I'll admit this is a tough one to demonstrate with true sincerity. She expects that you'll do silly romantic stuff when you're first dating because she knows that you believe it to be the gateway into her pants. How you'll "keep it up" (the romance, that is) can't really be determined until *after* the two of you have been going out for several months. Long term romance for her is a crapshoot just like the promise of continued hot sex is for you.

One thing you *can* do to give her a sense that you are a genuinely romantic guy is **touch** her a lot. Remember how we talked about the importance of touching her as soon as reasonably possible in order to express your interest in her as a man? Well, continued casual touching (arms, back, waist, etc...) shows her that *you never forget she is an attractive woman* and that the feel of her body next to yours is a wonderful thing. She will get the message that if you feel this much of a need to be close to her, then you'll probably do okay in the romance department in the long run.

Primary Emotional Need #4 – The Need to Show Off what a "Catch" You are to All Her Friends and Family. This is a tricky one that most women won't even admit to having, but oohhh it's there... you can bet on it. The need to *gloat* and show you off is her secret little evil delight that her "catty" side demands to be satisfied!

I'll never forget the first Thanksgiving that I spent with an old girlfriend of mine. All her sisters were there and every one of them was without male companionship because they were in various stages of break-up or divorce due to the fact that their husbands all happened to be drunks and losers. I was on my best behavior, and thoroughly impressed them all with my wit and charm. Well, evil cattiness silently abounded amongst the sisters on a very subliminal level that night, and my girlfriend was very pleased that she was able to show off how she was the *only* one who could get a really great guy to date her – unlike the worthless bums who'd failed her sisters. She won!

And so did I. I can't recall her being so happy and giddy and so willing to screw me every which way to Sunday for the next week or so as I did after that silly Thanksgiving! So don't ever underestimate how powerful her need to show you off to her friends can be. We guys often dream about having some cute eye-candy hanging on our arms to impress our friends, but I don't think this kind of showing off is as essential to us as it is for women.

Therefore, whenever you get that very first chance to go to some family function where the potential exists to impress her family and friends, *you have been served up an opportunity to score big time points with her that you must not blow!* She is taking a huge social risk showing you off like this... it is a massive PASS-FAIL test. **You must be on your best, classiest behavior and strive to impress the hell out of all of them.** If you successfully accomplish this feat you will have huge dividends coming your way!

If, on the other hand, you **FAIL** this pivotal test and embarrass her in any way, shape or form... your balls will turn bluer than glacial ice before you ever see any chooch for awhile. Understand?

How to Show Her that You can Deliver on this Need Big Time While you're Still in the Dating Stages: Always be and act *Classy*. This will get her thinking about how much fun it would be to start showing you off around her friends and making them all jealous. Some chicks get off on this more than sex I think. You might as well play it for all it's worth and let her use you for this devilish purpose. It won't be long before you get to use her for yours!

Remember... **FOCUS ON HER – ACTIVE LISTENING – BE DECISIVE – BE A CLASS ACT.** If you can skillfully demonstrate these things to her, you'll go a long way towards subliminally suggesting that you are the kind of guy who can satisfy her deepest emotional desires and provide what she's always been dreaming about in a relationship.

Keep in mind how insecure women are in a relationship. Are your eyes roving over to that blond sitting across the room? Show her early and often that you think she's the **hottest little piece of ass around.** She needs to always be reminded of this or she will begin to drift away from you emotionally. Watch for her to start nagging you about every little thing... that's the first signal that cracks are beginning to form in the relationship.

Your Four Primary Emotional Needs

Men also have Primary Emotional Needs which can only be satisfied within the structure of an *intimate* relationship. There are four considerable ones that especially need to be taken care of, or you will always retain some nagging sense of dissatisfaction with your relationships and the women who populate them. Let's have a look at these right now:

Primary Emotional Need #1 – The Need for Unconditional Acceptance. One of the saddest things you'll ever see is the guy who used to be your best pal and drinking buddy reduced to a pussy-whupped pile of dogshit by his incessantly nagging little bitch of a wife or girlfriend. What the fuck is wrong with these women that they can't just accept a guy for what he is and leave him the hell alone? They can't. Instead, as soon as they get married (and... **MAJOR RED FLAG:** even when *still dating*...) they go on a massive **reclamation project** to change and modify every little aspect of a guy's behavior until there's nothing left of the poor slob you once knew. Is this the goddamn price we have to pay for a regular slice of pussy?

I say NO!... Do NOT put up with any woman who tries to constantly push for you to make major changes in your lifestyle, dress, hobbies or circle of friends.

Sure I know there's going to have to be some compromise, and I am absolutely recommending that you do change some of your habits to accommodate any new relationship. This is all part of the fun and excitement and adventure of seducing and being with a woman... things ain't gonna be the same for you anymore! But there has to be some limit as to how much lifestyle modification you will accept. You'll need to determine what is personally acceptable for you to change about your present way of life, and then stick to it. Don't be afraid to set boundaries beyond which compromise is not an option any more. *Dominant males will not allow themselves to be bullied by women!*

Hey ladies if you don't like a guy the he is, *then go find one you do like!*

Ah, but there's the rub, isn't it? There *are* no guys that you actually like, are there? For certain women I'm convinced this is true. There are no men who some women seem to be able to tolerate in their natural, manly state. They have to change every little thing about them – the way they talk, walk, act in public and especially *dress*. These screwy airheads only want the most dominant male in the bunch and then when they get him, the idea becomes to completely tame him! Why? Maybe so he's less attractive to other women? "I bagged him, now all you other bitches stay away?" I don't know.

In any case, don't you stand for this kind of bullshit... or you will be a miserable, cowered, bastard as you fade away into the sunset. Sure you can probably stand to clean up your act a little and you should keep an open mind and take heed of her better suggestions, but just don't go off the deep end on me... caving into her every little demand to change this or that about yourself. *To hell with that!* There are plenty of reasonable women out there who don't think of men as restoration projects, and I suggest you must keep seducing away until you find one.

This probably all results from a "daddy hurt me" kind of deal where she's trying to reconstruct a wasted relationship with her father, *only this time she's going to fix everything and make it right.* I think you're nuts if you allow yourself to be the subject of this kind of twisted experimentation. Let her go find some other chump farther on down the food chain to hammer on, you must stand for a higher, *more dominant,* principle!

Early Warning Signs: She starts to **nag you** about all sorts of stuff, little things at first, *especially after you've begun having sex.* Some women think once they've 'given it up' they've purchased the right to start bossing you around. Horseshit. She's getting just as much fun out of the deal as you are, don't let her give you the attitude that she's doing you some kind of favor. Her nagging may even soon expand to include your friends – who of course are all just a bunch of stupid clowns that she 'wishes' you wouldn't spend so much time with.

Soon you will be locked at the hip and won't be able to go anywhere without her. *Can you say suffocation?* Don't let this happen to you... always hold onto the knowledge that there are plenty of fish to be had in this sea.

Primary Emotional Need #2 – The Need to have a True Friend at His Side. Not just a casual female buddy either but a *true confidante.* A man's circle of hard-core, solid friends tends to diminish when he gets older because we don't keep up our connections like women do. *So you'll need her to support you in the way in which a true friend would do when tough times arrive.* The same as you would do for her, right? And since you can't normally talk to your buddies about the kinds of things that you can tell a woman, you must have a sense that she's going to hold your discussions in confidence as well since these tend to be heavier issues.

You should also try to find a woman who will at least share in a few of your current interests. You can't expect her to love everything that you presently like to do with your same degree of enthusiasm, that's ridiculous... but you should be able to at least find some common ground with her.

Primary Emotional Need #3 – The Need for Respect. You need to know that your mate respects you and appreciates the things that you do for her. As a man you take great pride in fulfilling your woman's deepest needs and desires, make sure she shows you the respect that you feel you deserve for it. There's not much more that needs to be said about this... when you feel it you'll know it.

Primary Emotional Need #4 – The Need for Great Sex. Sex is extremely important to a man in a relationship, it's probably the main reason why we even bother at all! The key to any awesome sexual relationship is **mutual satisfaction**... if you take care of her the correct way, she will take care of you enthusiastically without having to be begged and cajoled into trying anything beyond the old tried and true missionary position. Enthusiasm is the real deal breaker here, because if you've got to drag her into every little sexual encounter by performing tricks for her (favors, doing shit you don't want to do, changing your behaviors, etc.) you are soon going to build up *massive resentment* and we all know where that leads to... no sex at all. Who the hell wants to give an orgasm to someone that we're always pissed off at?

The only way out of this trap is to never let it happen in the first place. Keep your sexual adventures sealed off as much as possible from the rest of the "real" world – create a "bubble" inside the bedroom where the concerns and anxieties of the outside world are shielded from affecting both your temperaments as much as humanly possible.

The "Right One", Defined

Alright, let's see if we can't pull this whole thing together into a coherent "philosophy of life" for you. Now that you understand something about the basic emotional needs of both men and women, it's easy to see how they could be fit together into a single package that would define the ideal personality that most of us would seek as a soulmate. The so called 'Right One'. Since this book is for guys, I'll lay out what I think are the **three most important characteristics** that any guy should be looking for in a woman:

1) *She should be someone who turns you on sexually* – Once again I harp on the importance of sexual attraction, since if you aren't really turned on by a woman right out of the starting blocks, just how bored do you suppose you'll be after a year... or *two*? This is why relationships grind to a halt and fall to pieces with the woman bitching that she never gets laid any more and the man looking to get laid, but somewhere else.

There are two considerations here: one, **body style** and two, seeing through your initial haze of horniness. The real deal breaker is body style... you've simply got to hold out for a girl whose body style is the kind that turns you on. Yeah I know she will change over time and there's nothing anyone can do about that (watch how fat your gut will get someday too), but if you've gone for a girl with the awesome body style right at the beginning, you will have given yourself the best possible chance of being able to remain sexually attracted to her over the long haul. The closer she is to your 'type' the longer it will take for her to morph into something you find unacceptable, and in fact she may *never* change so much that you find her unattractive.

Also be sure to target a body style that *you* find attractive no matter what it is, and don't worry about what your buddies think or what society seems to prefer. They're not the ones who will have to remain sexually excited by her over the years, so fuck 'em. If you like heavy ones or skinny ones then go for those. Choosing a partner for sex is an extremely personal decision, and you should keep your own counsel. Stay true to yourself and you'll be much happier in the long run.

The second thing to remember is that, in your initial **fog of horniness** soon after you've first met a chick, a lot of different types of women can give you a woody. There is a point where you'll fuck anything, and that's okay. Just remember that while she might be able to turn you on at first, will you have to struggle to get it up before too long? Only you can know this sort of thing for sure, but it's something that you should consider in the early stages in order to save yourself a lot of grief, heartbreak and tears later on. If you're cross-eyed with horniness it might be hard to ever imagine not being hot to jump her bones, but you know that there will come a day when that happens... especially it she's too far away from your body type to begin with.

2) She should be someone whose Four Primary Needs you feel enthusiastic and comfortable about fulfilling – The key word is *enthusiastic*... this woman should be someone whom you feel a steadily deepening affinity for. Someone that draws out the desire in you to fill those very basic needs for her – to be heard, to be romanced, someone to lean on, and a prize to be shown off – without her having to pout for it. All these expressions will be given by you freely and with a warm honesty because they come from the heart.

There is no better way to pave the pathway to future misery than to settle for someone that's below your threshold for happiness. That's why I talked about comfortable wimps and uncomfortable, tough MEN earlier in this book... it isn't easy to get a relationship set up the way it needs to be. You've got to suck it up and crash through all the bad feelings, knowing that someday it will all be worth it. Remember, the wimps will bail at the first sign of rough going and seek comfort. *Men will not settle for anything less than what they feel they deserve.* This is where you will earn your stripes in the war of love and romance.

3) She should be someone who seems ready, willing and able to fulfill YOUR Four Primary Emotional Needs – The best way to get this result is to hook up with a woman who **chooses you** (as opposed to you choosing her) during the early stages of the seduction. You almost can't go wrong in terms of finding a loyal partner if you allow yourself to be the "selectee" instead of the "selector" in the mating game, although of course this limits your action because it's a very passive way to approach things and to some extent places you in the role of the female, who must patiently await the arrival of the personality that will embody all those things which she desires in a mate. The danger is that this wait can exceed a human lifetime, and so contains a practical limit that must be balanced into the equation as well.

A further dilemma is that the woman who selects you with her flirtatious interest is often someone who is of no interest to you in a romantic sense. This is the age old quandary of the game of Love and Romance... unrequited love offered by one person, unreturned by the other. I'm sure you've run up against this particular wall several times in your life, most probably beginning in grammar school. Finding that perfect someone is the great quest of our lives, and it is by no means an easy task. Just look at how many people fail at it... look at the divorce rates, the broken families, the broken hearts. How many of your friends are just barely hanging on or suffering along with someone they've grown to dislike or even despise? People bounce from one relationship to another all their lives trying to find that special someone whom they can love and who without reserve will love them back just as powerfully.

The task of meeting the perfect mate is really no different than buying the perfect house or finding the perfect career for yourself... it's all a numbers game. Your chances of success increase in direct proportion to the sheer number of "items" that you consider for "purchase" before making your final selection. One of the things that you can do to help improve your odds is to project as big an image of male dominance as you possibly can. This will increase the number of women that you will have the opportunity to meet and date since they will be presenting themselves to you in regular fashion.

It's the *low status male* who gets so few chances with women that when one finally shows a meager interest he latches onto her like an old bulldog chewing on a pant leg. Seriously, what do you think the odds are of the first woman to come along in five or ten years that shows any romantic interest in you being the absolute perfect match? *How about zero?* There is no way that you can hit on the perfect woman for yourself with this **small of a sample** to work with unless you are extremely lucky (I'm talking winning-the-Lotto style luckiness) in which case your story is a freak of nature and should be written up in the newspaper when it happens. You simply won't live long enough to run enough women through the "relationship tester" to have any realistic chance of finding her with such an unfocused, hit-or-miss method. You would need to live several hundred years and possess the patience of Job to find your perfect mate by dribbling through one or two relationships per decade.

No, what you'll do instead is *settle*, and I already explained how that's just a fast track to unhappiness and bitterness.

So try your best to hold out for a girl who will gladly keep up her end of the deal and work to keep your four primary needs – to be accepted as you are, to be respected for what you do, to be a true friend and confidante, and to be enthusiastic about pleasing you sexually – *satisfied*. This is a formula for true love... love which can only flow from a balanced relationship wherein both partners care about pleasing the other one simply because they *like each other*. True "like" is not something that can be faked or forced either... it has to appear naturally from the chemistry that only occurs between **certain people** – the rhyme or reason for which continues to be as much of a mystery today as it ever has been throughout human history.

Getting Her Addicted to You

Once you finally break the intimacy barrier with a woman, all sorts of opportunities to form a powerful psycho-sexual bond between the two of you begin to present themselves. Getting a woman addicted to you is a seriously complex issue that could probably fill out an entire book on its own since it has to do with the creation of feelings of *trust and shared experience* and all that other good stuff. But I think that the foundational groundwork can be laid by showing her a good time in the sack, and specifically, becoming the guy in her life who can give her the **monster orgasm**. I'm not talking about your garden variety orgasm here, but one that is so deep and powerful she had no idea it was even possible to achieve such high levels of pleasure. And you're the man who brings her this great gift!

My secret isn't some sort of special 'Venus Butterfly' twisty tongue trick or any kind of physical technique at all – although you will have to provide some physical stimulation while doing it to make it work. It's highly unlikely that any other guy has figured this one out. **That means that it's very unique and will be associated only with you in her mind!** This tilts the relationship balance of power in your favor.

This simple pleasure enhancing maneuver makes use of one of the eye reading tricks that I showed you back in Chapter 5... but it uses it **in reverse.** Remember how we talked about provoking a woman to imagine something profound for the express purpose of watching how her eyes moved in order to get a clue about her preferred thinking style – visual, audio or kinesthetic? Then we attempted to match that style in order to create a feeling of immediate rapport? Well it turns out that the physical-mental link between eye movement and thought patterns runs in both directions. Not only do certain thoughts produce a particular kind of associated eye movement, but deliberately making the directional eye movement can stimulate the part of the brain that generates that specific kind of thought! Ah ha!... and doesn't that rarest of thought patterns – the *kinesthetic* sense – have everything to do with *feelings*? And not just emotional feelings, but physical ones too?

Oh yes it does. Surprising as it may seem, it turns out that physical sensation can be affected merely by keeping your eyes turned in a particular direction while being sexually stimulated. I know this for a fact because I've personally sent a few girls into orbit with this technique (and been sent there myself). Here's how it works...

Recall how kinesthetic individuals turn their eyes down and to their right while imagining something in their minds? They think in feelings... who knows (I'm not kinesthetic)... maybe they actually feel pleasure or pain when those thoughts are powerful enough? All I know is that the process works in reverse as well as forward. The trick is to utilize some kind of **device or prop** to get her eyes turned and held **down and to her right** while you are providing some manner of coital stimulation, either orally or with your cock. If you continue you to coach her along in this way, *she will have a blistering orgasm that will leave her utterly drained.*

And you will have become her new Superhero!

You have to put a little thought into this and get things arranged similar to the way a magician sets up a stage trick. What kind of prop makes this thing work? I like to use a candle. Let's say you're planning on having sex in your bed that night, and feel that the time is right to lay one of these mondo kinesthetic orgasms on her. Suppose you want to do it orally. Set up some pillows so that you can lay her stretched out with her head and feet pointed in a certain direction. Then, on the **right side of her body** (as she would be seeing it) and near the foot of the bed, set up a small table or footstool with a fancy candle on it. Splurge a few bucks and get one of those fancy, sculpted candles from an Arts & Crafts store or a specialty gift shop at the mall. Look for a scented one that doesn't smell too strong or perfumey. I would highly recommend *sandalwood* if you can find it... it gives off a very sexy, 'woodsy' scent which seems natural for a man to have in his home. In fact, I would suggest you make a serious effort to find this particular fragrance since it's just perfect for the erotic situation you're designing. When the two of you move to the bedroom that night and decide to get busy, light the sandalwood candle. Tell her you're setting a special mood. She'll love it.

More importantly, in the future she'll come to *associate the scent of sandalwood* within her subconscious mind with an array of warm, loving emotions that are *directly tied to you!* **This is a very powerful behavioral modification technique that can be used to effect a loving bond between two people.** Simply light the candle about every third time you make love... just enough to reinforce the cozy emotions without going overboard and making yourself seem weird or strange.

> **Please do not abuse the power of subliminal manipulation... you should only use this technique on a woman with whom you have serious romantic feelings. Play nice!**

Anyway... make sure you've arranged things so that she will be able to stare at the candle comfortably by glancing downwards towards her feet, without having to bend or strain her neck in any way. You don't want her to lose her **sensate focus** on the candle in order to keep the trance drifting along for as long as possible. You've got all the angles and positioning figured out in advance, right?

Later, when you're deep into stimulating her either orally or with intercourse (in the missionary position) and she's drifting off into sexual ecstasy, tell her to *watch the candle...* to stare at it and not look anywhere else. Tell her that the candle will hypnotize her and make her cum harder than ever before, but she must listen to you and do as you say. *Coach her along and make it into a game.* **She will have to turn her eyes downwards and to her right in order to look at the candle.** So what?... so this is the exact same eye position invoked by the kinesthetic thinker when they try to access remembered sensations or emotions. The same feeling point in the brain is being tickled! And I think this point is somewhere close to the brains' "ecstasy zone", wherever that is.

Every time that you get her to look at the candle, it won't be more than a few moments before she moans loudly with a jolt of ecstasy and throws her head back. *Keep coaching her to return her gaze to the candle.* But don't get all scientific and try to explain any of how this works to her, it will ruin the spell! **Just tell her it's your special magical sex trick.** Or make up some of your own custom bullshit... this is where you get a chance to go a little crazy!

When she gets close to cumming, this is where you really have to be firm in your commands for her to *watch the candle*. Make sure that she doesn't swing her head around towards it but **cuts her eyes down and to the right** to maximize the effect in her brain's pleasure center. *It's as though you've got your thumb dug into the sweet spot of that place inside her nervous system where her orgasm is generated, and you just keep pressing down on it without mercy!*

She won't be able to keep from squeezing her eyes shut and screaming like a banshee when she finally cums – but you can make it more intense for her each time if you can get her to keep looking at the candle as she gets closer and closer to orgasm... no matter how overwhelming the sensations become for her. Of course, there will come a point where she will blow her rocks uncontrollably. I hope you're prepared to have a thrashing, screaming wild animal clutching at you when it happens! **An orgasm this intense signals a complete surrender of all her inhibitions in your presence, and she will psychologically bond to you like a lost kitten.**

Women can sometimes come across as aloof when it comes to the sexual attention of men, but you must understand that their problem isn't finding sex (for most women, that's easy) but finding *quality sex with a man that they can feel totally free to open up with emotionally.* When you begin drawing this kind of immensely pleasurable response from a woman, almost against her will, you will have demonstrated beyond a doubt that she has stumbled upon sexual nirvana in your skillful arms.

At this point, the seduction has reached a pinnacle of consummation and her complete submission is all but assured. Beyond that you now have a ravenous sex / romance addict on your hands.

And you, my friend, are her drug of choice!

Your Perfect Pad for Shagging

You realize, of course, that the complete picture of seduction goes beyond just communicating your intentions as a dominant male on the prowl. At different stages along the way, you will slowly reveal more and more things about yourself and your lifestyle that will give her important clues as to what kind of man you are. One of those clues concerns the style in which you live and the look and feel of your apartment or home. Women will take the way in which you live into the calculus they use to determine if you're the kind of guy they want to hook up with for the longer term. It really is an important consideration for you in painting the overall picture of your desirability as a potential mate, so take heed.

Any woman that's worth your efforts is searching for a *man*, not an overgrown boy. The two are light-years apart, trust me. I've been both at different times in my life, and being a man is better. *You can score a much higher quality of woman if you adjust your image to that of a young* **man** *rather than an irresponsible boy.* The best women out there have outgrown their 'boy' phase and are looking for real men now.

A large part of that masculine character will reveal itself in how you currently choose to live. Women understand that things like a hot car and sharp clothes can be faked, but your living quarters will act as a kind of lie detector to separate the real men from the frat boys. They know you won't go through the effort of faking your living style just to look cool, it's too much trouble. But how you live proclaims a lot about your male status, dominant or otherwise. I would even go so far as to say that it can break or seal the deal.

There are two things to keep in mind when designing the look and feel of your living arrangements:

1) a woman should feel comfortable and welcome at your place,
but...

2) it should look like a *man* lives there.

You have to walk the delicate middle road somewhere between "bear-cave" and a place that suggests you might be moonlighting as an interior decorator. Know what I mean, sssss-sweetie? Rather than sit here and list everything that I think you should change about the way you're currently cribbing, I'll just paint a little contrast between how a man's approach to living differs from that of a boy's – and let you decide what kind of impression you're making with your present lifestyle. Then you can consider how you might wish to change some of those things in order to make your dominant male 'stock' begin to soar.

Inviting a woman to your apartment can be a pivotal moment in a seduction. It presents an opportunity to really move the needle on your "sexy guy" meter in a positive direction. When a woman enters your place for the first time, she's looking to discover what kind of guy you really are – man or boy...

Boys: Have posters of heavy metal bands and half-naked WWF Ring Girls on their walls.

Men: Have a few classy art prints hanging around. You can find inexpensive prints that look great just about anywhere. They only need to be interesting and non-offensive, and even better if they have a common theme that suggests a passionate interest of yours (imagine that!). Men also like to display a few photos of family members, friends and adventure memories in the halls and living room... but *NO ex-girlfriends or wives, please!*

Boys: Own a big, self-centered CD collection containing only the kinds of music (Metallica, Hole) *that **they** like*.

Men: Have a nice variety of CD's in their rack... rock, jazz, blues, rap, a bit of classical, and even something offbeat like reggae. This is to accommodate the varied tastes of the **different guests** they entertain from time to time (other than their usual football-drinking buddies who all think exactly alike).

Boys: Have nothing but beer (their own brand, of course) and Gatoraide in their fridge... okay, maybe some Pepsi too.

Men: Might have some wine (red table wines and white zinfandel), a classy beer (a mellow microbrew like Sam Adams, or something a little wilder like Corona), and a variety of soft drinks and juices. Why? Because, once again, he entertains people other than just his football bros.

Boys: Still sleep in the twin bed they've had since they were a kid. (I'll make no mention of the crusty bed sheets...)

Men: Sleep in a **full-sized bed** in order to accommodate the female company they have over from time to time *(yes indeed, this is what it suggests!)*

Boys: Are still getting mileage out of their ratty old the Star Wars comforter that they got for their 12th birthday.

Men: Own a dark solid comforter and bedding, use a cool top sheet and have two sets of pillows always made up and ready. *When she peeks into your bedroom, a woman should be able to imagine herself tucked in there with you, get it?*

Boys: Have their porno collection laying all over the place so their buddies will think they are grown up and cool.

Men: Will hide most of their nasty stuff but keep a few 'soft X' titles (Candida Royale, Playboy specialty tapes, or "hard R" movies) stored innocuously where she might find them one day when she's in a frisky mood. See how you can outsmart your opponent if you just use a little planning?

Boys: Have their X-Box on prominent display as the centerpiece of their home entertainment universe.

Men: Have a 20"+ TV, a stereo, a DVD, and something like a *backgammon board* under the couch. You should have some interesting things to do with her other than just veg out and watch tv all of the time.

Boys: Have mismatched chairs and an old, lumpy couch that they either got for free or paid $25 for at the flea market. And it stinks like old stale beer.

Men: Own a soft, comfortable sofa or love seat which is great for cuddling on those cold winter nights. And it's *clean* too... what a concept.

Boys: Houseplants? Isn't that totally gay?

Men: No, not really dude. Real *live* plants (the kind that you have to water now and then) add a touch of class and some atmosphere to your apartment. Women take notice of this kind of stuff when it comes to deciding whether she's dealing with a well balanced personality or not.

Boys: Since mommy's no longer around to yell or pick up after them, the bathroom generally looks like one of Osama bin Laden's hideaways shortly after a visit from a cruise missile..

Men: Have accepted the responsibility of cleaning up after themselves. This goes for their entire apartment, *but especially for the bathroom.* It should be clean, and the toilet should be spotless, at least when you know that female company will be visiting. Women grade highly on this particular test. Fresh towels in dark solid colors convey a "manly" impression that will get her thinking about what it might be like to stay over and share a bath with you. **Be sure to keep extra toilet paper and tissues in easy reach.** Women have a fetish about these products. I think it's genetic. You can't fight it so you may as well accommodate their toiletry-phillia and score the extra brownie points.

Boys: Maybe have a few wine coolers hiding in the back of the fridge somewhere behind the petrified stink-o cheese, I dunno.

Men: Always have at least one good bottle of *wine* chilling in the fridge because they know that most women enjoy wine. Almost any type of white zinfandel is easy to take even if you're not into wines and haven't acquired a taste for them yet. And having a set of wine glasses shows that you are a man of taste. Another radical idea is to have variety of other beverages like soda, milk, tea, and bottled water handy. It also doesn't hurt to have a stash of fancy Haagen Daaz ice cream or some other kind of decadent treat to really put her in a cozy mood when the moment seems right.

Boys: "You don't happen to have a few rubbers in your purse do you?... I think I ran out..."

Men: Take responsibility for their part of the birth and disease control bargain in a relationship. Always have a few different styles of condoms ready and waiting for deployment in the bedroom dresser.

Get the picture? If you saw yourself in the "boy" category way too much and not enough in the "man" category... well, I'm not your mother but you know what changes I would recommend you make. It doesn't take a ton of money or a major upheaval of your life to embrace these kinds of new habits. And the rewards will begin to show up in the extra regard that you will see from the women that you become involved with. Why is that? Because...

Boys: Are tolerated despite their childish ways.
Men: Are *respected*.

Play Nice You Evil Bastard

And so there you go... most everything that you need to know in order to gain the interest of a woman and to interact with her in a way that bestows upon you the highest chance for romantic success. I've poured out everything that I can possibly think might be of help to your Mighty and Noble Cause. But I get a sinking feeling that for some of you guys, I may have accidentally delivered the atomic weapon that you've been looking for in order to lay waste to all those who have wronged you.

Look, I hope that this book has been of genuine help in overcoming the greatest obstacle that has been keeping you from the arms of some hot chick for too many of your precious years... the fear of rejection. As our old Hall of Fame coach Marv Levy (Buffalo Bills 1986-1997) said during one of his speeches:

"Expect rejection, but expect even more strongly to overcome it. There will be many 'failures' sprinkled among the successes you enjoy. Any such failure becomes just one bad time at bat if you refuse to let it defeat you."

Wise words. And it truly captures the crux of the Life Challenge facing any man. But a determination to look Fear straight in the eye won't always be enough. That's why I tried to provide you with the twin towers of knowledge and confidence building techniques to help you disable those fears.

But all that good stuff aside, I'd like to kick around one final topic, and that's the larger issue of your overall intentions. By that I mean simply... how do you intent to use this information? The social skill set that you will soon be able to employ in your own self-interest is very powerful. You can bet that the vast majority of men have no clue about the existence of many of the things that I've discussed with you in this book (male dominance, eye-reading cues, importance of the first kiss, etc.) and neither do most *women* for that matter. Oh sure a lot of people have a good intuitive sense of these things, and they're the one's we call 'naturals', but they probably never thought the entire subject through to the very fine degree that you and I have just finished doing. And that's both good and bad, because I'm afraid that some of you guys could be ready to go off the deep end on me. Why?

Revenge.

You've been hurt. You are a rejected, low status male who's been shit on all his life from every corner of society... schoolmates, neighborhood bullies, bosses, so-called 'friends', and especially... *women*. The rage of the rejected male burns bright in you, and there's the temptation, maybe even the determination, to make 'em all pay dearly. I hope you understand that you now have the power to turn your social life around in a positive direction for possibly the first time ever, but I know that you could also be plotting just how many hearts that you can break for a change.

My advice: Remember the creed of the High Status Male and try your damndest *not* to be petty. Make one of the aspects of your new character a determination to **rise above the need to get even with anyone.** (Or an entire *gender* for that matter!) I don't know what your life was like growing up... maybe one of emotional deprivation, or perhaps over on the *opposite* end of the spectrum – the life of the spoiled brat. Adolescents can't learn to become emotionally resilient if they don't get any practice at having their desires frustrated once in a while. If your parents protected you from failure and disappointment at every turn of your life, then you may've simply gone into shell shock at the moment of your first flat out rejection by a girl... *and still haven't recovered!*

Whatever your reasons were for feeling that you needed the help I've presented in this book, I only hope that you won't let them turn you into a vengeful seeker of female scalps for your trophy case. Hey, if you have to go through a few women for practice before you feel the time is right to zero in on your perfect soulmate, then go for it. I laid out what your criteria for happiness must be and how you should stand up for your principles like a man and not compromise. Just remember though that you're playing with people's emotions. Yeah I know women have mercilessly fucked with yours all your life – but like I said, this is your golden opportunity to demonstrate that you're above and beyond all their bullshit.

Remember that in Love, just as in office politics... your **success** is the sweetest form of revenge!

*   *   *

The most completely wasted years of my life were from the age of 18 to 24.

At a time in your life when you should be getting a good grip on the balls of the world, I had collapsed into a complete and total shell of shyness and was working my way through what would end up almost being a wholesale withdrawal from the human race.

As all my friends, one-by-one, began to 'normalize' and take up with girlfriends (even the ones who, like me, had never seemed to have any luck with girls during their early teens), I began to realize with a mounting panic that something was seriously wrong with me. I had somehow grown extremely fearful of approaching a woman in any kind of social setting, and the strangest part was that I was otherwise a very outgoing and humorous kind of guy. The sort of guy that you imagine would be something of a natural with women. Sure I was kind of short (5' 6"), but I was well proportioned and athletic for my size. Lots of short guys were able to find girlfriends. But I had developed some kind of *phobia* and, back then, there was no thought of seeking any kind of help. Me?... crazy? *You're nuts!*

And yet there I was, unable to even look a waitress in the eye when ordering a meal at a restaurant... unwilling to go out with my friends to clubs and bars anymore because the frustration of being so deeply dysfunctional was too painful to bear... unable to speak up and say anything to a woman because I was deadly afraid that it would come out utterly stupid and make me look like a fool for even trying to reach out and make contact.

I was unable to take a pretty girl off a pedestal long enough to even see her as human – incapable of comprehending the dark cloud of shame that had wrapped itself around my heart and taken control of me. Never catching a lucky break, never winning at any chance I did manage to take... always meekly laying down my timid bet of 'scared money' and immediately watching it snatched away from me. Seeing the fine line between 'losing' and being a 'loser' becoming blurred until there was no distinction to be made. I had reached rock bottom off the tail end of what seemed like a pretty average, happy and normal adolescence that was never fouled by any sort of trauma, even a mild one. So what the hell was wrong?... And why?

Maybe I did have a bit of luck after all, in retrospect. I was saved at the brink of the Deep End by stumbling into an association with a bunch of guys that had rented a cottage on the lake near a small beach hangout. It turned out to be a complete *Animal House* sort of arrangement with much drunken partying and all the hilarious shit that goes along with it. I was pretty much half *forced* into a one-night stand with some girl while wandering around in a loaded daze one night. It grew into my first real relationship at the age of 26. We spent many happy years together that I will never forget before finally parting ways, but even during this and a subsequent long relationship, I never really did get any sort of clear understanding as to what the hell was wrong with me.

It actually wasn't until I happened across John Bradshaw's work on *Healing the Shame that Binds You* did I finally start to put the pieces of the puzzle together. It took a lot of introspection and some other research be able to step back and finally see the complete overall picture that I've tried to present to you in this book.

I burden you with this sad tale of woe only to demonstrate that no matter how hopeless you might feel your situation is, it isn't. You couldn't be as bad as I was at that time in my life, you just couldn't be. If I would've know this stuff when I was 18 or 20 I could have recovered years of my life – the best years – from the miserable pit of loneliness and isolation into which I ultimately lost them.

So *don't give up,* and don't let your cynical, thick skin stop you from taking what I've shown you to heart and using it, really using it, to help turn your life around. You still have plenty of time... even if your 60 years old reading this! I don't care. It's the truth articulated as best I can make it in a way that I hope is unique enough to be helpful to as many of you guys out there as will ever need it.

On that heartfelt note I will take my leave of this long-winded treatment on a subject that is pivotal to any real chance of happiness that you or I can ever hope to find. Without a woman in your life, all your other accomplishments will seem hollow and pointless. I don't need to tell you this, you already know it I'm sure.

If you have any questions or comments about *Without Embarrassment*, please feel free to e-mail them to me. I would be thrilled to hear from all you grunts laboring out in the field! Tell me your problems, mistakes and victories; give me your cherished war stories, both the good and the bad. I'll try to answer as many of your communications as humanly possible, and I'll post the best stuff on the website so everyone can learn from them. Don't worry, I'll keep all your names and e-mail addresses unpublished and confidential.

Now off with you young Jedi... and let *your* Social Adventure begin!

 Capturing a woman's heart can be a highly hit-or-miss proposition, even in the best circumstances. It requires a blend of the man making all the correct signal moves, and the woman allowing events to unfold without throwing up roadblocks at every turn.

For men it's all about getting that perfect combination of attitude and appearance – which is our so-called **Male Display** – working just right for us. It is within this display that we advertise the suitability of our genetic heritage for the creation of new life. This is the information women are compelled to seek about us. Make this work for yourself and you will create a steady stream of romantic opportunities coming your way that will NOT require a massive display of courage to take advantage of.

And that's the central focus of my new book… **She's Yours For The Taking: A Man's Guide to the Seduction and Sexual Enchantment of Women** is a brilliant collection of strategies and operational techniques designed to lure women into your world by feeding them the proper romantic signals they crave every step along the way. Once women get the idea that you understand the game on their terms – worlds of possibly will begin to open up for you.

Best of all, the romantic skills I teach in SYFT will become more refined as you use them and will continue to serve you for a lifetime as you move through life's phases.

You'll see that it's a better way – a *real* way – to bring fascinating women falling like pretty little snowflakes into your life. For complete details, please visit: www.highstatusmale.com

Without Embarrassment

Appendix A : *Cayman Magic*

Cayman Magic
by Mike Pilinski

David idly picked away at the label of his sweaty bottle of *Corona*. He delighted in the healthy and gratifying ache along the top of his shoulders, a recollection still lingering in his body from an afternoon spend water skiing along Seven Mile Beach. It was a fading recollection though, gradually being massaged away by the robust Mexican brew he'd come to love since arriving on Grand Cayman only... what was it? Five days *already*? Christ, it wouldn't be long before he was brushing the goddamn snow off his windshield again.

His mind recoiled at the sudden intrusive thought of those gray days, and quickly shoved them away like a dog shakes off water. It was a million miles away and didn't exist any more, he told himself. At least not for another...

Stop. No more thinking of such things. He was here to forget and it would all stay forgotten no matter what it took. Shit, maybe it was time to have Roger fix him up a double of that candy he called Yamacn' Rum. There would be no more meddlesome visions of any dreary northern winters after he "kissed the 'cane", he smiled to himself. David looked up and spotted Roger jabbering away with a couple of his buddies down at the far end of the bar, the three of them engrossed with something they'd apparently discovered in the want ads of the afternoon paper. Some gem of an old '78 Camaro junker flown over from Cuba or Mexico – *"never seen da win'er..."* – no doubt.

"Caaawww... Caaawww!..." came the shrill cry from behind his left ear somewhere, followed by the now-familiar *wee-ohh, wee-ohh* double whistle. Sharp as a sudden gust from a piccolo. David swivelled around to see the grandiose white macaw that carried the bar's namesake *Calico Jack* just as he spread open his wings to their impressive full three foot expanse. Seeing he had an audience, Jack casually proceeded to splay apart the feathers on his crown in a show of fallow vanity. Heck, what self-respecting tropical bar was complete without a tropical mascot?

"Ay Jack, you'n finally awake?" Roger shouted to his stretching bird, then with a startling dexterity that would've been the envy of any table magician, dug a peanut out of the snack bowl sitting atop the polished ebony bar and with almost no detectable movement of his hand, flicked the morsel across the hazy room towards the posing macaw. The peanut landed on the sand-covered plank floor and the pampered bird plopped off his t-bar perch and scooped it up in a single move. With an easy flutter of his oversized wings he levitated back atop the perch and went to work noisily cracking the nut within his beak. The downwash from his wings swirled the sand into a pair of perfect spiral patterns.

David let his eyes roll lazily around the cozy tropical barroom. Frail tendrils of blue cigar smoke suspended themselves like dead jellyfish in the warm rays of the evening sunlight – angling through foggy, sandblasted windows. He and Roger and his two pals had the place all to themselves for now, but it was early yet – still daylight – and that would change in about an hour or so when mobs of tourists began to drift in from the packed resorts, red-faced after a long afternoon vegetating on the beach or getting cleaned out in the casinos up in George Town.

As if she'd read his mind, "Mrs. Roger" (he was embarrassed to admit to himself that he hadn't yet discovered her name) suddenly emerged from behind the kitchen door next to the bar and began earnestly wiping down the circular redwood tables that were lined up along the back wall, a lofty show of cleanliness in anticipation of the forthcoming crowds. She smiled as she passed by his stool and David nodded a return hello. The smell of fresh cut pineapples followed her around the room. Under his wife's keen eye, Roger suddenly got busy polishing some neglected shot glasses that were piling up in the sink. David smiled and swigged his spicy beer.

Calico Jack's was conveniently situated within 'staggering distance' of the Sunset House Resort where he was staying for the week, here on the far western end of Grand Cayman Island. Genuine and unsullied with the crass Disney-like fakery of the pseudo-tropical bars that were attached directly to the resorts, Jack's was truly a native hangout. Locals actually spent their afternoons here, as they had been doing for nearly a hundred years. Yes, Calico Jack's had been alive and partying long before the mega-resorts had exploded onto this out-of-the-way little island that had become a sort of Mecca for scuba divers and holiday seekers from around the world. That explained how the bar had acquired such a seemingly impossible prime location snuggled among the multi-million dollar strip of wealthy beachfront hotel properties. It was *grandfathered* in!

And no amount of money had ever been able to dig ol' Roger or his father, who'd run the place for 45 years before him, out of this precious spot. Hell, why should he move? The resorts had brought an instant 1000% free increase in business. And bartending wasn't exactly back-breaking work. Where was he supposed to go and piss away the million bucks they'd waved under his nose anyway? He already was living in paradise.

Grand Cayman was itself the largest member of a rather isolated group of modest islands in the Caribbean sea -- technically not a part of either the windward or leeward chains like Barbados, Antigua or the Virgin Islands that were so familiar to global vacationers. Cayman was an old British protectorate – hiding a little over four hundred miles due south of Miami and about halfway between Jamaica and the southern coast of Cuba. The sister islands of Little Cayman and Cayman Brac were about 90 miles to the east and accessible only by air shuttle, making it something of a special project to contemplate a visit. Not a problem, David hadn't budged from the western end of Grand Cayman since he'd arrived four days ago, and was only now beginning to realize that he probably wouldn't be venturing much farther for the rest of his two week stay. The mellow tropical hug of his new gilded lifestyle had swallowed him whole and he willingly let it. All his adventure plans were gradually vanishing into the hazy heat of the days and the sweaty steel beat of the nights.

Mrs. Roger finished up and returned to the kitchen. The two dozen or so red snappers readying in the broiler undoubtedly needed her attention. She was all towering hair and clattering jade bracelets as she airily swept past him, humming some unknown tune. Seeing that he was free at last, Roger abandoned the glasses in the sink and returned to his buddies... laughing and joking in their near-unintelligible island accents. They were staring out the beach-side window at something. David finished his *Corona* and tipped the bottle playfully in Roger's direction. The sturdy Cayman islander grabbed another from the cooler and opened it with a movement so deft it was hard to tell if it had actually happened or if David had only imagined it. He reached over and exchanged David's empty and somehow managed to slide a fresh napkin under the new bottle with more of the same bartender's aplomb that continued to fascinate him. David flipped him a five and waved off the change. Roger smiled, a clear acrylic replacement tooth shining like a lighthouse beacon from his upper palate.

"You should go out on de deck, Captn'..." Roger suggested in a smoke-worn, gruff voice, "much nicer breeze out there. The pelicans come in around dis time. Fun to watch." David was somewhat reluctant to move since his fun-tired ass had all but melted into the bar stool by now, but Roger seemed strangely insistent. "Go on, mon. Go git some fresh air. Too much smoke in here." His eyes sparkled. Suddenly catching on, David figured that Roger and his mates probably want some privacy in order to sneak in a few tokes before the wife returned from the kitchen.

So, taking the hint, he nodded and casually began making his way towards the beachfront patio through the rear french doors. He slid aside a battered screen and stepped outside. The deck was about twenty by thirty feet of sun-bleached gray wood with little post tables scattered around, just enough to accommodate several drinks and a few sticky elbows. Wood railing, woven with fisherman's netting and some worn out dock rope, encircled the entire patio to keep the drunks from tumbling over the three foot drop onto the sand and suing Roger out of business.

He immediately saw her leaning against the far railing, looking out across the beach in the direction of the surf. Her floral print sundress was being tickled by the sea breeze into the gentlest of oscillations all down along her hemline. One leg was bent at the knee – a corkwood pump sandal rocking back and forth off the end of her heel strap. Her hair was a dark red color that was exaggerated by the crimson light of the failing sun. It was cut in that shaggy high-fashion model style that David loved. Her profile was cherubic, cute. He felt his heart clutch up in his throat. Every once in a while a guy stumbles across that certain kind of look that really just does it for him. Well, he was looking straight at his "look" right now.

David was frozen in place. This was the kind of woman that really pissed him off in a way because she intimidated the hell out of him. The higher the stakes the greater the fear. And the biggest prize created the biggest stakes. He knew this was all just his own subjective interpretation of things, but that didn't make it any less real in his mind where it counted the most. In fact, it made it worse because his fear could very well seem puzzling to her. A lot of women couldn't "take their own temperature"... meaning that they were often unaware of just how powerful an effect they could have on certain men. It was very difficult to play it cool in these kinds of circumstances. What the hell should he do? Go back inside and stick his head in his beer or hang out here and maybe take a run at it? Shit. Can you say *nerve-wracking?*

He had to remember that the only way to do this right was to just make a game of it and not try to imagine any specific outcome, otherwise the pressure would be too great and he would come off like an asshole and make a fool of himself... every man's deepest dread. She was probably on vacation like he was and just kicking back, no worries, no expectations. A perfect state to be approached by a friendly, flirtatious guy, right? Women love being hit on as long as the guy shows a little class and doesn't come on like a desperate freight train. He figured he should at least give it a shot. If nothing else it would make a fine memory for the two of them to carry home.

David took note of the fact that she was wearing a small shell necklace that she might've picked up locally. There was a volleyball game going on about thirty yards down the beach that she seemed to be casually watching, another conversation topic that might get things started. There wasn't much else going on around them to dig into, except for the beautiful sunset that was gathering impetus out over the Caribbean Sea. In the tropics, though, gorgeous sunsets were a dime a dozen and not really noteworthy. Unless it was your first day in paradise.

David took a deep breath and steadied himself. Did he need another beer? No, the head was still in the neck of the bottle. That was plenty and he didn't want to start getting sloppy and stupid anyway. Maybe later. He deftly maneuvered himself into position along the edge of her field of vision and pretended to take an interest in the volleyball game. There was only one other couple on the patio but they were seated at a table near the back door of the bar and engrossed in conversation, unaware of David and this very pretty girl. He casually turned in her direction and almost on cue she looked his way and caught his eye. Without thinking he smiled at her and she did the same. *Whew... good reflex!* he thought to himself. The last thing he would've need was to lock up into a panicked fear face.

But now he had only moments to act! Once the first acknowledgment of each other had been made, he knew there was only a brief opportunity to make a move or she would be able to sense his timidity... and that wasn't good. Confident men seized the lucky breaks life dealt them without hesitation, and he knew that this alone could be a powerful turn-on to many women. David's heart was racing. If he thought about it for too much longer he would freeze up and not be able to say anything. Already his critical judgement was beginning to tighten around his brain like a heavy noose, squeezing the life out of his wit and courage. The eye contact and trade of smiles had short-circuited the luxury of taking his sweet time and pondering the situation to death. He could already feel the pregnant moment beginning to slip through his fingers like the blonde beach sand piled up all around them. This was not the kind of stress he needed on his vacation.

Perhaps he should've done a few shots of that Yamacn' rum after all!

"Hi," he heard himself say, almost like he was listening to a recording off the radio. She tilted her head and tossed him an innocent, unassuming little smile that pretty much consummated the complete destruction of whatever higher brain function he may've had left. She was stunning. And friendly. He was surely gonna blow it.

"Hello," she responded casually. Like they were old friends.

"Looks like you've cornered your little piece of paradise..." David said in his friendly, *guileless* manner.

"Yes, it is beautiful. Like a painting" She had a cute, buttery voice.

He wrinkled his nose in feigned uncertainty. "I don't suppose a guy with a K-mart Hawaiian shirt fits into that painting very well..."

She laughed, then flashed him a pinch-lipped smile. "I

shouldn't be one to talk," she says, grabbing the conch necklace and holding it up, "me with my K-mart beads!"

David chuckled and stepped closer, taking up a spot on the railing about six feet away. "Oh wow," he pretended to smack his head "and I was just about to ask if those were from Tiffany's in George Town. Thought they might be the genuine conch pearls." She giggled and shook her head. Did she get the joke? Conchs don't make pearls. Or maybe they did? Yikes. Maybe he better go back to biology class before making any more dumb jokes!

"Actually I found them on Cardinal street... in the local flea market, she said, coming to his rescue, "But they're just the cheap ones."

"They'll make a wonderful souvenir."

"Yes," she said pensively, "I suppose they will"

David turned to face her and introduced himself. As he shook her hand, he gave it a gentle little turn to the right so that her hand was above his just before he released and let it slide free. Her eyes sparkled. "I'm Nikki."

"Glad to meet you Nikki."

They exchanged a little bit of information about where they were both from. David had escaped the nasty core of a dread Buffalo winter by joining some business friends on a week's vacation, who were graciously putting him up at their villa on Jackson Point. It turned out that Nikki hailed from nearby Pennsylvania and was staying at a local resort.

"So how have you been spending most of your time here?" he asked her, "hanging out on the beach?"

"Actually, I've learned how to scuba dive..." she said, her eyes lit up with excitement.

"Oh that's cool," he responded, "I hear this place is a paradise for divers. That's all you see are dive shops and reef tours all over the place. I was half-tempted to walk into one the other day and sign up for one of their quickie courses..."

"That's what I did. It's not as scary as it looks. It's something I always wanted to try." Her hair seemed to sparkle in the fading sun. Her pale skin painted orange. David was having a hard time not just staring at her like a work of art.

"Was it one of those one-hour certifications?"

"Yes. You get some instruction in the pool to become familiar with the equipment and how to breathe correctly so that you don't hurt your lungs. Mostly you have to know to exhale whenever you rise to the surface, and how to clear you ears when you go down so that they don't pop. The rest of it is pretty easy."

"Did they take you out in the ocean?" he wondered.

"Oh yes! We went right over there," she pointed with her long slender arms out towards the falling sun, "to *Annie's Reef,* which is just about a half mile off shore. They took fifteen of us out on the *Lazy Polly*, you may've seen it..."

"Oh yeah I did... that 25 footer in the Jackson Marina right down the road. Those are dive boats?" David asked. He turned to face her and stepped closer along the rail. She mirrored his movement with a casual and friendly ease.

"Yes. Many of them. The dive shop owns three of them I think."

"The reef dive must have been cool..."

"It was awesome." her deep brown eyes drove deep into his soul, "it was like being inside a gigantic aquarium. The fish were all different colors, and many of them were striped. We saw a school of giant blue angelfish that were about a foot long, and a couple of small lemon sharks. I touched one of them."

"The shark?" he gasped.

She nodded and put her hands in front of her mouth. "On the tail fin. I don't know what made me do it. I just wanted to know what it felt like. I was afraid it was going to turn around and bite me, but it didn't... *thank God!*"

David laughed. "Sounds like quite an adventure for your first dive."

Nikki then went on to describe how breathtaking the ancient coral forests were, and how the clear ocean water gave the illusion that you didn't even feel as though you were down very deep, although they had been as far below the surface as fifty feet at one point.

"There's a few shipwrecks not far from here that you can dive on too, so I've heard anyway..." David said. Mrs. Roger passed by the door and David motioned for her to bring them another Corona and a glass of white Zin for Nikki.

"Yes, the *Balboa* and another one, I forget what it's called."

"The Cale, or something like the that?"

"The *Cali*! It's an old Mexican freighter I think," she replied. They held eyes for a long moment until Roger's wife stepped between them with a tray and their drinks. David paid and tipped her generously. Nikki thanked him and insisted she could pay for her own, but David wouldn't hear of it. The issue was dropped immediately and their conversation about the local dive spots continued for a few minutes longer.

They watched the sun swell into a red, oblong ball and shimmy its way down into the aquamarine sea. In silence they shared this magnificent visual dreamscape. "Gone to west," David finally said, mimicking Elmer Fudd's silly voice. Nikki giggled at his playful stab at a turn of childish humor.

From that point on, everything that happened seemed almost magical. She reached over and touched the back of his hand for just a second or two while describing a small fight that had broken out between two of the guys they were watching play volleyball farther down the beach. Evidently everything had worked out alright because the guys were on the same team now, laughing and kidding around. When David looked out and described the pair of clouds that were hanging perfectly still over the still-blazing horizon as looking like a pair of radiant ocean liners, he turned to see her gazing at him with her head slightly tilted coyly to one side. Like a painting.

Their conversation continued for nearly another hour as the twilight faded into the soft tropical evening. It remained upbeat and interesting, not too personal, and just a bit self-revelatory, but no crazy deep secrets. David kept them focused in the present with the goal of creating a warm memory of this moment that perhaps they would both be able to keep forever. He surely would. His tone of delivery was soft and flirtatious, a slight pause hanging before every response to her many questions about him. There was a kind of a laid-back lethargy to his words that Nikki soon experienced to be hypnotic. Even his movements had somehow become fascinating to watch.

Made comfortable by the ease with which they were connecting, Nikki suggested a walk down the beach to where some friends were having a clambake.

"Over where that bonfire is going?" David asked, pointing.

She nodded. "That's them."

They turned to face each other. Surrendering to an urge that he made no attempt to control any longer, he reached over and brushed a strand of her auburn hair aside and looped it back over her ear. She smiled at him and looked down, softly... like a dream. They set their empty drinks aside and made their way towards the rear entrance of the bar. It was a different world than the one David had left only what?... was it two hours ago already? Whatever. The place was filling up with boisterous tourists and the air was split with the hammering thump of steel reggae coming from the eight speakers that encircled the perimeter of the room. He spotted Roger and his friends still hanging out at their private corner of the bar, smoking thick, foul cigars and drinking shots of rum.

"Hold on one second Nikki," David shouted to her above the din. He drove his way through the crowd towards Roger, pulled a $20 dollar bill from his wallet as he approached and palmed it down onto the bar in front of him. Roger raised an eyebrow, his plastic tooth glinting like a sapphire in the hollow glow of a nearby Budweiser sign.

"One good tip deserves another," David told him.

Roger glanced at the bill and laughed. "Gets mighty cold in Buffalo dis time of year boss. Come back and visit me before you leave, right?"

David nodded, "Sure will."

As David and Nikki walked past the feisty Calico Jack on their way to the beach, the battered old macaw cackled and whistled his avian farewell.

Outside again, the night air clung to them like sweet honey. A gentle sea breeze made Nikki's sundress dance like a billowing cloud in the old pale mercury streetlight. David reached for her hand, making a hook of his index finger. They met halfway and locked fingers as they set off down the beach, guided by the billowing bonfire in the distance. Beckoning them towards... who could say for sure?

In the east, looking out across the far side of Cayman island in the direction of Africa, an orange, surreal-looking three-quarter moon had just cleared the horizon on the start of its timeless arc across the night sky.

*   *   *

On Closer Examination...

Alright, now that you've suffered through my humble little attempt at a Harlequin romance, let's briefly run through the essay once more – only this time annotated in a way that I hope will demonstrate a few simple lessons in the art of seduction. This innocuous bit of fiction has been deliberately loaded with many of the crucial elements necessary to create a great first approach and conversation by the main character, David. It sets the stage perfectly for a complete seduction, if he were to choose to pursue it with that ultimate goal in mind. (Alas, we'll never know... since it was just a "day in the life of..." sort of deal). That's okay, because I wrote Cayman Magic not so much to entertain as to *teach*.

So let's go ahead and dissect this story right now to get a better understanding of the logic behind David's actions and Nikki's reactions. I've focused on depicting the "pickup" phase of the seduction because that's the part that gives guys like us the most trouble, and the reason why so many of us fail to ever make any headway with women. The opening first third of the story is just fluff to set up the situation and the tropical setting, so we'll skip ahead to the part where David first sees Nikki standing on the patio deck of Calico Jack's and is debating with himself whether or not to approach her. You know too well this agonizing moment or fear and uncertainty, I'm sure.

What I'll do now is reprint portions of the story and insert my comments and annotations after each segment that requires further explanation of the characters' motives and responses. I want you to see how this story is really nothing more than an example of how many of the concepts in this book would play themselves out in an actual real life interaction between two people. **Similar situations that, hopefully, you too will find yourself engaged in very soon!**

David was frozen in place. This was the kind of woman that really pissed him off in a way because she intimidated the hell out of him. The higher the stakes the greater the fear. And the biggest prize created the biggest stakes. He knew this was all just his own subjective interpretation of things, but that didn't make it any less real in his mind where it counted the most. In fact, it made it worse because his fear could very well seem puzzling to her. A lot of women couldn't "take their own temperature"... meaning that they were often unaware of just how powerful an effect they could have on certain men. It was very difficult to play it cool in these kinds of circumstances. What the hell should he do? Go back inside and stick his head in his beer or hang out here and maybe take a run at it? Shit. Can you say *nerve-wracking?*

He had to remember that the only way to do this right was to just make a game of it and not try to imagine any specific outcome, otherwise the pressure would be too great and he would come off like an asshole and make a fool of himself... every man's deepest dread. She was probably on vacation like he was and just kicking back, no worries, no expectations. A perfect state to be approached by a friendly, flirtatious guy, right? Women love being hit on as long as the guy shows a little class and doesn't come on like a desperate freight train. He figured he should at least give it a shot. If nothing else it would make a fine memory for the two of them to carry home.

Remember what I said about the power of **assuming?** Assuming is the cornerstone of the kind of powerful male attitude that is required to make a killer first impression with any woman. The whole concept of attitude, in turn, centers around the notion of **empowering mental belief systems vs. disempowering belief systems.** If you fill your head with disempowering thoughts and beliefs, i.e., *I'm too short, she probably has a boyfriend, I'm not her type, she's probably just waiting for her girlfriends to show up and party with her, I don't know what to say that would sweep her away, etc. etc.* – you will absolutely clog your mind with negative confidence and paralyze yourself to take any type of action. Even a simple hello can become impossible to negotiate in this kind of depleted mental state. The resulting fear will protect you until the moment of opportunity safely slips away and you are free to continue walking around in your social shell again, which is exactly what your over-protective unconscious mind wishes to happen.

Well, your male power to act in the presence of an attractive woman flows from your ability to contain just the *opposite* sort of assumptions in your mind, **empowering thoughts,** necessary to boost your confidence. I'm not talking about some kind of mental sleight of hand – nor is self pep-talking a form of "cheating" (hell, having those sort of impossible rules lodged in your head are in fact *themselves* a form of disempowering mentality!). We **need positive self-talk** to move us along in stressful moments whenever risk-taking is required in order to achieve a goal that has any real importance to us. For instance, if an upcoming job interview is causing you anxiety, you do what it takes to mentally prepare yourself, quell the fear, and then go do the damn interview. Whatever it takes to advance your career is fair game. Who cares what anybody else thinks? They do the same things, or worse.

So if there's no shame in adopting self-talk therapy to help yourself get past any other type of stressful situation in life, why shouldn't the same be true when preparing to approach an attractive women with romantic intent? This could turn out to be a life-altering event, and thus it is distressing – and thus... well, you must do whatever it takes to get yourself up for the task instead of mentally self-sabotaging and tearing yourself down!

Some of the positive things that David could be saying to himself when wrestling with the idea of hitting on Nikki are: **SHE HAS NO BOYFRIEND... SHE WANTS TO BE APPROACHED BY A MAN... I'M AN ALRIGHT LOOKING GUY... THERE'S NO PRESSURE... FLIRT FOR FUN... NO MEMORY... NO SHAME.** See? If he assumes all these things to be true, they will be reflected in his attitude and he will be giving off potent, non-verbal dominant male signals that will make him seem light-years more attractive to any woman. Same body, different attitude, vastly different results. Prepare yourself, but don't fall into the trap of over-thinking everything to death either or paralysis will set in and the opportunity to act will quickly disappear (which might be what you secretly wish to happen, so beware of your secret subliminal fears!)

David took note of the fact that she was wearing a small shell necklace that she might've picked up locally – a good complimenting point. There was a pick-up volleyball game going on about thirty yards down the beach that she seemed to be casually watching, another conversation topic that might get things started. There wasn't much else going on around them to dig into, except the beautiful sunset that was gathering impetus out over the Caribbean Sea. In the tropics, though, gorgeous sunsets were a dime a dozen and not really noteworthy. Unless it was your first day in paradise.

Notice how, before charging in like a bull elephant, David spends a moment (despite his anxiety) carefully taking note of something either about **her or their surroundings** that he can either comment on or compliment her on. It is critical that you learn to think on your feet like this... your display of clever observation and pre-thought comes across as being very classy and is highly impressive. *Nothing is more of a turn-off to women than some canned opening line that you obviously memorized out of some shitty "pick-up book" that you probably bought from one of my competitors!* (Serves you right ya bastard...)

Your approach should 1) sound unrehearsed (a simple "hello" is best, really), 2) be relevant to your surroundings or the events going on around you (no super-clever "head scratchers"), and 3) be non-phoney sounding. Do not come on with some kind of *fake personality,* even if you're only joking. She might not "get" your lame attempt at humor.

Your opening remark should be genuine, interesting, possibly complimentary (only **one** compliment uniquely targeted to her, not a "generic" compliment) sexually neutral, and set a positive tone for the following conversation. Being playfully flirtatious, creative and demonstrating a bit of clever humor doesn't hurt either, but don't overdo it... especially the humor aspect. You don't want to turn into a jokin' asshole at any cost! Spontaneity is definitely a High Status signal.

If all this sounds like a tall order, don't panic. It's easier to actually *do* than to read about – just use your common sense. Flirt, but in a friendly way with no hard-driving goal "to score" obvious (but always keep an optimum outcome that you would like to achieve in the back of your mind).

David took a deep breath and steadied himself. Did he need another beer? No, the head was still in the neck of the bottle. That was plenty and he didn't want to start getting sloppy and stupid anyway. Maybe later. He deftly maneuvered himself into position along the edge of her field of vision and pretended to take an interest in the volleyball game. There was only one other couple on the patio but they were seated at a table near the back door of the bar and engrossed in conversation, unaware of David and this very pretty girl. He casually turned in her direction and almost on cue she looked his way and caught his eye. Without thinking he smiled at her and she did the same. "Whew... good reflex!" he thought to himself. The last thing he would've need was to lock up into a panicked fear face.

Remember how important it is to train yourself to *catch her eye* and not look away like a low-status shy guy? You must practice this all the time with old people, dogs, or even those psychos at the morning bus stop if you have to in order for it to become a natural reflex. Have you practiced today? Then get busy... and don't forget to smile! (Okay, you are excused from having to smile at the bus stop psycho)...

But now he had only moments to act! Once the first acknowledgment of each other had been made, he knew there was only a brief opportunity to make a move or she would be able to sense his timidity, and that wasn't good. Confident men seized the lucky breaks life dealt them without hesitation, and he knew that this alone could be a powerful turn-on to many women. David's heart was racing. If he thought about it for too much longer he would freeze up and not be able to say anything.

Already his critical judgement was beginning to tighten around his brain like a heavy noose, squeezing the life out of his wit and courage. The eye contact and trade of smiles had short- circuited the luxury of taking his sweet time and pondering the situation to death. He could already feel the pregnant moment beginning to slip through his fingers like the blonde beach sand piled up all around them. This was not the kind of stress he needed on his vacation. Perhaps he should've done a few shots of that Yamacn' rum after all.

Timing is everything, especially at the opening bell. A pause of more than a few seconds can make all the difference between her hanging around and turning away. David knows that he has only a few seconds to act or the essential spontaneity of the moment will vanish. Any action he then takes afterward will seem to have come at the end of a long internal struggle with fear that will only serve to diminish his status. What to do? **ASSUME** that she will like you and then act like it! Pretend in your mind that she's an old friend who will be happy to see you if you must. Lie to yourself. Anything. *Act!*

"Hi," he heard himself say, almost like he was listening to a recording off the radio. She tilted her head and tossed him an innocent, unassuming little smile that pretty much consummated the complete destruction of whatever higher brain function he may've had left. She was stunning. And friendly. He was surely gonna blow it.

"Hello," she responded casually. Like they were old friends.

"Looks like you've cornered your little piece of paradise..." David said in his friendly, guileless manner.

"Yes, it is beautiful. Like a painting" She had a buttery voice.

David makes use of his prior observation of her necklace to get her talking about herself a little... maybe not in the smoothest way possible, but in real life that's how it goes sometimes. You can't make everything come out perfect like a Hollywood script. The trick is to stay light on your feet and keep things moving forward as best you can.

She knows that this is a stressful time for you and will cut you some slack as long as you don't say something patently offensive. Don't obsess about any small goof-ups, just roll right over them and keep talking. Remember, what you say will be almost instantly forgotten anyway... it's *how* you say it -- your attitude, your assumptions – that she's subliminally picking up on. David also keenly swerves away from getting too stupid with the jokes.

"Actually I found them on Cardinal street... in the local flea market, she said, coming to his rescue, "But they're just the cheap ones."

"They'll make a wonderful souvenir."

"Yes," she said pensively, "I suppose they will"

David turned to face her and introduced himself. As he shook her hand, he gave it a gentle little turn to the right so that her hand was above his just before he released and let it slide free. Her eyes sparkled. "I'm Nikki."

"Glad to meet you Nikki." *(The Handshake Trick!)*

They exchanged a little bit of information about where they were both from. David had escaped the nasty core of a dread Buffalo winter by joining some business friends on a week's vacation, who were graciously putting him up at their villa on Jackson Point. It turned out that Nikki hailed from nearby Pennsylvania and was staying at a local resort.

"So how have you been spending most of your time here?" he asked her, "hanging out on the beach?"

Notice how David asks an open-ended question (one that **can't** be answered with a simple yes or no and thus bring the conversation to a screeching halt) and then *LISTENS carefully to her response.* If she gives him some clue as to what is interesting and exciting to her in her life at this moment, does he roll right over it and start to brag about what a great guy he is and how many rich friends he has and how bright and shiny his new Corvette is?... **NO!** *David picks up on the clue and turns the conversation in that direction.* He draws her out and shows some genuine interest in what she's into. In this case, he's soon to discover that it's Nikki's new found enjoyment of scuba diving. *Get a Life Line!*

People love to talk about themselves, and are endeared to anyone who shows any little bit of interest in the things that make up their world. The key here is *genuine interest...* if your approach seems like that of a slick phoney who's just pretending to be interested in what she's saying to get into her pants, she'll pick up on that sort of bullshit and shut your ass down fast.

Instead, demonstrate your legitimate interest by lingering on the subject for awhile and asking a series of relevant follow-up questions. Bring some of your own views or curiosities into the discussion. You may be attracted to her body, but you must be interested in her person. How long do you listen? Allow the topic completely exhaust itself naturally before moving on.

Then look for another LifeLine! That's right... let *her* do most of the actual talking if she's willing to. Let your moves and attitude communicate to her non-verbally the critical things that you want her to understand about the feelings you're having about her right now. Women are not like lunk-headed men who have to be smashed in the face with something before they get it... they think intuitively and tease all the hidden meanings out of the seemingly innocent expressions, attitudes and body postures. Especially those coming from the men who are expressing an interest in them!

"Actually, I've learned how to scuba dive..." she said, her eyes lit up with excitement.

"Oh that's cool," he responded, "I hear this place is a paradise for divers. That's all you see are dive shops and reef tours all over the place. I was half-tempted to walk into one the other day and sign up for one of their quickie courses..."

"That's what I did. It's not as scary as it looks. It's something I always wanted to try." Her hair seemed to sparkle in the fading sun. Her pale skin painted orange. David was having a hard time not just staring at her like a work of art.

"Did they take you out in the ocean?"

"Oh yes! We went right over there," she pointed with her long slender arms out towards the falling sun, "to Annie's Reef which is just about a half mile off shore. They took fifteen of us out on the Lazy Polly, you may've seen it..."

David maintains a captivated attitude towards her throughout their conversation. He projects no tendency towards having any sort of ulterior motive. Sure he's interested in meeting and talking with her, but why not? She's a pretty girl, and no dominant male makes excuses or apologies for his desires as a man.

He just strives to express them in the most classy, impressive way possible!

Nikki might've been a bit nervous at the outset of their encounter, but David's limited stabs at humor and his choice of interesting conversation topics have very subtly endeared him towards her. He's also being careful not to say anything socially offensive or sexually callus, which can easily burst the delicate bubble of trust that's already begun to develop between them.

Remember though that you don't need to hammer a woman with blatant sexual comments in order to communicate your amorous interest. Trust me, she knows. Yet some men are so afraid of being misinterpreted as a "buddy-buddy wimp" that they'll risk making complete fools of themselves with lewd commentary just to *insure* that a woman makes no mistake that he's after her tail. While their desire to stay out of the friends zone is laudable, their method of achieving it is so ham-handed that it destroys any real chance of seduction with all but the most sluttiest types of women who will fall for even a brazen come-on. I'm assuming that you'll eventually want to do better than that, right?

The *classy* way to demonstrate your sexual interest in a woman is with non-verbal cues (deep eye contact, tonally modulated voice, mirrored body movements, etc.) and brief, inoffensive touches. In the game of seduction, women read *between the lines* (i.e., your attitudes and the underlying assumptions that you hold about yourself which create them) in order to get a sense of a man's dominant male status and thus, his attractiveness. Inappropriately premature dirty talk is a clear low status signal to her. It screams: *"...Hey, get a load of me baby, I know all about how to have hot sex with a woman... even though I look like I don't know how to open a condom wrapper..."* A truly sexy, dominant male knows he projects plenty of sex appeal to women (with his **attitude!**) and therefore doesn't have to go around broadcasting it like a complete asshole.

"Oh yeah I did... that 25 footer in the Jackson Marina right down the road. Those are dive boats?" David asked. He turned to face her and stepped closer along the rail. She mirrored his movement with a casual and friendly ease.

"Yes. Many of them. The dive shop owns three of them I think."

"The reef dive must have been cool..."

"It was awesome." her deep brown eyes drove deep into his soul, "it was like being inside a gigantic aquarium. The fish were all different colors, and many of them were striped. We saw a school of giant blue angelfish that were about a foot long, and a couple of small lemon sharks. I touched one of them."

"The shark?" he gasped.

She nodded and put her hands in front of her mouth. "On the tail fin. I don't know what made me do it. I just wanted to know what it felt like. I was afraid it was going to turn around and bite me, but it didn't... thank God."

David laughed. "Sound like quite an adventure for your first dive."

Nikki then went on to describe how breathtaking the ancient coral forests were, and how the clear ocean water gave the illusion that you didn't even feel as though you were down very deep, although they had been as far below the surface as fifty feet at one point.

"There's a few shipwrecks not far from here that you can dive on too, so I've heard anyway..." David said. Mrs. Roger passed by the door and David motioned for her to bring them another Corona and a glass of white Zin for Nikki.

"Yes, the Balboa and another one, I forget what it's called."

"The Cale, or something like the that?"

"The Cali! It's an old Mexican freighter I think," she replied. They held eyes for a long moment until Roger's wife stepped between them with a tray and their drinks. David paid and tipped her generously. Nikki thanked him and insisted she could pay for her own, but David wouldn't hear of it. The issue was dropped immediately and their conversation about the local dive spots continued for a few minutes longer.

They watched the sun swell into a red, oblong ball and shimmy its way down into the aquamarine sea. In silence they shared this magnificent visual dreamscape. "Gone to west," David finally said, mimicking Elmer Fudd's silly voice. Nikki giggled at his playful stab at a turn of childish humor.

Once you've got a toehold of familiarity established between the two of you, a little bit of goofy humor is okay. But don't lead off with it unless you're a really smooth guy with the jokes because she doesn't know you yet... are you just kidding or what? How's she supposed to know? She doesn't, so use humor more like a spice. Save your routine for open mike night at Chuckles.

From that point on, everything that happened seemed almost magical. She reached over and touched the back of his hand for just a second or two while describing a small fight that had broken out between two of the guys they were watching play volleyball farther down the beach. Evidently everything had worked out alright because the guys were on the same team now, laughing and kidding around. When David looked out and described the pair of clouds that were hanging perfectly still over the still-blazing horizon as looking like a pair of radiant ocean liners, he turned to see her gazing at him with her head slightly tilted coyly to one side. Like a painting.

Their conversation continued for nearly another hour as the twilight faded into the soft tropical evening. It remained upbeat and interesting, not too personal, and not too self-revelatory. David kept them focused in the present with the goal of creating a warm memory of this moment that perhaps they would both be able to keep forever. He surely would. His tone of delivery was soft and flirtatious, a slight pause hanging before every response to her many questions about him. There was a kind of a laid-back lethargy to his words that Nikki soon experienced to be hypnotic. Even his movements had somehow become fascinating to watch.

Made comfortable by the ease with which

they were seeming to connect, Nikki suggested that they take a walk down the beach to where some friends of hers were having a clambake.

Very interesting... Made comfortable, a woman will frequently take the lead in pushing a new relationship along to it's next level. Recall what I said before about escalation and how important it is that every seduction hit its mark and keep moving along. You must escalate before things get too stale – but at the same time you want to display the patience to experience all of these steps in their time (eye contact ; smiling ; teasing and flirting ; first words ; interested & safety issues ; open ended questions ; exchange of names ; sincere compliments ; connecting common interests through conversation ; humor ; eye reading & establishing rapport ; minor self-revelation ; touching ; gazing ; mirroring ; asking for contact information or making a date) and so on.

David's laid back sex appeal and his High Status Male confidence suggests the perfect mix of empathy (*good listening skills, genuine interest*) and ego drive (*no attempt to apologize for his male drives and desires*) that a woman loves to see in a man. The careful pace of any seduction is a form of hypnotic suggestion that places Nikki into a kind of trance... where she willingly submits to David's gentle advances.

"Over where that bonfire is going?" David asked, pointing.

She nodded. "That's them."

Notice that David does *not* suggest going back into the bar for more drinks, instead of meeting up with her friends at the clambake where she's more likely to lose her undivided focus on him. That's because this type of tired, worn-out old "get-her-hammered" ploy triggers all sorts of potentially *negative* dating associations that can break the aura of connectedness that's beginning to grow between them. This time it's different – David is not the insecure and jealous type but open to letting her express herself, and that intrigues her into hanging out with him for a while longer, if for nothing more than merely to see what comes next.

They turned to face each other. Surrendering to an urge that he made no attempt to control any longer he reached over and brushed a strand of her auburn hair aside and looped it back over her right ear. She smiled at him and looked down, softly... like a dream.

Don't forget the power of touch! Even just innocently touching her hair can be enough to turn loose a cascade of emotions that will leave the two of you closer even after a mere instantaneous event. Keep the touch brief, and pick a moment that feels just right. Timing is everything with this powerful escalation.

They set their empty drinks aside and made their way towards the rear entrance of the bar. It was a different world than the one David had left only what?... was it two hours ago already? Whatever. The place was filling up with boisterous tourists and the air was split with the hammering thump of steel reggae coming from the eight speakers that encircled the perimeter of the room. He spotted Roger and his friends still hanging out at their private corner of the bar, smoking thick, foul cigars and drinking shots of rum.

"Hold on one second Nikki," David shouted to her above the din. He drove his way through the crowd towards Roger, pulled a $20 dollar bill from his wallet as he approached and palmed it down onto the bar in front of him. Roger raised an eyebrow, his plastic tooth glinting like a sapphire in the hollow glow of a nearby Budweiser sign.

"One good tip deserves another," David said.

Roger glanced at the bill and laughed. "Gets mighty cold in Buffalo dis time of year boss. Come back and visit one more time before you leave, right?"

David nodded, "Sure will."

As David and Nikki walked past the feisty Calico Jack on their way to the beach, the battered old macaw cackled and whistled his avian farewell.

Outside again, the night air clung to them like sweet honey. A gentle sea breeze made Nikki's sundress dance like a billowing cloud in the old pale mercury streetlight. David reached for her hand, making a hook of his index finger. They met halfway and locked fingers as they set off down the beach, guided by the billowing bonfire in the distance. Beckoning them towards... who could say for sure?

In the east, looking out across the far side of Cayman island in the direction of Africa, an orange, surreal-looking three-quarter moon had just cleared the horizon on the start of its timeless arc across the night sky.

So there you have it. My imagining of how a cool, classy first encounter with a woman would go off in a perfect world. Of course, the world is far from perfect and all sorts of things could've gone wrong with this deal. In reality, Nikki could've been uninterested in meeting David for any number of reasons... she might've been engaged or married – or had personal problems that were keeping her stuck in a foul mood. Or maybe David just might've been her "anti-type" – the kind of guy whose *looks just turned her off* no matter how charming he might've been. In other words, there are many, many factors that could've caused David to be *rejected* that were (and will always remain) completely out of his control.

This is why I say that it's important to score yourself **on your performance,** which is totally **under your control,** and NOT on all the various X-factors like those I just listed above which are *not* under your control.

In other words, if you try your best to do everything that you can to present yourself as a dignified, dominant male – then you have *no right to beat yourself up* if the results of the approach do not go down as you would've liked them to. So endeavor to become as skilled as you can at those things about your **attitude and actions** that give you the best chance to succeed with women... and release yourself from bearing responsibility for those aspects of the seduction which no one but Fate alone has any control over. Remember that it takes two to tango – she has to be willing to meet you halfway or no seduction will never get off the ground. Acting under the **assumption** that she will respond favorably to your advances is the single most important thing to remember because *that* more than anything else will minimize your chances of being rejected. The Arrogance of that old Assumptive Attitude we talked about before.

Any man can always be rejected by the whim of a woman, no matter how overwhelming his persona or charm. As long as you always remember to score **your performance** and not *her* reaction – you can hold your head high and move on to your next seduction with the sort of pride that will all but ensure an eventual conquest.

Appendix B: The 7 Mega-Rules

The 7 Mega-Rules of Men / Women Relations

1) In the Mating Game...
...it's the Women Who Choose the Men – and not vice-versa

"Men get rejected most often when they fail to get a GO signal from a woman *first* before approaching her in a romantic context. Society's illusion would have you believe that men control the game of Seduction. They do **not** – they need to know how to *Recognize & React* instead."

2) A Mans' Demeanor Reveals His Status...
... Among Other <u>Men</u>

"High status males act **gracious and welcoming** because they have nothing to prove – whereas low status males are often mean, sarcastic and even cruel. The more nasty the man, the lower his perceived status among men."

3) Your Apparent Position on the Male Dominance Scale is the Sole Determinant of your Attractiveness to Women... Period!

"Women do not grade men on their physical looks in the same manner that men rate women... instead, you are graded on where you *appear to rank among other males* in terms of socio-economic status, power, intelligence, wealth, etc. Lucky for you, this can be *faked* far more easily than physical unattractiveness can be hidden!..."

4) <u>Assuming</u> is the Key to the Dominant Male Attitude

"What you assume to be true makes a vastly more powerful statement than anything you could ever say with mere words. You cannot hide your assumptions since your actions and behaviors are all based upon them."

5) Men Must Always Be the Ones to Initiate:

A) The First Words
B) The First Kiss

"The male role in the Dance of Seduction is actually rather limited... since much of it is controlled by the woman, *with the exception* of these two crucial actions which must originate from the man. That's because they both act as signals of his romantic/sexual desire, which a woman must be able to witness before she can consider submitting to him."

6) The Best Way to Communicate Your Availability to Women...
...is Via Other Women

"The most effective way to communicate your "market possibilities" to any woman is via **female proxies** in the form of her girlfriends and / or other female associates at work, etc. You do this by socializing and dating around within that social "pack" and developing a *name and reputation* for yourself as a player. Learn to harness the willingness of other women to gossip about you!..."

7) The Partner who expresses the <u>Least</u> Interest in a Relationship...

...<u>Controls</u> that relationship

"The only kind of relationship that can stand the test of time is one in which the partners both love and respect each other **equally**. If one partner has less interest in things then the other partner will tend to "kiss his or her ass" in order to get them to change – but this only creates a *loss of respect* which will grow into *resentments* after a while. This will either kill or otherwise greatly diminish the quality of the sexual aspect of the relationship. Time to pull the ripcord when this happens, and preserve your self-respect and/or your sanity."

Appendix C: The Dominant Male Test

Test time kids! Sharpen your pencils and no more talking!

Here's a little quiz that you can take to help you get a feel for just where you're scoring on that all important "Male Dominance Scale" that lurks within the minds of most eligible women out there. Answer the following 25 questions **honestly** in terms of how you think *you would most likely react* to the described situations – not what you "think" would be the right answer (I'll admit that some can be guessed at, but is this what **you** would really do?). No one's going to see the results but yourself, so there's no reason to cheat... unless of course you can't stand to know the truth about yourself. In that case, your station in life is pretty much destined to remain the same. Remember that you must face down your delusions in order to bring about any significant change in your life.

Okay, print out this test and circle the answer that most likely describes your reaction (choose only **one** answer) for each question. Then check **Appendix D** for how to figure your score, an explanation of the overall scoring results, and a little tutorial after each question explaining how and why the dominant male acts differently from the weak submissive one.

Have fun!...

1) You're driving your car in fairly heavy traffic with your date, late for a movie, when someone cuts in front of you and steals your parking spot. You have to hit your brakes fairly hard and as a result have to waste time driving around looking for another spot. How would you react?

A) Pound the steering wheel and swear the sonofabitch upside down and backwards.
B) Sit there quietly stewing but not mention it
C) Shake your head in disgust, but make a joke about it.
D) Use the opportunity to rub your date's inner thigh.

2) At a family gathering... your sister Kathy, yourself and your cousin Mark are all sitting on the couch having a few beers. Your sister, who understands football from a girls' perspective (so-so), excitedly begins to describe a touchdown play to Mark, a big time Steelers fan, that the two of you saw at last night's home game. Do you...

A) Look at Mark while she's describing the play and roll your eyes?
B) Let her tell the story her way, and then fill in any technical details that Mark might find interesting afterwards?
C) Cut her off and tell the story your way, using football jargon that only a couple of NFL-savvy guys like you and Mark would understand?
D) Try to slip your hand under your sister's ass while she's distracted?

3) It's the first day in your new math class. Time to pick a seat. Where do you sit?

A) In the front row.
B) In the back third of the class, where you're not likely to be noticed.
C) In the far rear corner where you can inflict the greatest amount of damage when you open fire.

D) In the front third of the class near a cute girl.

4) A co-worker whips up a one-page flyer for next month's office picnic on his word processor during his lunch break. He hands you the flyer and asks what you think. What's your reaction?

A) You glance at it briefly and tell him it looks fine.
B) You point out two spelling errors.
C) You compliment him on his dedication to the Cause, then make a couple of suggestions for improvements.
D) You turn him into the boss for using company resources.

5) You're out driving around with your buddies and you see a shabby old man with a brown paper bag, obviously drunk, weaving around on the sidewalk minding his own business. Do you...

A) Ignore him?
B) Seize the opportunity to make a nasty joke?
C) Think "Holy shit... *dad!*..."
D) Roll down your window, shout "Hey, you stupid fuck!..." and spit at him for the amusement of your friends?

6) You spot a cute girl at a friend's party standing alongside a guy who you *think* is probably her brother... but you're not absolutely certain. You've seen a similar couple hanging around the neighborhood, and maybe you're confusing the two -- in which case the guy is almost certainly her boyfriend. It's 50-50. You really want to meet her though, and this would be the perfect opportunity. Do you...

A) Ask all your friends to see if anybody knows what the deal is with her.
B) Stay right where you are and do nothing.
C) Walk over and introduce yourself, then try to determine if

they're brother and sister by striking up a conversation.
D) Keep trying to catch her eye, and then smile & wink at her every time that you do.

7) You're out at a fancy restaurant with a date and the waitress goofs up your order big time, how would you react?

A) Give her a dressing down and embarrass her.
B) Make a joke about it and let her know that it's ok.
C) Insist on seeing the manager.
D) Ask her if she'd like to meet you later for a few drinks.

8) How do you typically act around your male friends?

A) Like a tough guy, with f-words flying every few seconds.
B) By verbally sparing with them – half-jokingly putting them down all the time.
C) Like myself... based on however I feel that day.
D) Quiet, always hanging around in the background. I just like to observe their antics for my amusement.

9) You are hanging out with a small group of people at a social setting. An attractive woman you've never seen before is standing nearby, but neither of you have acknowledged each other's presence except for some brief eye contact. Are you most likely to...

A) Wait for her to say something to you first?
B) Introduce yourself and shake her hand?
C) Wait for someone in the group to formally introduce the two of you?
D) Show her your Gene Simmons tongue waggle next time you catch her eye?

10) You look out your living room window and see two dudes talking out in the street. One of them is leaning up against your new car parked out front, and he's wearing a belt with a big buckle that looks like it could scratch the paint job. Do you...

A) Go outside and ask him to "...not lean on my new car 'cause the bank still owns it..." in a non-threatening way?
B) Charge outside and scream "Hey dude, get the fuck off the car!..."
C) Sneak around from behind and sucker punch him in the head?
D) Say nothing, go back to the couch and continue watching *Friends* re-runs?

11) How scared are you of your boss?

A) Terrified, I can't even look him in the eye.
B) I'm respectful, but not scared.
C) I am the boss (or I work for myself).
D) Fuck him, that stupid cocksucker.

12) You're picking up your date at her house for an evening out at the new downtown nightclub. Her ten year old son is having a mood and giving her grief. How do you react?

A) Grab the kid by the hair and slap him?
B) Take her son aside and talk about sports or his favorite hobby for a few minutes?
C) Invite him to go along with the two of you for a few drinks?
D) Say nothing, then tell your date (later on) that she should learn how to control her kid better?

13) How would you describe humor as a component of your personality?

A) I sometimes get too wild and nutty, especially when I'm out

drinking with my friends.
B) I'm an opportunist, I pick my spots for a clever comment now and then.
C) I like to make fun of all the assholes I see hanging around, or the stupid jerks that I hate.
D) I joke around and act funny *constantly*.

14) When you leave the house – whether its to go to work, grab a bite to eat by yourself, or just take a quick run over to the laundromat – how do you usually dress?

A) In whatever I happen to be wearing
B) I put on a shirt and tie
C) In my flasher raincoat
D) Casual but clean

15) You're talking to a girl you know from work during a happy hour get together with a small group of co-workers from the office. Would you place your hand casually on her forearm while the two of you are engrossed in an animated conversation, and let it linger there for a few seconds?

A) No way, I'm not getting a sexual harassment grievance filed against me!
B) Sure, why not? She's cute, and I find her attractive.
C) Probably not. I wouldn't want her to get the wrong idea.
D) Only as a distraction while I try to work my other hand under her skirt.

16) Can you accept the generosity of another person – a man or a woman – gracefully?

A) Only with great difficulty.
B) No way, I don't want to owe anyone anything. Better that they owe me.
C) Sure, why not.

D) What are you talking about? No one is ever generous to me.

17) If someone were to present an idea or dream of their's to you, would you tend to encourage or discourage it?

A) Encourage it, with some advice or reservations if I saw the need for it.
B) Discourage it. I hate listening to other people's stupid plans... none of it ever works out anyway. So why waste my time?
C) Encourage it wholeheartedly.
D) I'd tell them about *my* dreams instead.

18) Your enjoying a quick sandwich on your lunch break, sitting outside on a bench in front of the office building, reading a paper. You look up for a moment and catch the eye of a cute girl about twenty feet away looking back at you. Give me the first thing that just popped into your mind right now... Do you...

A) Quickly look away, then peek back in about a minute to see if she's still watching you?
B) Smile warmly for a second, then look away casually after about 3 seconds?
C) Hold her eye, nod, wink and raise your Pepsi can in a toast?
D) Bug your eyes and give her your best maniacal Charlie Manson glare?

19) Tomorrow is the birthday of one of the cute girls you work with at the office. You'd like to get more involved with her on a personal basis outside of work, but you're not sure if this is a good opportunity to make a move or not. What do you plan to do?

A) Nothing, totally ignore her and the fact that it's her birthday.
B) Get her a light-hearted, romantic birthday card.
C) Buy her a dozen red roses.

D) Dress up like a clown, bring her a cake and sing for her.

20) How tall are you?

A) Over six feet.
B) Between 5'8" and six foot tall.
C) About 5'7" or shorter.
D) Don't call me a fuckin' midget... *I'm a dwarf!*

21) If you get an opportunity during a business meeting or a social gathering to shake hands with an attractive woman after being introduced by someone, do you...

A) Try to squeeze her hand real hard to impress her with your strength?
B) Hold just her fingertips and give her a little 'baby shake' so that you don't hurt her?
C) Give her a firm shake almost like you would a man?
D) Give her the old 'sweaty limp fish' handshake?

22) How many people in your life (subordinates) do you have the power to give orders to?

A) None.
B) Less than five.
C) Dozens.
D) Not even my dog listens to me.

23) You step into an express elevator and find yourself alone with an attractive woman. You're both riding to the top floor, which will take about a minute. Do you...

A) Look straight ahead and not say anything?
B) Drop trou and ask her to smoke your bone?
C) Make some small talk with a flirtatious gleam in your eye?
D) Make some curt, clipped small talk to relieve the tension?

24) You've invited a young lady over for a casual dinner at your place, which you'll prepare and cook after she arrives. She offers to help out with the vegetable chopping for the salad. What would be your likely reaction?

A) Thank her but insist that you do everything yourself.
B) Welcome her help and let her go to work.
C) Insist that she do nothing but sit there while you run over every few minutes to check that her wine is full and everything is ok.
D) Tell her that you don't let anyone handle the cutlery except for you and Mother.

25) If you had a weird personal habit – like for instance a funny, jerky laugh – would you feel free to express it in a public place, such as a restaurant?

A) No way!
B) No, I would always control such a laugh.
C) I might. It would depend on the mood I was in and the situation.
D) Sure, why not? How can I tell if I have a stupid laugh anyway?

Okay, pencils down. Did you answer every question as honestly as you could? If you did, then you'll find that you have performed a very revealing self-analysis that will give you an accurate insight into just what kind of image you are projecting to women. This "image" is highly subliminal, and speaks to her unconscious assessments of your value to her as a potential mate. This translates directly into your chances of having your romantic advances either accepted or rejected.

Now go to Appendix D to determine your score... and to find out just a little bit more about how your HSM/LSM status among your fellow men either helps or hurts you in the grand, never-ending competition for the ladies.

Without Embarrassment

Appendix D : Scoring the DM Test

Scoring the Dominant Male Test & Interpretation of Results

Alright, now it's time to see just how much of a babe magnet you really are. Following are all the "scores" for each answer of the *Dominant Male Test* that you just took back in Appendix C. Review which letter answer **A - D** you picked for each of the 25 questions, and write in the appropriate numerical score next to it. When you're finished collecting the individual scores, **add them up into a final overall sum** and refer to the scoring ranges at the end of this section. There you will find an interpretation of what your final score reveals about your ranking as a dominant male (or not!).

This is will be a very clarifying look into the psychological mirror that can aid you in developing a more attractive personality to present to women. This will show you where you might be going wrong with them by presenting a new spin on your current behavior patterns. Guys don't get any instruction on this sort of thing... we just stumble and fumble our way into whatever sort of relationships we can find. But this kind of self-insight is crucial to your long-term success with women... you have to *Know* before you can *Grow*!

Anyway, the format for this scoring sheet is as follows:

I've repeated the question so you can refer to it quickly and easily without having to constantly page back to Appendix C. Then I repeated the 4 possible answers followed by a numerical score in parentheses (X) for that particular answer. Whatever letter that you selected as your most likely response, write that corresponding number down on your score sheet.

The best answer for each question (reflecting the most likely behavior or some characteristic of the dominant male) is 10 points. There's usually a joke answer mixed in with each multiple choice selection just to see if you're still awake. I placed the joke answer in *italics* and gave it a value of zero (0). If you picked the joke answer because you're too much of a stiff to appreciate my awesome humor, then zero's exactly what you deserve! ;-)

I also make use of two acronyms: **LSM** means Low Status Male, and **HSM** conversely means High Status Male of course.

Finally, I give you my all important **Comments** for each of the selections. This is important stuff – it's where I teach the lesson contained in each question and distinguish for you the differences between the actions of the dominant and submissive males. ***Read these comments carefully and understand that your scores will improve as you become more familiar with the material in this book and take many of the changes I discuss to heart.***

*   *   *

1) *You're driving your car in fairly heavy traffic with your date, late for a movie, when someone cuts in front of you and steals your parking spot. You have to hit your brakes fairly hard and as a result get stuck driving around looking for another spot. How would you react?*

A) Pound the steering wheel and swear the sonofabitch upside down and backwards. (2)
B) Sit there quietly stewing and not mention it (5)
C) Shake your head in disgust, but make a joke about it. (10)
D) *Use the opportunity to rub her inner thigh. (0)*

Your Score : __10__

Comments:

A) One of the hallmarks of the low status male (LSM) is his **rage**. Having been relegated to the low end of the scale by most of the other men he's encountered in his lifetime, the LSM harbors within him a deep, latent, seething rage that's very difficult for him to control. He tends to be short tempered and nasty. Road rage is pretty common, but the LSM's is especially virulent because it acts as a momentary pressure relief valve for all his hidden, *subducted rage* which he is normally too scared to vent at the people he's really mad at in life.

B) This 'quiet stewing' -type of response can be a genuine display of calmness or it could be just an expression of willful self control. Which is it for you? If B was your answer to Question 1, then ask yourself if you would have genuinely *not* been all that enraged by the situation, or are you just good at "holding it in" (until the next serial murder maybe?). If it really wouldn't have angered you too much, then increase your score to an 8. If you probably would have been struggling with your urge to vent, then keep it a 5 (...hey, don't get mad at me...). *The tense silence would also be a downer to the playful and upbeat mood that you should be trying to create on the date.* She's not just staring dumbly out the window while all this happens... she's **gaging your reaction** to see just how potentially violent (and thus how low status) you are.

C) This best response demonstrates the calm demeanor of the high status male (HSM), and his ability to stay light on his feet in a conversational sense. It's okay to pass judgement on what a fool the guy was, but he also used the opportunity to make a joke about it and laugh it off, and thus transformed a potential negative event into a positive one. You can be sure that the woman took notice and excitedly moved him up a notch in her mind. The HSM does not carry around a great deal of latent rage with him, so his reactions to minor transgressions of this sort do not release a flood of strong emotions. It takes more to provoke him.

D) Only a truly clueless Romeo would choose this answer, and for that you get the goose egg (zero points).

2) At a family gathering... your sister Kathy, yourself and your cousin Mark are all sitting on the couch having a few beers. Your sister, who understands football from a girls' perspective (so-so), excitedly begins to describe a touchdown play to Mark, a big time Steelers fan, that the two of you saw at last night's home game. Do you...

A) Look at Mark and roll your eyes? (5)
B) Let her tell the story her way, and then fill in any technical details that Mark might find interesting afterwards? (10)
C) Cut her off and tell the story your way, using football jargon that only a couple of NFL-savvy guys like you and Mark would understand? (2)
D) *Try to slip your hand under her ass while she's distracted and cop a feel?* (0)

Your Score : 10

Comments :

A) LSM's have a tendency to act like "know-it-alls" in order to make themselves appear superior to other people, and thus possess a basis for putting them down... even women (hell, even your own *sister!*). **It's just another manifestation of their inferiority feelings.** That you were doing it indirectly behind her back makes you marginally better that the guy who chooses (C), and that's the only reason you get a 5.

B) HSM's are secure in their knowledge and thus can step aside and allow others to have their moment. They are generous and will be sensitive to the feelings of other people, especially loved ones. The HSM knows how to make the description of the touchdown complete without having to put down his sister's more limited knowledge of the game in the process. **Dozens of accumulated little slights like these are where the resentments between people take root and fester.** The story gets transferred to Mark accurately, and (more importantly) no one's ego had to get bruised along the way.

C) Unlike this rude prick, who's need to try and crawl his way up the Status Ladder at every opportunity far exceeds any desire he might still have left to keep things civil between himself and his sister (or anyone else for that matter). Score a 2, know-it-all.

D) Yeee-haaa!... incest is the best ain't it!

    3) It's the first day in your new math class. Time to pick a seat. Where do you sit?

A) In the front row. (5)
B) In the back third of the class, where you're not likely to be noticed. (3)
C) *In the far rear corner where you can inflict the greatest amount of damage when you open fire.* (0)
D) In the front third of the class near a cute girl. (10)

    Your Score : _10_

Comments :

A) Close but no cigar. At least you feel unafraid to engage the subject and risk being picked on to give an answer now and then.

B) Another mark of the LSM is his desire to hide from attention and disappear in a group.

C) Ok, ok... I know it's politically incorrect and tasteless to say such a thing nowadays. So just shoo... ah, never mind.

D) Just like a great pool player, the HSM is always **looking to**

set up his next shot. Pool shot, I'm talking about a pool shot now... aw forget it. Go to the next one.

    4) A co-worker whips out a one page flyer for next month's office picnic on his word processor during his lunch break. He hands you the flyer and asks what you think. What's your reaction?

A) You glance at it briefly and tell him it looks fine (7)
B) You point out two spelling errors (2)
C) You compliment him on his dedication to the Cause, then make a couple of suggestions for improvements. (10)
D) *You turn him in for using company resources.* (0)

    Your Score : _____

Comments :

  A) Not bad, maybe some resentment. Not really the perfect reaction though.

  B) **The LSM is quick to criticize** and point out other people's shortcomings. It's all part of his never-ending quest to keep fighting his way up the status ladder by openly demonstrating his 'superiority' to other people (men especially, but not exclusively) . Why? Because he knows that he's nowhere near the top and has no real chance to get there *doing something openly courageous*, so he takes little sneaky shots at everyone else all the time. His is a war of constant mental attrition that he's fighting endlessly.

  C) With nothing to prove because he's secure in his position in life, the HSM passes out the compliments with ease. Can you say **charisma**, boys and girls?

  D) This is supposed to be the zero points joke answer, but I gotta wonder 'cuz I've seen this happen...

5) *You're out driving around with your buddies and you see a shabby old man with a brown paper bag, obviously drunk, weaving around on the sidewalk minding his own business. Do you...*

A) Ignore him? (10)
B) Seize the opportunity to make a nasty joke? (3)
C) *Think "Holy shit... dad!..."* (0)
D) Roll down your window, shout "Hey, you stupid fuck!..." and spit at him for the amusement of your friends? (1)

Your Score : _10_

Comments :

A) Our secure HSM has nothing to prove.

B) An opportunity to proudly show off that you have a higher status than a homeless drunk. Wow, how impressive.

C) Joke (I hope...)

D) This prick is even lower down the food chain that the guy who chooses B, he likes to use the **hostile wit**... which is a way to express anger and hatred at someone through the use of *twisted humor*. You need lots of head work if this was your answer. I know, I used to be this way big time.

6) *You spot a cute girl at a friend's party standing alongside a guy who you think is probably her brother... but you're not absolutely certain. You've seen a similar couple hanging around the neighborhood, and maybe you're confusing the two -- in which case the guy is almost certainly her boyfriend. It's 50-50. You really want to meet her though, and this would be the perfect opportunity. Do you...*

A) Ask your friends to see if anybody knows what the deal is with her. (5)
B) Stay right where you are and do nothing. (2)
C) Walk over and introduce yourself, then try to determine if they're brother and sister by striking up a conversation. (10)
D) Keep trying to catch her eye, and then smile & wink at her every time that you do. (2)

    Your Score : __2__

Comments :

  A) Not quite right, too sneaky. Probably what most guys would do though.

  B) This is too intimidating a situation for the LSM. He's paralyzed to act.

  C) Only a confident HSM would have the courage to do something like this, but really, it's not a huge social risk so long as you play it cool and try not to be too obvious about what you're doing. It is a party after all – you're just making the rounds and being friendly, right? Good cover.

  D) This ought to be the zero joke question, but I'm not all that sure about some of you guys...

    7) You're out at a fancy restaurant with a date and the waitress goofs up your order big time, how would you react?

A) Give her a dressing down and embarrass her. (2)
B) Make a joke about it and let her know that it's ok. (10)
C) Insist on seeing the manager. (1)
D) *Ask her if she'd like to meet you later for a few drinks.* (0)

    Your Score : __10__

Comments :

A) Here we go again with the LSM trying to boost his own frail ego at the expense of others. One of the things that women look for on a date is how the guy they're with treats "the little people", i.e., valets, waitresses, etc. whose job it is to kiss the public's ass. This puts them at an unfair disadvantage to their customers, but the LSM happily exploits this artificially-created differential in social power to make himself feel like a big guy. It's all bullshit though, and the woman knows it. Even worse for the poor LSM chump, she also knows that this is how you'll be treating *her* after she's given you sex. Except that, if she's smart, you'll never be getting any.

B) This shows that you have no desire to seize on another person's mistakes to put them down or embarrass them. It's called being *magnanimous*, and is something that only the gracious person **operating from a position of power** can do. It signals HSM all the way very brightly.

C) This is even worse than response **A** because it exposes a malicious desire to really harm someone, or even get them fired. This is a real nasty, bitter LSM who's been shit on all his life from every direction and so is looking for any chance to give it back wherever and whenever he can regardless of the circumstances or how bad it will make him look.

D) What can I say? Some of you horndogs are just too smooth for me. Why don't you write your own book?

8) How do you typically act around your male friends?

A) Like a tough guy, with f-words flying every few seconds. (2)
B) By verbally sparing with them -- half-jokingly putting them down. (2)
C) Like myself... based on however I feel that day. (10)
D) Quiet, always hanging around in the background. (5)

Your Score : __5__

Comments :

A) This is an example of the false bravado that the LSM likes to wrap himself up in. It's easy to play tough with your friends because they understand that it's all bullshit designed to make you feel good about yourself, and that if any of them ever challenged you, you would quickly move back to the bottom of the pecking order where you belong. They know it and so do you.

B) Same thing.

C) The HSM is secure in his identity and self-worth and therefore free to act however he wants to around his friends. They **respect** him for it.

D) This demonstrates a classic case of something called the **Disabled Will,** which I will talk about more in Chapter 4. It manifests itself in the form of an arrogance and a false feeling of superiority to everyone else. This is because the person with the disabled will can only think of himself in two ways: either god-like and supreme, or as a worthless worm. There is no middle ground with this type of guy, no healthy sense of shame to ground him. Bad stuff.

9) *You are hanging out with a small group of people at a social setting. An attractive woman you've never seen before is standing nearby, but neither of you have acknowledged each other's presence except for some brief eye contact. Are you most likely to...*

A) Wait for her to say something to you first? (2)
B) Introduce yourself and shake her hand? (10)
C) Wait for someone in the group to formally introduce the two of you? (5)
D) *Show her your Gene Simmons tongue waggle?* (0)

Your Score : 10

Comments :

A) Afraid of being rejected? I know the feeling.

B) The best move to make. It demonstrates a willingness to take a social risk which impresses the hell out of women because... that's right, it's the mark of the HSM!

C) This is the safe move that most guys would wait for. It's not the best way to make that high status impression that B gives you though.

D) I... want to rock 'n roll all night... and party ev-ery day!

10) *You look out your living room window and see two dudes talking out in the street. One of them is leaning up against your new car parked out front, and he's wearing a belt with a big buckle that looks like it could scratch the paint job. Do you...*

A) Go outside and ask him to "...not lean on my new car 'cause the bank still owns it..." in a non-threatening way? (10)
B) Charge outside and scream "Hey dude, get the hell off the car!..." (5)
C) *Sneak around from behind and sucker punch him in the head?* (0)
D) Say nothing, go back to the couch and continue watching Friends re-runs? (2)

Your Score : 10

Comments :

A) The best way to defuse a situation like this. It shows courage without issuing a direct challenge. The HSM doesn't go looking for a fight everywhere but will stand up for his rights when he has to.

Guys respect that. (Except for serious LSM's who will have to take every threat as a call to fisticuffs since their weak egos cannot survive the thought of them having backed down from anyone. And don't forget the simmering rage aspect of his character either.)

B) This works too I suppose, but it also shows you off as the LSM who takes every little transgression in life as a life-or-death challenge to his flimsy ego (see above). Relax already.

C) In your dreams, Rambo.

D) Don't want to miss a chance to check out Jennifer A's nips?

11) How scared are you of your boss?

A) Terrified, I can't even look him in the eye. (2)
B) I'm respectful, but not scared. (8)
C) I am the boss (or, I work for myself). (10)
D) Fuck him, that stupid cocksucker. (2)

Your Score : _____

Comments :

A) This is a very meek, cowered male. You're so far down in the pecking order that you actually fear being in the presence of a clearly more powerful, dominant male.

B) This an alright answer. It shows that you are not so far away from being a top male in your own mind that you can't stand toe-to-toe with your boss. Someday you may even challenge for his spot.

C) Best answer, the dominant male is in charge... either of other people or simply his own destiny.

D) This is the same as A with a splash of good old LSM rage

mixed in.

12) *You're picking up your date at her house for an evening out at the new downtown nightclub. Her ten year old son is having a mood and giving her grief. How do you react?*

A) *Grab the kid by the hair and slap him?* (0)
B) Take her son aside and talk about sports or his favorite hobby for a few minutes? (10)
C) *Invite him to come along for a few drinks?* (0)
D) Say nothing, then tell your date (later on) that she should learn how to control her kid better? (2)

Your Score : 10

Comments :

A) A joke (I hope)

B) This is a great opportunity for you to show a little class and score some points with her. Talking to the boy might be all he needs to change his temperament somewhat. It also shows that you're not afraid to get involved in her life a little bit.

C) Joke #2

D) The LSM loves to criticize, doesn't he?

13) *How would you describe humor as a component of your personality?*

A) I sometimes get too wild and nutty, especially when I'm out drinking with my friends. (5)
B) I'm an opportunist, I like to pick my spots. (10)
C) I like to make fun of all the stupid jerks that I hate. (2)
D) I joke around and act funny *constantly*. (2)

Your Score : __10__

Comments :

A) It's not bad to be humorous, better than being a serious sour-puss, but you have to know how to balance it with some reserve. An ok answer, 5 points.

B) Humor is best used in a *clever* fashion, and *sparsely*. Especially around women. Part of the gift is knowing when to pick your moments, and then resisting the urge to beat the joke to death in order to milk out every last possible laugh.

C) This is the old hostile wit again, a tricky way in which the LSM tries to gain a higher status over someone by putting them down with mockery. But hey, it's just a joke, right? No need to punch in my cowardly little face, right?

D) Hey... you're what I call a ***jokin' asshole!*** The kind of guy who never stops with the hilarity. Did you ever notice that a guy's ability to be funny is inversely proportional to the amount of time he spends *trying* to be funny? Just a thought for you there, Shecky.

14) *When you leave the house – whether its to go to work, grab a bite to eat by yourself, or just take a quick run over to the laundromat – how do you usually dress?*

A) In whatever I happen to be wearing. (5)
B) I put on a shirt and tie. (2)
C) *In my flasher raincoat.* (0)
D) Casual but clean. (10)

Your Score : __5__

Comments :

A) The HSM is always aware that the opportunity to meet an

attractive woman can occur *when you least expect it,* so he tries to be presentable. If this isn't your attitude yet, then you're still not quite there.

B) What are you, Mr. Rogers or something?

C) I love the double-breasted red vinyl myself...

D) Like a good Boy Scout, you should always be prepared.

15) *You're talking to a girl you know from work during a happy hour get together with a small group of co-workers from the office. Would you place your hand casually on her forearm while the two of you are engrossed in an animated conversation, and let it linger there for a few seconds?*

A) No way, I'm not getting a sexual harassment grievance filed against me... even if it is after hours. (2)
B) Sure, why not? She's cute, and I find her attractive. (10)
C) Probably not. I wouldn't want her to get the wrong idea. (5)
D) *Only as a distraction while I work my hand up her skirt.* (0)

Your Score : 5

Comments :

A) This is just an excuse to cover your fear of being rebuffed. Sorry.

B) As a dominant male and a master seducer, you realize that the positive non-verbal communication conveyed by a simple, casual touch can be very powerful.

C) Refer to Comment A.

D) Too smooth. Just too smooth.

16) *Can you accept the generosity of another person – a man or a woman – gracefully?*

A) Only with great difficulty. (5)
B) I don't want to owe anyone. Better they owe me. (2)
C) Sure, why not. (10)
D) *No one is ever generous to me.* (0)

Your Score : 5

Comments :

A) One of the characteristics of the HSM is a recognition that other people gain pleasure from giving gifts now and then, and that to deny them this pleasure does not endear them to you but in fact *makes them resentful.* **You have to be secure in your own self worth in order to accept a gift graciously without feeling that you're always being manipulated.** If the simple act of receiving a gift still makes you uncomfortable in any way, then you're not in the optimum place that you want to be yet.

B) This kind of paranoid suspicion is the domain of the LSM, because he's a **control freak**. Due to the fact that the LSM has so little genuine authority in life, he's constantly seeking to control and manipulate others whenever he can as a form of psychological compensation. *Therefore, he's always* **suspicious** *that others are trying to do the same thing to him, and is wary of their motives.* This notion that there's some kind of Grand Cosmic Ledger out there where score is being kept as to "who owes whom" for every little favor or slight, is an especially certain tip-off that an LSM is in the house. No one gives you anything without expecting something back, he reasons, and is therefore fanatical about making sure that other people are always **indebted to him** and not vice versa. He sees any attempt at generosity as an evil ploy designed to tip the balance sheet against him, and so is generally resentful and rejecting of these offers – which he views as threats. As long as you owe *me*, then I am superior to you. See how it works in his mind?

C) The HSM is secure with his position in life and does not feel threatened by the generosity of others. He accepts gifts as graciously as he gives them and makes no attempt to keep any kind of 'score'.

D) Again, I hope this is a joke. If not, then the negative energy you radiate must truly be off the charts.

17) If someone were to present an idea or dream of their's to you, would you tend to encourage or discourage it?

A) Encourage it, with some advice or reservations. (8)
B) Discourage it. I hate listening to other people's stupid plans... none of it ever works out anyway. Why waste the time? (2)
C) Encourage it wholeheartedly. (10)
D) I'd tell them about my dreams instead. (2)

Your Score : _____

Comments :

A) The HSM does not feel threatened by the dreams or aspirations of the people that he knows because he's secure in his own life and career path. This is a good answer, although the need to point out your 'reservations' might be interpreted as demonstrating a bit of envy, so the best answer is C.

B) The LSM is often very jealous of other people's plans to get ahead in the world because he knows that his own deep-seated fears keep him handcuffed with failure. If his friends reveal their dreams to him, his **petty jealousy** often provokes him to try and derail their success in whatever way that he can, usually by discouraging or mocking those dreams and ideas. Since he already feels himself to be way down in life's pecking order, the last thing he needs is to see more people getting ahead of him, especially his own friends whom he imagines himself superior to! *Their potential advancement threatens his delusion of superiority.*

C) Best answer, total encouragement without any desire to hold the other guy back in any way. Making people feel good about themselves by bolstering their egos in this manner is what creates the attractiveness factor that we call **charisma**. *Women especially love guys who give off charisma!*

D) This is another variation of response B spiked up with a need to show off and prove that "mine is bigger than yours". All manner of braggarts, know-it-alls, criticizers and control freaks will also practice sabotaging the dreams of other people since it leaves them farther behind and makes them look bad when those people succeed. Unable to compete because their own fear of taking any sort of risk in life cripples them so completely, they resort to using various manipulations in order to try and hold others back at any cost.

18) Your enjoying a quick sandwich on your lunch break, sitting outside on a bench in front of the office building, reading a paper. You look up for a moment and catch the eye of a cute girl about twenty feet away looking back at you. Give me the first thing that just popped into your mind right now... Do you...

A) Quickly look away, then peek back in about a minute to see if she's still watching you? (2)
B) Smile warmly, then look away casually after about 3 seconds? (10)
C) Hold her eye, nod and raise your Pepsi can in a toast? (5)
D) *Bug your eyes and give her your Charlie Manson glare?* (0)

Your Score : _____

Comments :

A) This kind of shyness is common, indeed almost reflexive, but is something that the successful HSM has learned to overcome. This draws a low score, unfortunately.

B) Because the HSM has a track record of success when it comes to meeting and seducing women, he has learned to seize such moments as the perfect opportunity he needs to get the ball rolling on yet another seduction. Only a man with powerful social skills acts like this, and women notice it immediately and are very impressed by it.

C) This might work if you can pull it off in a humorous way, it's certainly better than looking away and doing nothing, but you lose points because acting goofy like this creates a built-in excuse for explaining away a rejection to yourself later on. You're not taking a full risk like the HSM would be inclined to do.

D) Don't forget to brush the hair away from your forehead so she can see the cute little hand-carved swastika too.

19) *Tomorrow is the birthday of one of the cute girls you work with at the office. You'd like to get more involved with her on a personal basis outside of work, but you're not sure if this is a good opportunity to make a move or not. What do you plan to do?*

A) Nothing, totally ignore the fact that it's her birthday. (5)
B) Get her a light-hearted, romantic birthday card. (10)
C) Buy her a dozen red roses. (2)
D) *Dress up like a clown, bring her a cake and sing for her.* (0)

Your Score : 10

Comments :

A) Acting aloof can be an effective ploy in the dance of

seduction, but it has to occur after some degree of interest has first been established. Otherwise it could be interpreted to be, well... disinterest. You might be afraid of being rejected too, so this is a tough call. Five points, and that might even be too much.

B) Perfect! Enough to establish some interest without going overboard like the nut case in response C. An appropriate way for the HSM to seize this golden opportunity to get things perking.

C) Way overboard and totally inappropriate. The poor girl must be thinking psycho-nutzoid-stalker... *run!*

D) And don't forget the balloons... I love balloons!

20) How tall are you?

A) Over six feet (10)
B) Between 5'8" and six foot tall. (8)
C) About 5'7" or shorter. (2)
D) *Don't call me a fuckin' midget... I'm a dwarf!* (0)

Your Score : __10__

Comments :

A) Your physical stature has an effect on how both men and women perceive you in terms of your ranking on the dominant male scale. Your behavior can compensate for or even completely eliminate height as a factor... but unfortunately, that doesn't help you make a great first *visual* impression on many people. Being six foot tall or more is the best.

B) This range is ok, your height is not a negative issue.

C) Height becomes a negative issue in this range (my problem!). You have to work harder on your **style** to overcome a height disadvantage. I score a 2, too. But hell, I played basketball by learning how to become a good outside shooter. You just have to discover a strategy to compensate for your "shortcomings".

D) Ah, political correctness...

21) If you get an opportunity during a business meeting or a social gathering to shake hands with an attractive woman after being introduced by someone, do you...

A) Squeeze her hand to impress her with your strength? (2)
B) Hold her fingertips and give her a little 'baby shake'? (2)
C) Give her a firm shake almost like you would a man? (10)
D) Give her the old 'sweaty limp fish' handshake? (1)

Your Score :

Comments :

A) "Ya... I vil crush yoo 'cause yoo are veek!"

B) This is wimpy and disgusting, don't do it.

C) Fully engage her hand until the webs between your fingers touch, then shake firmly but without crushing... and remember to hold eye contact and smile. Then, use the little subliminal **handshake trick** that I show you in Chapter 5 to really pique her interest!

D) *Yeeesh!* Gives me the creeps just thinking about it.

22) How many people in your life (subordinates) do you have the power to give orders to?

A) None. (2)
B) Less than five. (5)
C) Dozens. (10)
D) *Not even my dog listens to me.* (0)

Your Score : 10

Comments :

A) Not too good. Everyone bossing you around all the time eventually turns you into a hateful LSM. You're the bottom of the barrel and it will show itself in your shy, cowered attitude around women. (And you won't even realize it, that's the worst part).

B) Not bad, at least you have some authority in life. Take on more responsibility at work and your legion of subordinates will likely grow in the future. This too will show up, but in a male *dominant* attitude.

C) You're the boss, excellent! And it shows in your assumptions and attitudes around others. Women *notice* you.

D) It's really bad when all the non-human species begin losing respect for you too.

23) You step into an express elevator and find yourself alone with an attractive woman. You're both riding to the top floor, which will take about a minute. Do you...

A) Look straight ahead and not say anything? (2)
B) *Drop trou and ask her to smoke your bone?* (0)
C) Make some small talk with a gleam in your eye? (10)
D) Make some small talk just to relieve the tension? (5)

Your Score : 10

Comments :

A) While the tension builds to unbearable levels? This is typical, rejection-fearing LSM behavior.

B) Hey, just like in your favorite porno flick! Works every time!

C) Perfect. *The HSM is not afraid to take a bit of a social risk.* All you need to do is say something light-hearted to get a flirt going and then she what happens. At the onset of any seduction (the "pick-up" phase) you only need to communicate two things to her, that you are 1) safe, and 2) interested in her.

D) Not bad – better than standing there like a petrified log, but without any focus or goal in mind you're not likely to ignite any sparks either. The HSM immediately seizes on these kinds of opportunities to meet women in everyday life because he knows that their guard is down and they can be far more receptive to your approach. This kind of chance encounter can prove to be ten times more effective than anything you could ever drum up in a bar or nightclub where the women think that every word out of your mouth is pure bullshit.

24) *You've invited a young lady over for a casual dinner at your place, which you'll prepare and cook after she arrives. She offers to help out with the vegetable chopping for the salad. What would be your likely reaction?*

A) Thank her but insist that you do everything yourself. (3)
B) Welcome her help and let her go to work. (10)
C) Insist that she do nothing but sit there while you keep running over every few minutes to check that her wine is full and everything is ok. (1)
D) *Tell her that you don't let anyone handle the cutlery except for you and Mother.* (0)

Your Score : _____

Comments :

A) This is out-of-control *controlling behavior*, a hallmark of the LSM who – because he lacks any real authority in life – seeks to obsessively control anyone and everyone that he possibly can who has the misfortune of entering into his sphere of influence.

B) The HSM, on the other hand, is **confident and secure** and doesn't feel threatened by other's efforts to help him. He accepts their help with grace and good cheer.

C) This is serious, psychopathic control freak behavior. Might be time to see a shrink.

D) Maybe she'd like to stay over and have a shower too... eh Norman?

25) *If you had a weird personal habit – like for instance a funny, jerky laugh – would you feel free to express it in a public place, such as a restaurant?*

A) No way! (3)
B) No, I would always control such a laugh. (10)
C) I might. It would depend on the mood I was in and the situation. (5)
D) Sure, why not? How can I tell if I have a stupid laugh anyway? (2)

Your Score : 5

Comments :

A) One of the dangers of being single and socially isolated is that, over time, you'll tend to slip into behavior patterns that others instantly recognize as weird. This is deadly because women pick up these signals and sense your lack of romantic experience, setting you up for rejection. Although answers A and B seem the same, **A** suggests that you are covering up the weird habit (the laugh) out of shame and shyness, and so it scores lower.

B) Here you are attempting to control a weird personal habit out of a deeper sense of self-awareness. You have an understanding of just exactly how you are projecting yourself to other people, and are managing your behavior in order to make the best possible impression that you can.

C) This answer is not as good because it shows that you have an incomplete understanding of how you are viewed by others, unlike answer B.

D) Here you are completely *oblivious* to the image that you are projecting to others around you. This indicates that your isolation has pulled your persona down into the state of full blown weirdness, which is the principle danger of extended social withdrawal. Your isolation now feeds on itself and runs like a perpetual motion machine.

*   *   *

Alright, add up all your individual scores into a **single number.** This is your Final Score. The best you can do on this test is 250 (highly unlikely) and the worse is around 20 (also unlikely unless you deliberately blew the test off and picked all the joke answers). Whatever score you did get will fall into the following ranges, and they will provide you with a fairly good idea of just where you currently fit in along the Male Dominance Scale that women weigh so heavily when judging your attractiveness:

196

SCORING & INTERPRETATION OF RESULTS

250 - 200 – You're getting laid more than any man can imagine! Where the hell do you find time to read? You should be out there teaching the rest of us how it's done.

200 - 150 – You've got most of the personality traits and behaviors of a natural seducer already pretty much down. I still think you can use the information in this book to hone your craft somewhat – since there's always something to learn no matter how good you are at anything. Hey if you're not moving forward, you're moving backward... there's no standing still in life. I envy a guy like you... if I could have ever scored this well without years of research and self-training on this subject I highly doubt I would have had the motivation to write this book. Would've been too busy beating the babes back with a stick!

150 - 100 – I suspect this is the scoring range where most of my readers will be found camping out. You've got some of this 'male dominance' stuff figured out but your knowledge is incomplete and your seduction skills are not as sharp as you would like them to be. You will definitely improve your luck with women by carefully studying the techniques found in this book and putting them into action in your life.

One of the problems that we have with the topic of seduction as men is that we don't talk and strategize among ourselves and learn from each others' successes and failures. Why? Because one of the great 'macho codes' of guys is that you are just supposed to somehow *know* all about picking-up women after having passed a certain age (just like you're supposed to know all about sex!)... without anyone actually telling you how it's done. *As if it were all some sort of instinct!* When it comes to the topic of women, about the only thing guys do is brag and tell bullshit stories to each other which is less than helpful to say the least. It only makes the lesser among us feel worse about ourselves and less confident.

But humans are complicated animals who operate on **learned knowledge** and not on instincts. Plus, our mating rituals consist of a highly complex interplay between intellectual events and biochemical drives that conform to – and yet *change with* – the popular cultural norms of the day. There's a lot to know about women in terms of effectively meeting and mating with them – it's not something that you just wake up one fine morning and find yourself suddenly skilled at. Witness all the goofy behaviors men affect around women trying to get noticed by them, or all the lame 'raps' they lay on them in a desperate attempt to get in their pants. These are the product of the unskilled working in an information vacuum.

Women, on the other hand, actually trade notes with each other about their romantic dealing with men all the time. Hell, they've probably been obsessing about it since they were teenagers! That's because women have *far less shame* attached to the idea of interpersonal communication. They read articles in Cosmo and study books about relationships. They spend hours working on cosmetics and clothes... doing the things that they know will make them more attractive to men (who want to see a sexy visual from girls). In other words, they put *time into studying the topic* of seduction from their perspective.

There's no shame in being ignorant about a subject that you were never taught anything about. There *is* shame (stupidity, really) in choosing to **remain ignorant** when knowledge is finally available. So don't reject the knowledge in *Without Embarrassment* before giving it a full workout – have some faith in yourself and stay the course. Take this test over again a year from now and you'll be amazed at the improvement a little self-awareness can make in your life!

100 - 50 – You really need some help. Don't go crazy and throw in the towel though because that's been one of your problems all along. *Your frustration has maxed-out and filled you with impatience and anger.* Take a deep breath and relax – knowledge and a little bit of courage will propel you into a new life faster than you might imagine. Once you break the cycle of hopelessness that commands your consciousness, you will begin to make stunning improvements in your self-image and on the impression that you make on women.

Less than 50 – I can't believe anyone could actually score this low. You must've screwed with the test. What the hell are you afraid of? Honesty will set you free.

Made in the USA
Lexington, KY
26 July 2011